African American Biographies

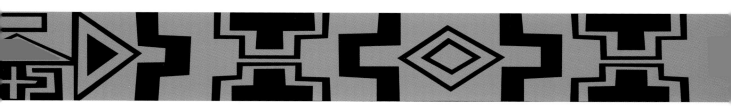

Volume 3

Cleaver, Eldridge—Edmonds, Kenneth "Babyface"

GROLIER

an imprint of

■SCHOLASTIC

www.scholastic.com/librarypublishing

First published 2006 by Grolier,
an imprint of Scholastic Library Publishing,
Old Sherman Turnpike
Danbury, Connecticut 06816

© 2006 The Brown Reference Group plc

Set ISBN 978-0-7172-6090-4
Volume ISBN 978-0-7172-6093–5

Library of Congress Cataloging-in-Publication Data
African American biographies.
    p. cm.
    Includes index.
    Contents: v.1. Aaliyah–Blyden, Edward W.—v.2. Bond, Horace
Mann–Clarke, John Henrik—v.3. Cleaver, Eldridge–Edmonds, Kenneth
"Babyface"—v.4. Edwards, Herman–Greener, Richard—v.5. Greenfield,
Elizabeth–Jacobs, Harriet—v.6. Jakes, T. D.–Loury, Glenn C.—v.7. Love,
Nat–Oliver, Joe "King"—v.8. O'Neal, Shaquille–Satcher, David—v.9.
Savage, Augusta–Tyson, Cicely—v.10. Tyson, Mike–Zollar, Doris
    ISBN 978-0-7172-6090-4
    I. African Americans—Biography—Juvenile literature. I.
        Scholastic Library Publishing

E185.96.A439 2006
920'.009296073–dc22
[B]

                        2005050391

For information address the publisher:
Grolier, Scholastic Library Publishing,
Old Sherman Turnpike,
Danbury, Connecticut 06816

FOR THE BROWN REFERENCE GROUP PLC

Project Editors: Sally MacEachern, Aruna Vasudevan
Design: Q2A Solutions
Picture Researcher: Laila Torsun
Index: Kay Ollerenshaw
Design Manager: Lynne Ross
Production Director: Alastair Gourlay
Senior Managing Editor: Tim Cooke
Editorial Director: Lindsey Lowe

Academic consultants:

        Molefi Kete Asante, Professor,
            Department of African American
            Studies, Temple University
        Mario J. Azevedo, Chair and Frank Porter
            Graham Professor, Department of Africana
            Studies, University of North Carolina at
            Charlotte
        Scott M. Lacy, University of California Faculty
            Fellow, Department of Black Studies,
            University of California
        Mawusi Renee Simmons, Development
            Consultant and Museum Docent, University
            of Pennsylvania Museum Philadelphia,
            Pennsylvania

Printed and bound in Singapore

ABOUT THIS SET

This is one of a set of 10 books about the African Americans who have helped shape the past of the United States and who play a vital part in the nation's life today. Some were leaders of the abolitionist movement against slavery in the latter half of the 19th century; others excelled in their fields despite being born into slavery themselves. The abolition of slavery after the Civil War (1861–1865) did not mark the end of the prejudice that prevented most black Americans from fulfilling their potential, however. During the first half of the 20th century the African Americans who made their names in the arts, entertainment, sports, academia, or business remained exceptions who reached prominence as the result of a determined struggle to overcome discrimination and disadvantage.

The civil rights advances of the 1950s and 1960s removed legal and institutional barriers to African American achievement, but pioneers in many fields still faced greater difficulties than their white peers. By the start of the 21st century, however, black Americans had become prominent in all fields of endeavor, from space exploration to government.

This set contains biographies of more than a thousand of the many African Americans who have made a mark. Some are household names; others are largely—and unjustly—overlooked or forgotten. Their entries explain not only what they achieved, but also why it was important. Every entry has a box of key dates for quick reference. Longer entries also include boxes on the people who inspired great African Americans or people they themselves have influenced in turn. Most entries have a "See also" feature that refers you to related articles elsewhere in the set. If you want to find out more about an individual there are suggested books and Web sites. Addresses may change, however, and the accuracy of information on sites may vary.

Throughout the set are a number of guidepost articles. They provide an overview of particular aspects of African American experience, such as the civil rights movement or the Harlem Renaissance of the 1920s, and help place the individuals featured in the biographies in a wider context.

The biographies are arranged alphabetically, mostly by last name but also by stage name. Each volume contains an index that covers the whole set and will help you locate entries easily.

CONTENTS

CLEAVER, Eldridge
Social Activist, Black Panther

Eldridge Cleaver rose to prominence in the late 1960s as the minister of information for the controversial Black Panther Party, an Oakland-based political group that combined revolutionary speeches with social initiatives designed to aid the African American community. His 1968 book, *Soul on Ice*—based on essays written while in prison (*see box*), presented a powerful statement of the degradations faced by urban black Americans and vocalized the philosophical viewpoints defining the black power movement of the late 1960s and early 1970s.

Early life
Born Leroy Eldridge Cleaver in Wabbaseka, Arkansas, on August 31, 1935, Cleaver moved as a youth first to Phoenix, Arizona, and later to Los Angeles, California, where his family settled in the Watts district. Cleaver's mother worked as a teacher, while his father was a railroad dining-car waiter and nightclub musician.

In trouble with the law as a teenager, Cleaver was convicted of theft and possession of marijuana; he was sentenced to time in reform school and prison. In 1958, following his conviction for assault with intent to kill, Cleaver was sentenced to between two and 14 years in prison. He was paroled in 1966, after serving time in California's notorious Folsom and San Quentin prisons.

Black Panthers
Soon after he left prison, Cleaver joined the recently founded Black Panther Party led by Huey P. Newton and Bobby Seale. The Panthers' goals included protesting police brutality and improving the social conditions faced by Oakland's African American community.

As the group's minister of information, Cleaver was a powerful and sometimes outspoken voice for the cause. He felt that African Americans needed better political organization in order to deal with white society from a position of power. Fellow Panther David Hillard commented, "I thought Eldridge was the reincarnation of Malcolm X. I'd never heard such power, such eloquence."

As the Panthers began to receive national media attention, Cleaver became a recognized and important figure in the 1960s protest movement. In 1968 he was the presidential candidate for the radical Peace and Freedom Party. When he was invited to speak at the University of California, Berkeley, an outraged Ronald Reagan, then the governor of California, said, "If Eldridge Cleaver is allowed to teach our children, they may come home one night and slit our throats."

A change in direction
On April 6, 1968, Cleaver's life took a sudden turn as the nation's cities exploded with racial violence in the aftermath of the assassination of Martin Luther King, Jr., two days earlier. Tensions were high and Cleaver and seven other Panthers became involved in a gun battle with the Oakland police: The shootout lasted for over an hour and a half. By the time the Panthers were forced to surrender, 17-year-old party member Bobby Hutton was dead, and Cleaver had been shot in the leg. The surviving Panthers were arrested and charged with the murder of a police officer killed during the confrontation. Released on bail, Cleaver fled the country with the help of student radicals from the militant Weather Underground

▲ *Eldridge Cleaver in 1968, the year he ran for the presidency, was wounded in a shootout with the Oakland police, and jumped bail to flee the country.*

INFLUENCES AND INSPIRATION

Cleaver's experiences while in prison profoundly changed the remainder of his life. Using his time to pursue an education, Cleaver was strongly influenced by the political writings of Karl Marx, Thomas Paine, W. E. B. DuBois, Vladimir Lenin, and Malcolm X. They motivated Cleaver to put his own ideas and thoughts on paper and to write the essays that became the basis for *Soul on Ice*, an autobiographical account of African American rage against a society that was completely controlled by whites. Credited with inspiring the black power movement, the book was praised by some commentators for the valuable insight it gave into the black view of U.S. life. "You don't have to teach people to be human," Cleaver wrote, "you have to teach them how to stop being inhuman."

Cleaver and the legacy of the Black Panther Party continue to be a controversial and inspiring aspect of African American history in the early 21st century. In 2001 Kathleen Cleaver, Eldridge's former wife and a member of the original Panther leadership, organized the International Black Panther Film Festival to promote films that examined and encouraged active resistance to oppression just as the Panthers did. Speaking about her ex-husband's complex legacy, Cleaver said, "I think he was so very, very controversial that he inspired so much, either anger or rage, or admiration or love."

organization, beginning a seven-year political exile that would take him to Mexico, Cuba, Algeria, and France. His wife, Kathleen, later joined him.

Disillusionment

Cleaver left the United States disillusioned with the injustices of the U.S. system. However, as he observed the realities of life in other parts of the world, his views gradually began to modify. He converted to evangelical Christianity and adopted a fervently anticommunist political stance. Writing in the *New York Times*, Cleaver described the political system in Cuba as "voodoo socialism" and argued that "with all its faults the American political system is the … most democratic in the world." In 1975 Cleaver returned to the United States to face the murder charge against him in Oakland. With the help of his wife, who mounted a campaign to protest his innocence, Cleaver's charge was reduced to assault; he pleaded guilty and was placed on probation. When asked why he had returned to the United States,

Cleaver responded, "I found the systems of dictatorship and communism to be absolutely unacceptable."

Following his return to America Cleaver became more conservative in his political outlook. At different times he advocated the teachings of the Reverend Sun Myung Moon, the leader of the Unification Church, and experimented with Mormonism. In 1986 Cleaver was unsuccessful in his bid to become the Republican nominee for one of California's seats in the Senate. He remained committed to improving the lives of poor African Americans, however. In the 1990s he became a vocal critic of the African American community's leadership, which he felt was too concerned with maintaining its own power and not focused on the needs of its constituency.

In the mid-1980s Cleaver became addicted to crack-cocaine and was arrested for drug possession in both 1988 and 1992. After being attacked by a fellow addict in 1994, Cleaver tried to beat his addiction; he also tried to reestablish relations with his family, from whom he was estranged. He was arrested again for drug possession, however; he died from a heart attack on May 1, 1998.

KEY DATES	
1935	Born in Wabbaseka, Arkansas, on August 31.
1967	Marries Kathleen Neal on December 27.
1968	Publishes collection of autobiographical essays *Soul on Ice*; wounded in gunfight with Oakland police on April 6; flees to Mexico in November.
1998	Dies in Los Angeles, California, on May 1.

See also: Civil Rights; Cleaver, Kathleen Neal; DuBois, W. E. B.; King, Martin Luther, Jr.; Malcolm X; Newton, Huey; Seale, Bobby

Further reading: Cleaver, Kathleen, and George Katsiaficas (eds.). *Liberation, Imagination, and the Black Panther Party.* New York, NY: Routledge, 2001.
http://www.pbs.org/wgbh/pages/frontline/shows/race/interviews/ecleaver.html (PBS interview with Cleaver).

CLEAVER, Kathleen Neal
Civil Rights Activist, Attorney

Kathleen Neal Cleaver is a civil rights activist, attorney, writer, and educator. The former wife of Black Panther leader Eldridge Cleaver, she has dedicated her life to fighting discrimination.

Kathleen Neal was born in Dallas, Texas, on May 13, 1945. Her father, Ernest, taught at Wiley College and Tuskegee Institute in Alabama before joining the Foreign Service. The Neal family spent several years abroad in countries such as India and Sierra Leone.

Cleaver returned to the United States to finish her education. She became heavily involved in the civil rights movement while studying at prestigious Barnard College, New York, but in 1966 she left to work full time for the Student Nonviolent Coordinating Committee (SNCC). There Cleaver became aware of the Black Panther Party (BPP), a nationalist party with a radical approach to social change. She met its minister of information, Eldridge Cleaver, and moved from New York to San Francisco to be with him. The couple married on December 27, 1967. Kathleen Cleaver became the BPP's national communications secretary; she helped organize a campaign to get Huey Newton, the BPP's minister of defense, released from jail. She was also the first woman to sit on the BPP's decision-making central committee.

Exile

The Cleavers' life changed radically following the events of April 6, 1968. Eight BPP members, including Eldridge and Bobby Hutton (1950–1968), were traveling in two cars when they were allegedly ambushed by the Oakland police. A shootout left Cleaver wounded and Hutton dead. Cleaver was arrested and charged with attempted murder, but he fled the country. Kathleen later joined him in Algeria.

In 1971 Kathleen returned to New York to establish the Revolutionary People's Communication Network, formed by the Cleavers after a disagreement between Eldridge and Newton. She set up the Eldridge Cleaver Defense Fund after her husband returned to the United States to face his attempted murder charge, which was dropped after he pleaded guilty to assault. The couple divorced in 1987.

Cleaver graduated in history in 1983 and law in 1988. She clerked for black jurist A. Leon Higginbotham and joined a New York law firm. The author of several books, Cleaver also speaks on civil rights and race issues.

KEY DATES	
1945	Born in Dallas, Texas, on May 13.
1967	Marries Eldridge Cleaver.
1983	Graduates from Yale University with BA in history.
1987	Divorces Eldridge Cleaver.
1988	Graduates in law from Yale University; begins to teach at Emory University, Atlanta.

See also: Civil Rights; Cleaver, Eldridge; Higginbotham, A. Leon; National Organizations; Newton, Huey

Further reading: Cleaver, Kathleen, and George Katsiaficas (eds.). *Liberation, Imagination, and the Black Panther Party.* New York, NY: Routledge, 2001.
http://www.lacitybeat.com/article.php?id=661&IssueNum=36 (Interview with Cleaver).

▲ *In 1968 as the BPP's national spokesperson, Kathleen Cleaver made speeches across the country.*

CLIFTON, Lucille
Writer

A celebrated poet and children's writer, Lucille Clifton first came to prominence during the 1960s, when she was associated with the black arts movement, the literary school sometimes referred to as the "spiritual sister" of the black power political trend. Clifton's spare and deceptively simple poetry explores the humanity and dignity of ordinary African American urban life. Her work often celebrates family relationships and their place within an evolving black American history and community.

An extraordinary woman
Born in Depew, a suburb of Buffalo, New York, on June 27, 1936, Thelma Lucille Sayles was the daughter of a steelworker and a launderer who was also an amateur poet. She was encouraged to write from a young age.

From 1953 to 1955 she studied drama at Howard University, Washington, D.C., where she met Fred James Clifton. The couple married in 1958. Lucille Clifton also studied at Fredonia State Teacher's College, New York, in 1955. While she was establishing a reputation as a poet, Clifton held several state and federal government jobs, including that of literature assistant in the Office of Education in Washington, D.C.

Like other African American poets involved in the black arts movement, Clifton wanted to create a distinctive black poetry that employed the rhythms of ordinary, working-class black experience. In 1969 *Good Times*, her first book of poetry, was published; the *New York Times* chose it as one of the 10 best books of the year. Subsequent collections included *Good News about the Earth* (1972), *An Ordinary Woman* (1974), and *Quilting: Poems, 1987–1990* (1991).

Family and history
Clifton's work explores many different issues. She often draws on her own personal experiences and has written about being a daughter, wife, and mother. Clifton has also produced "sorrow songs" in which she mourns the death of friends and loved ones. Other poems reflect African American life "in the inner city/ or/ like we call it home." Clifton has also drawn on African American heritage and history. In *Generations: A Memoir* (1976), for example, she recounted the stories of her ancestors, including her great-great-grandmother, who was abducted from West Africa and brought to America

▲ *Lucille Clifton has said that "the proper subject matter for poetry is life."*

in 1830 as a slave. Clifton has written many children's books. The most famous feature Everett Anderson, a young African American boy living in the inner city.

Clifton has been nominated for the Pulitzer Prize several times, and she has served as poet laureate for the state of Maryland. In 1991 she became distinguished professor of humanities at St. Mary's College in Maryland. *Blessing the Boats: New and Selected Poems, 1988–2000* won the National Book Award in 2003.

KEY DATES	
1936	Born in Depew, New York, on June 27.
1969	Publishes *Good Times*.
1991	Appointed distinguished professor of humanities at St. Mary's College of Maryland.
2003	*Blessing the Boats: New and Selected Poems, 1988–2000* wins the National Book Award.

Further reading: Bloom, Harold. *Black American Women Poets and Dramatists*. London: Chelsea House Publications, 1995.
www.poets.org/poet.php/prmPID/79 (Biography and poems).

CLINTON, George
Musician

Widely regarded as the leading figure in the creation and development of funk music, musician George Clinton has enjoyed a career that has spanned a half-century. Clinton, sometimes called Dr. Funkenstein, was known for his often outrageous costumes, colorful hairstyles, and extravagant stage shows. His influence extends far beyond funk music—his work has been sampled by many rap bands and has been cited as an influence by bands such as the Red Hot Chili Peppers and Rage against the Machine.

The road to success

George Clinton was born in Kannapolis, North Carolina, on July 22, 1941, the youngest of nine children. Clinton's family moved to Plainfield, New Jersey, when he was a young child. Music was an obsession from an early age. He learned to sing as a child. After two short-lived jobs as a hairdresser, where he was responsible for straightening hair, and as a worker in a hula-hoop factory, he formed his first band in 1957. The doo-wop group, inspired by Frankie Lymon and the Teenagers, was called the Parliaments after a brand of cigarettes. They performed in the Newark area before recording "Poor Willie" in 1958. The band recorded several other songs but remained largely unsuccessful commercially. They moved to Detroit in 1963, where they came to the attention of Berry Gordy, head of Motown.

The Parliaments released several records and had hits with the 1967 "[I Wanna] Testify," which reached No. 5 on Billboard's rhythm and blues (R&B) chart and the Top 20 on the pop charts. Clinton changed the sound and mood of the band in 1967, adding loud horns and electric instruments to create a hard rhythm that became known as funk. He said, "Do, Bop! Bahm, Do Bop!… and ballads like 'Everything's gonna be everything baby'…. Doo Wops! That's how we began. By the time we had our first hit on Motown, Doo Wop was getting old. We changed to blues

▼ *Known for his extravagant appearance George Clinton has influenced many bands.*

INFLUENCES AND INSPIRATION

Although George Clinton has influenced many musicians, he has often credited musician Jimi Hendrix (1942–1970) with being his own inspiration. Hendrix became famous for his legendary expertise with the electric guitar. As a young musician Hendrix worked with such greats as Sam Cooke, Little Richard, and Ike and Tina Turner. His solo work combined a mixture of acid rock, psychedelic blues, and a raw, hungry voice. Clinton was a huge Hendrix fan. In the 1970s Clinton's band Funkadelic melded Hendrix's style with other of his favorites such as "Godfather of Soul" James Brown. Hendrix also influenced the band's style of dress and stage performance. Clinton said, "First we were straight. Straight suits and clean. Then we took it to exaggeration. We wore sheets, we wore the suit bags our suits came in. And it was funny to us, 'cause we came from a barbershop, we knew how to make it look cool, so you never felt uncool. We had fun doing it. Plus, I knew Jimi Hendrix did it. To me that's the ultimate, Jimmy James."

for a bit. That was my mother's music. And then everyone was playing rock." Gordy hired Clinton to write songs for Motown stars, including the Jackson 5 and Diana Ross.

The road to Funk

In 1969 Clinton formed Funkadelic using many of the members of the Parliaments. The band mixed elements of James Brown, Jimi Hendrix, and Sly and the Family Stone with outrageous live performances, shocking drug-induced lyrics, and blaring electronic and brass sections. They claimed to be African Americans from other planets, and their costumes often reflected a space-age theme. In a very astute move, in 1970 Clinton formed a new band called the Parliaments, made up of the same musicians, which performed a more accessible style of music than Funkadelic. When it became known that the two bands were essentially the same, they were often called Parliament Funkadelic or P-Funk.

Clinton's long multicolored dreadlocks, his teetering platform boots, his wild costumes, and outrageous stage shows made him famous. In 1975 Parliament sold a million copies of two albums, *Chocolate City* and *Mothership Connection*. Other recordings included *The Clones of Dr. Funkenstein* (1976) and *Gloryhallastoopid* (1979).

Funkadelic were prolific through the 1970s. Their most popular song, "One Nation under a Groove" (1978), sold a million copies. Not content with the two bands, Clinton created spinoffs Bootsy's Rubber Band (named for Bootsy Collins, who joined Clinton in 1972) and Brides of Funkenstein. Clinton's bands dominated black music through the decade, with over 40 R&B hit singles and three platinum albums. A high point of Clinton's career was the massive world tour he undertook from 1978 to 1979, the Parliafunkadelicment Mothership Connection Tour, which brought his unique blend of soul, funk, and jazz to hundreds of thousands of fans.

New interests

For most of the 1980s complicated legal actions with his record company prevented Clinton from playing in either Parliament or Funkadelic. Instead, he became interested in the music industry's new technology of remixing and sampling. In the late 1980s he started to tour again, working as a producer for bands such as the Red Hot Chili Peppers in the 1990s. In 1996 Clinton reunited with former members of Parliament and Funkadelic and released T.A.P.O.A.F.O.M. In 2005 he embarked on a new tour and released *How Late Do U Have 2BB4UR Absent?*

See also: Brown, James; Gordy, Berry; Hendrix, Jimi; Jackson 5; Ross, Diana

Further reading: Rickey, Vincent. *Funk: The Music, The People and The Rhythm of the One* (with an introduction by George Clinton). New York, NY: St Martin's Griffin,1996.
http://www.georgeclinton.com (Clinton's official site).

KEY DATES

1941	Born in Kannapolis, North Carolina, on July 22.
1957	Forms a doo-wop band, the Parliaments.
1967	Develops musical sound that becomes funk.
1969	Forms Funkadelic.
1978	Undertakes Parliafunkadelicment Mothership Connection Tour.
2005	Clinton begins new tour.

COACHMAN, Alice
Athlete

Athlete Alice Coachman's achievements have been enormous: As the first African American woman to win an Olympic gold medal, Coachman inspired generations of young women athletes, including Florence Griffith-Joyner and Jackie Joyner-Kersee. In 1952 Coachman was also the first black female athlete to sign an endorsement deal with a multinational corporation, Coca-Cola.

Early life

Born in Albany, Georgia, on November 9, 1923, Coachman was the daughter of Fred "Doc" and Evelyn Coachman, and was one of 10 children. Coachman was raised primarily by her maternal great-grandmother and grandmother. Coachman was a born athlete but found herself the victim of a Georgia segregation policy that denied African Americans access to public sports facilities and school athletic competitions. Undeterred, Coachman found other ways in which to train, creating track-event equipment such as hurdles and high jumps from rope and sticks; she used local dirt roads as running tracks, often training barefoot. In 1938 she attended Madison High School, where she had access to good equipment and attracted the attention of Coach Henry E. Lash, who encouraged her to pursue her dreams of becoming a world-class athlete.

Making an impression

In 1939 Coachman won a scholarship to Tuskegee Institute in Tuskegee, Alabama. The institution was one of the few black educational facilities to take women's athletics seriously. Trained by Cleveland L. Abbott (*see box*), Coachman excelled at athletics. In her first year she broke Amateur Athletic Union (AAU) and collegiate records for the women's high jump. At Tuskegee she won 10 AAU high-jump titles, nine consecutively, and also held national titles in 50-meter and 100-meter sprints and

▼ *Alice Coachman (right) attends the 1948 Olympics in London, England, with high jumper Emma Reed (left) and sprinter Nell C. Jackson (center).*

INFLUENCES AND INSPIRATION

Alice Coachman influenced generations of female athletes. Before Coachman, track-and-field competition was seen as a predominantly male domain; the women who dared to compete were often derided as being "muscle molls" or amazonian types. Coachman's achievement in the 1948 Olympics gave many female athletes the opportunity to pursue their dreams. Her success also gave many black Americans added pride in their race.

Coachman attended Tuskegee Institute in Alabama, one of the few places to take women's athletics seriously. She was coached by the legendary Cleveland Leigh Abbott, who was a big influence on the young Coachman. Abbott spent 32 seasons as athletic director, track and field, and football coach at Tuskegee. Under Abbott, who was a graduate of South Dakota State College, the institution's team dominated the national track circuit, winning

14 national outdoor titles, nine consecutively. With Abbott's help Coachman won nine national high-jump titles in a row. Nicknamed "Tuskegee Flash," she was also the first African American to be selected for the All-American team. Coachman acknowledged how much she and other female athletes owed to Abbott. In 1994 she established the nonprofit Alice Coachman Track and Field Foundation to help young athletes and former Olympians.

---

4 x 100-meter relay. In 1946 Coachman had the distinction of being the first African American chosen to join the All-American Team. She also played basketball and helped Tuskegee to three championship wins.

An Olympic dream

There was no denying Coachman's talent; following trials in the high jump, she joined the U.S. Olympic team to compete in the 1948 Games held in London, England. She was one of nine black American women on the 12-member U.S. track and field team.

Despite suffering from a twisted ovary that caused her considerable back pain, Coachman jumped 5 feet 6⅛ inches (1.68m), setting both a U.S. and world record. Coachman also became the first black American woman to win a gold medal; she beat Britain's favorite, Dorothy Tyler. Audrey Patterson became the second African American woman to win an Olympic medal when she picked up a bronze in the 200-meter sprint.

National recognition

Coachman returned from the Olympics a national hero. Her success, combined with that of Patterson, helped raise the profile of black female athletes, and many schools set up track-and-field programs. African Americans were still treated unequally, however, and Coachman was unable to attend the ceremony honoring her achievement held in Albany, Georgia, owing to state segregationist policies.

Following her return to the United States, Coachman retired from sports competition. In 1949 she was awarded a degree in home economics and science from Albany State College, Georgia, after which she taught physical education in several high schools and colleges. In 1975 Coachman was inducted into the National Track and Field Hall of Fame. She was honored as one of the 100 Great Olympians at the 1996 Olympic Games in Atlanta. Coachman's career has inspired many black American female athletes.

KEY DATES

1923 Born in Albany, Georgia, on November 9.

1939 Attends Tuskegee Institute in Alabama.

1946 First African American selected for the All-American team.

1948 Wins a gold medal in high jump at the Olympics Games held in London, England.

1949 Earns degree in home economics and science.

1975 Inducted into the National Track and Field Hall of Fame.

1994 Establishes the nonprofit Alice Coachman Track and Field Foundation.

See also: Griffith-Joyner, Florence; Joyner-Kersee, Jackie

Further reading: Plowden, Martha Ward. *Olympic Black Women.* Gretna, LA: Pelican, 1996.
http://nj.essortment.com/biographyofali_ruom.htm (Biography).

COBB, Jewel Plummer
Scientist, Educator

Jewel Plummer Cobb is one of the most noted African American scientists of her generation; her specialty is cell biology.

Jewel Isadora Plummer was born in Chicago, Illinois, in 1924. Her grandfather was a freed slave who managed to obtain the education necessary to become a pharmacist. Her father, Frank V. Plummer, became a physician after graduating from Cornell University. Her mother, Carriebel, was a physical education teacher

Early interest in science
Plummer's early interest in science was fostered both at home and at school. She first enrolled at the University of Michigan but had to live in segregated accommodations. She decided to leave and went on to gain her BS degree in 1944 from Talladega College in Alabama and her MS degree from New York University in 1947. In 1950 she was awarded her PhD by New York University; her dissertation was on the mechanisms of pigment formation. Cobb did her postdoctoral research at the National Cancer Institute in Bethesda, Maryland.

A leading expert in melanomas
Plummer married Roy Cobb in 1954 and returned to New York University, where she continued the research that was to make her name. Cobb was particularly interested in melanin pigment-producing cells and the types of cancer associated with abnormal growth of these cells, the melanomas. Cobb became one of the major researchers in this aspect of cancer biology, with many publications to her name, including nearly 50 books.

Melanin is a dark pigment found in skin, feathers, and scales that helps protect the skin from the dangerous rays of the sun and absorbs heat from sunlight. Although in the Unites States fewer than 5 percent of skin cancers are melanomas, they are responsible for three-quarters of skin-cancer deaths. Melanomas are always malignant.

Supporting women
Cobb's interest in biology extended to teaching cell biology and pathology, and also to promoting and supporting scientific careers for women, particularly minorities. From 1960 to 1969 Cobb was professor of biology at Sarah Lawrence College. She was appointed professor of zoology at Connecticut College in 1969, becoming dean. In 1976 she moved to Douglass College, the women's college of Rutgers University, as dean and professor of biology.

In 1981 Cobb became president of California State University at Fullerton, where she worked to enhance the university's reputation for diversity and research. As a senior academic, ultimately trustee professor of California State University at Los Angeles, she wrote and campaigned against racial and sexual discrimination in science and the universities. Cobb retired from Fullerton in 1990 but continued her research on cell biology. She is quoted as saying that she would like to be remembered "as a black woman scientist who cared very much about what happens to young folks, particularly women going into science."

Cobb has received 22 honorary doctorates. In 1989 Douglass College at Rutgers dedicated the Bunting-Cobb Math and Science Hall in honor of Cobb and microbiologist Mary Ingraham Bunting, both former deans of Douglass. In 1991 California State University at Fullerton dedicated the Jewel Plummer Cobb Residence Halls in Cobb's honor. In 1993 Cobb received the Lifetime Achievement Award from the National Science Foundation for contributions to the advancement of women and underrepresented minorities.

KEY DATES	
1924	Born in Chicago, Illinois, on January 17.
1950	Awarded PhD in cell physiology from New York University.
1981	Becomes president of California State University, Fullerton.
1990	Retires from California State University, Fullerton.
1993	Receives Lifetime Achievement Award for contributions to the advancement of women and underrepresented minorities from the National Science Foundation.

Further reading: Ambrose, Susan A., Barbara B. Lazarus, Indira Nair, and Deborah A. Harkus. *Journeys of Women in Science and Engineering: No Universal Constants.* Philadelphia, PA: Temple University Press, 2000.
http://www.historywomen.com/Admire20.html (History's Women page on Cobb).

COBB, William Montague
Physical Anthropologist

During William Montague Cobb's long and distinguished career as a physical anthropologist he helped disprove scientifically many of the prejudices surrounding the physiognomy of African Americans.

Cobb was born in Washington, D.C., on October 12, 1904. He attended Dunbar High School, an elite preparatory school for African American boys. In 1925 Cobb graduated from Amherst College, Massachusetts, and received a scholarship to study biology. This led him to study for a medical degree at Howard University and then to postgraduate work in physical anthropology.

Teaching anatomy

In 1932 Cobb graduated from Western Reserve University in Cleveland, Ohio, the first African American to receive a PhD in physical anthropology, which is the study of human remains with an emphasis on the interaction between biology and culture.

In the 1930s many white Americans believed that the growing dominance of African American athletes in competitions was due to racial anatomy. As professor of anatomy at Howard University, Cobb collected about 700 skeletons. He also measured African American Olympic athletes and compared them to average African American and European American skeletons. He was able to prove that there were no differences, and thus that racial biology and behavior are not fixed. Cobb also worked hard to disprove views about the social inferiority of African Americans. He tried to prove that racial segregation and inequality affected black health, and as a result adversely affected the finances of the nation.

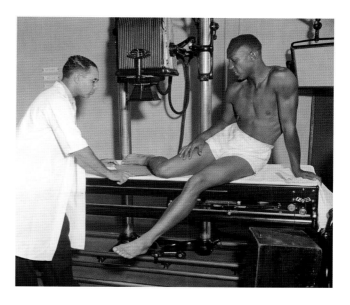

▲ *William Montague Cobb examines champion athlete Jesse Owens in an attempt to find out what makes him so fast—race or stamina.*

Cobb remained at Howard University until his retirement. In 1949 he became chair of the department of anatomy and in 1973 distinguished professor emeritus. While at Howard Cobb worked tirelessly to promote racial integration in hospitals and medical schools. In 1957 he established the Imhotep National Conference on Hospital Integration, which met annually until 1963. In 1964 he became president of the National Medical Association.

In 1976 Cobb was elected president of the National Association for the Advancement of Colored People (NAACP), a position he held until 1982. Cobb continued to work well into his eighties. During his life Cobb received over 100 awards and published more than 1,000 articles countering the myths surrounding the biological racial inferiority of African Americans. He died in 1990.

See also: Owens, Jesse; Segregation and Integration; Slavery

Further reading: Harrison, E. and F. V. (eds.). *African American Pioneers in Anthropology.* Chicago, IL: University of Illinois Press, 1998.
www.nmanet.org/pr_101204.htm (Biography).

KEY DATES

1904   Born in Washington, D.C., on October 12.

1929   Awarded a medical degree from Howard University College of Medicine.

1932   Becomes first African American to receive a PhD in physical anthropology.

1949   Becomes chair of the department of anatomy at Howard University.

1987   Presents his last professional paper.

1990   Dies in Washington, D.C., on November 20.

COCHRAN, Johnnie
Attorney

Johnnie Cochran was a highly successful defense lawyer known as the "attorney to the stars." Cochran's rallying cry was "An injustice anywhere is a threat to justice everywhere." In 1994 he became a household name when he defended the former football player O. J. Simpson, who was accused of murdering his wife, Nicole Brown Simpson, and her friend Ron Goldman.

The road to success

Johnnie L. Cochran, Jr., was born in Shreveport, Louisiana, on October 2, 1937. His father owned an insurance company, and his family was well-off. Cochran was raised in Los Angeles, California, where he later studied business administration at UCLA. One of Cochran's heroes was the Supreme Court judge Thurgood Marshall, and he was inspired to study law at Loyola Marymount University, graduating in 1962. After being admitted to the bar in California in 1963, Cochran became a deputy city attorney for the criminal division. He was involved in some high-profile celebrity cases, including the 1964 prosecution of the comedian Lenny Bruce on obscenity charges. In 1966 he cofounded the law firm Cochran, Atkins, and Evans; his cases included defending the former Black Panther Elmer Geronimo Pratt against a murder charge in 1972. Although Pratt was found guilty, Cochran continued to fight for his release: The decision was reversed in 1997.

In the late 1970s Cochran became the first black assistant district attorney of Los Angeles County. In 1981 he returned to private practice and established the Cochran Firm, which specialized in entertainment law, criminal defense, public financing, and personal injury litigation. Although Cochran specialized in police brutality cases, he became known for his work defending celebrities such as the musicians Tupac Shakur and Michael Jackson.

▲ *Johnnie Cochran became an international celebrity as a result of the O. J. Simpson trial of 1994.*

In 1994 Cochran achieved international recognition during the televised O. J. Simpson trial. Cochran skillfully used errors made by law-enforcement officers, racist comments, and civil liberty violations to help acquit Simpson. *The National Law Journal* subsequently named Cochran "America's Trial Lawyer of the Year." In the years before his death of a brain tumor in March 2005, Cochran became a popular public speaker and hosted several legal programs on television.

See also: Jackson, Michael; Simpson, O. J.; Shakur, Tupac; Supreme Court; Marshall, Thurgood

Further reading: Cochran, Johnnie, Jr., with Tim Rutten. *Journey to Justice.* New York, NY: Ballantine Books, 1997. www.cochranfirm.com (The Cochran Firm site).

KEY DATES	
1937	Born in Shreveport, Louisiana, on October 2.
1962	Graduates in law.
1966	Establishes Cochran, Atkins, and Evans.
1981	Sets up the Cochran Firm.
1994	Defends O. J. Simpson in his murder trial.
2005	Dies in Los Angeles, California, on March 29.

COKER, Daniel
Educator, Antislavery Campaigner

Daniel Coker was an author, educator, and colonist. He was born into slavery as Isaac Wright in Frederick County, Maryland, in around 1780. His mother, Susan Coker, was a white indentured slave, and his father, Edward Wright, was a black slave. After receiving several years of schooling, Coker escaped to New York City and changed his name.

Religious orders
While in New York City Coker joined the Methodist Church and was ordained as a lay minister. In 1801 he returned to Baltimore, then home to one of the largest populations of free African Americans. Initially Coker kept secret his return because he was still a slave. Despite qualifying as the first licensed African American minister, he hid until Quaker abolitionists bought his freedom in 1802. From then to 1816 Coker became the first African American teacher at the African School attached to the Sharp Street Church.

Once free, Coker began to preach in public against the mistreatment of African Americans and slavery. In 1810 he published *A Dialogue between a Virginian and an African*

▼ **Daniel Coker became the first licensed African American minister and then a missionary in Africa.**

Minister, a treatise against slavery. He also advocated the withdrawal of African Americans from the predominantly white Methodist Church and the formation of their own church. In 1814 his congregation bought its own church.

A new church
Two years later Coker attended a conference held by black church leaders that concluded in the formation of a central church to which all black Methodist churches would belong, the African American Methodist Episcopal Church (AME). Coker was elected the first bishop of AME, but he refused the position. Instead, Richard Allen, another high-ranking minister, became bishop. On April 17, 1818, for reasons that are unclear, Coker was expelled from the church, but he was given back his job the following year.

Life in Africa
In 1820 Coker sailed to Africa as a missionary. He wrote an account of the trip, but only the first volume was published. He arrived in Liberia later that year. Sickness and the inhospitable living conditions soon took their toll on Coker's fellow colonists, and Coker was left in charge. However, conditions in Liberia were too difficult, and he moved to Sierra Leone, where his wife and children joined him. Coker established a church in the capital, Freetown. He is thought to have died in 1846.

See also: Allen, Richard; Religion and African Americans; Slavery

Further reading: www.genealogyforum.rootsweb.com/gfaol/resource/AfricanAm/Coker.htm (Biography).

KEY DATES	
1780	Born a slave in Frederick County, Maryland.
1801	Becomes first African American licensed minister in Baltimore.
1810	Writes the first published antislavery treatise by an African American.
1816	Forms African American Methodist Episcopal Church.
1820	Sails for Africa, first to Liberia then to Sierra Leone.
1846	Dies in Sierra Leone at about this time.

COLE, Johnetta B.
Educator, Intellectual

Johnetta Cole has had a distinguished career as a scholar, college and university teacher, and administrator. She became the first African American woman to serve as president of Spelman College, Atlanta, Georgia. Cole once observed that "When you educate a man, you educate an individual, but when you educate a woman, you educate a nation." These words describe her life mission. A passionate advocate for educational opportunities for people of color and women, she is president emerita of Spelman College and professor emerita of Emory University, Georgia. She also holds important positions on corporate, government, and community bodies.

Early life
Johnetta Betsch was born on October 19, 1936, into a relatively wealthy family in Jacksonville, Florida. Cole began her college studies at Fisk University, Nashville, Tennessee, at age 15 and completed her undergraduate degree at Oberlin College, Ohio. She earned her MA and, in 1967, her PhD in anthropology from Northwestern University, Chicago.

Cole has taught anthropology, women's studies, and African American studies at Washington State University, the University of California, Hunter College, the University of Massachusetts, and the City University of New York. She has also published widely for both academic and general audiences. Her more popular books include *Conversations: Straight Talk with America's Sister President* (1992) and *Dream the Boldest Dream: And Other Lessons of Life* (1997).

Historic milestone
Cole made educational history in 1987 when she was appointed the seventh president of Spelman College, the first African American woman appointed to the position. Cole was fondly called "Sister President" by her students, and her tenure is remembered for the way in which she raised the profile of this historically black college. In 1996 *Money Magazine* made Spelman the seventh-ranked college of any kind in the United States

In 1992 Cole acted as coordinator for education, labor, and the arts and humanities on President-elect Clinton's transition team. Although it seemed likely that she would be picked for the cabinet, her outspoken opposition to the U.S. embargo on Cuba caused Clinton to change his mind.

After retiring from Spelman College in 1997, Cole taught at Emory University and then became president of Bennett College for Women, Greensboro, North Carolina. She also acted as a diversity adviser for Wall Street companies. In 1998 Bill Clinton appointed her to the Commission on the Celebration of Women in American History. In 1999 Georgia governor Roy Barnes appointed her to his Education Reform Study Commission. In May 2004 Cole became the first African American to serve as chair of the board of the United Way of America. The United Way movement brings communities together to focus on their needs and build partnerships to achieve them. Cole has more than 50 honorary degrees to her name and has received numerous awards. In recognition of her community work, the United Way of Atlanta set up the Johnetta B. Cole Society of Leadership.

Cole has three sons from her first marriage and is married to Arthur Robinson, Jr.

KEY DATES	
1936	Born in Jacksonville, Florida, on October 19
1967	Awarded PhD.
1970	Begins teaching at the University of Massachusetts.
1987	Becomes president of Spelman College.
1990	Wins the American Woman Award from the Women's Research and Education Institute.
1992	Coordinator for President Clinton's transitional team.
1999	Awarded Eleanor Roosevelt Val-Kill Medal; appointed to Education Reform Study Commission.
2001	Awarded Alexis de Tocqueville Award for community service by the United Way of America.
2004	Awarded Joseph Prize for Human Rights by Anti-Defamation League.

See also: Historically Black Colleges and Universities

Further reading: Cole, Johnetta. *Conversations: Straight Talk with America's Sister President*. New York, NY: Random House, 1994.
http://www.wrei.org/about/award_cole.htm.(Biography on Women's Research and Educational Institute site).

COLE, Natalie
Singer

Natalie Maria Cole, daughter of the musical legend Nat King Cole, is an accomplished singer and performer. In her 30-year career she has had a number of songs top the Billboard and pop charts, several gold and platinum albums, and numerous awards, including Grammys and Soul Train and American Music awards.

Cole was born on February 6, 1950, and made her first professional singing appearance at age 10 in a musical beside her father. By age 12 she was lead singer of her own teenage band. Cole's father died when she was 15, a loss that affected her deeply.

From the start Cole's singing career was set to soar. Her debut album, *Inseparable* (1975), went gold and won two Grammys. Her next album, *Natalie* (1976), also went gold, while *Unpredictable* (1977) went platinum.

See also: Cole, Nat King

▼ **Natalie Cole sings at the New Victoria Theatre, London, England, on September 30, 1976.**

Between 1975 and 1978 five of Cole's singles from these albums topped the Billboard rhythm and blues (R&B) charts. She won a second Grammy in 1977.

Following her initial success, Cole's fortunes took a downturn during the early 1980s. Her marriage ended, and she developed a dependency on alcohol and drugs. The albums she released did not sell well. She made a comeback with *Everlasting* (1987) and *Good to Be Back* (1989), singles from which reached the Top 10 of the pop charts. In 1991 she released *Unforgettable, With Love,* a collection of her father's greatest hits, including "Unforgettable," which she sang as a duet with him thanks to digital remastering. The album was a huge success, selling over 10 million copies and winning seven Grammys.

Cole was honored with NAACP Image Awards in 1976, 1977, and 1992, and with the American Music Award in 1978 and 1992. In 1992 she began to develop a TV acting career, appearing in *Lily in Winter* (1994), *Always Outnumbered* (1998), and *Freak City* (1999). In 2000 her autobiography, *Angel on My Shoulder*, was published. In 2002 Cole released the album *Ask a Woman Who Knows*.

See also: Cole, Nat King

Further reading: Cole, Natalie, with Digby Diehl. *Angel on My Shoulder: An Autobiography*. New York, NY: Warner Books, 2000.
http://www.nataliecole.com/ (Cole's official site).

COLE, Nat King
Musician, Actor

From the late 1930s through the 1940s Nat King Cole was the remarkable jazz-swing pianist who led the popular King Cole Trio and "sang a little." In the 1950s and 1960s he became internationally popular for his smooth, velvety voice and romantic hit songs, such as "Unforgettable" and "Mona Lisa."

Early life

Nathaniel Adams Coles was born in Montgomery, Alabama, on March 17, 1919. Some sources give his birth date as 1917. His father, Edward, was a Baptist minister, while his mother, Perlina, was the soprano soloist and director of the choir in her husband's church. When Coles was four, the family moved to Chicago, where he grew up.

From an early age Coles could sing "Yes, We Have No Bananas" while playing the piano. He made his first public performance as a pianist at age four in the Regal Theater in Chicago. His mother, who was his first music teacher, wanted him to become a classical pianist. At age 12, Coles began playing the organ and singing in his father's church. But he was more interested in jazz, which displeased his parents because of its association with nightclubs. By age 14 Coles was playing piano in his own band; a year later he dropped out of high school to concentrate on music full time. Coles was a fan of musicians such as Louis Armstrong and Duke Ellington, but it was jazz pianist Earl "Fatha" Hines (1903–1983) who mainly influenced him.

In 1936 Coles moved to Los Angeles, California, where he formed a group with guitarist Oscar Moore and bassist Wesley Prince, which later became the King Cole Trio. The band reportedly did not need a drummer—which was unusual for jazz bands at the time—because Cole maintained such a consistent rhythm with his piano playing. The trio gradually built up a following on the club circuit at a time when larger bands and singers were more popular. Coles made several important changes, dropping the "s" from his last name and adding the new middle nickname "King," which came from the nursery rhyme "Old King Cole."

Although the trio was mainly an instrumental group, Cole sometimes sang to add variety to the sound. He was an unwilling singer who did not think he had much vocal talent. He continued to think so even after he became famous for his distinctive voice. In a 1954 interview with

▲ *Nat King Cole had a modest opinion of his voice and was surprised by the success of his singing.*

the *Saturday Evening Post* he said: "My voice is nothing to be proud of. It runs maybe two octaves in range. I guess it's the hoarse, breathy noise that some like."

Recording contract

In 1943 the King Cole Trio signed with Capitol Records. By that time Wesley Prince had been drafted into the military and was replaced by Johnny Miller (1915–1988). In 1943 they released "Straighten Up and Fly Right," a song written by Cole and based on one of his father's sermons. It became one of the biggest hits of 1944, selling more than 500,000 copies. It appealed to both black and white audiences, and crossed the barrier between jazz and pop music. The band's success continued with the hits "Get Your Kicks on Route 66" and "For Sentimental Reasons."

The trio had even bigger success with "The Christmas Song," recorded in 1945 but a huge hit in the winter of 1946–1947. It was the trio's first recording with a string section and the first to emphasize Cole as a singer rather than a singing pianist. As he became more of a pop singer, dedicated jazz lovers increasingly condemned him for selling out.

INFLUENCES AND INSPIRATION

Cole is considered to have had one of the 20th century's most distinctive singing voices. He was a pioneer who paved the way for African American performers, especially musicians. In the 1960s and 1970s Cole's daughter Natalie revived interest in his music and became famous by singing his songs. His catalog continues to sell in excess of one million albums every year.

Cole's influence as a vocalist has been far-reaching. He had an impact on artists such as Miles Davis and was a primary influence on the career of Marvin Gaye.

Cole's skill on the piano and his open and fluid style left a legacy for fellow musicians, influencing a generation of artists, such as Art Tatum and more recently the jazz performer Diana Krall (1964–).

Cole prepared the way for the musical style of bebop, which is characterized by songs with a fast tempo and intricate melodies. He influenced pianists in the 1950s such as Oscar Peterson (1925–), Bud Powell (1924–1966), Bill Evans (1929–1980), and Ray Charles, who once said: "I was trying my best to sound like Nat King Cole. I slept Nat King Cole. I ate Nat King Cole. I drank Nat King Cole."

KEY DATES

1919   Born in Montgomery, Alabama, on March 17.

1936   Forms a band with guitarist Oscar Moore and bassist Wesley Prince that later becomes the King Cole Trio.

1950   The ballad "Mona Lisa" reaches No. 1 and sells three million copies.

1956   Becomes the first African American to host his own TV show.

1965   Dies in Santa Monica, California, on February 15.

After the release of the single "Nature Boy" in 1948 the trio broke up, and Cole became a solo artist. In 1949 he released "Mona Lisa," which reached No. 1 on the pop charts. It sold over three million copies, making him the bestselling African American recording artist of his generation. Cole soon became an international star, releasing such hits as "Too Young," "Unforgettable," and "Lazy, Crazy, Hazy Days of Summer." In 1948 he became the first African American jazz musician to have his own radio show.

Mixed response

As a leading African American entertainer during a time of great social upheaval in the United States, Cole did not escape racial prejudice. In 1949 he and his wife bought a house in the white Hancock Park area of Los Angles, but neighbors formed an association to prevent them from moving in. In early 1956 a group of white men physically attacked him on stage in Birmingham, Alabama. Civil rights activists sometimes criticized Cole for not taking a more aggressive stance against racial prejudice, and he was also condemned by some for regularly performing in venues with segregated audiences. Cole sued segregated hotels and challenged segregation when he thought he could win, but as an artist he also felt responsible to all his fans.

In 1956 Cole became the first African American host of a network television series with *The Nat King Cole Show*, which debuted as a 15-minute weekly program on November 5. The show was expanded to a half hour in July 1957. It received good ratings but failed to attract national sponsors and was canceled that December.

Cole also acted in movies and got his biggest role in 1958 playing the part of "father of the blues" W. C. Handy in the film *St. Louis Blues*. His last acting role was in *Night of the Quarter Moon* in 1959.

The final years

In the early 1960s Cole played successful concerts in Latin America, Japan, and Europe, including a Royal Command Performance for Queen Elizabeth II in London, England.

Cole enjoyed over 100 pop chart singles and more than 24 chart albums over a period of 20 years, enough to rank him behind only Frank Sinatra (1915–1998) as the most successful pop singer of his generation.

In 1964 Cole was diagnosed with lung cancer. After unsuccessful treatment, he died on February 15, 1965.

See also: Armstrong, Louis; Charles, Ray; Cole, Natalie; Davis, Miles; Ellington, Duke; Gaye, Marvin; Handy, W. C.; Tatum, Art

Further reading: Epstein, Daniel Mark. *Nat King Cole*. Boston, MA: Northeastern University Press, 2000.
http://www.nat-king-cole.org/ (Biography).

COLE, Rebecca J.
Doctor

Rebecca Cole was the second female African American physician in the United States. The few records that remain of her life reveal that Cole's 50 years of medical practice focused on helping poor and destitute women and their children.

Early life
Cole was born on March 16, 1846. At a time when education for women and African Americans was difficult, she managed to overcome barriers to fulfill her desire to become a physician.

In 1863 Cole completed her secondary education at the Institute for Colored Youth (now Cheyney University), the first coeducational institution for blacks in Philadelphia. She went to the Woman's Medical College (WMC), an institution set up by radical Quaker physicians in 1850 as the Female Medical College of Pennsylvania. Intended to challenge the male-dominated medical field in Pennsylvania, it was the first women's medical college in the world. In 1867 it changed its name to the Woman's Medical College, and from 2002 it became the Drexel College of Medicine. Cole graduated in 1867, becoming the first African American woman to receive a medical degree from the WMC. Her medical thesis was on the eye.

New York Infirmary for Women and Children
Cole's career now benefited from the efforts of a pioneering white doctor. Elizabeth Blackwell (1821–1910) was the first woman to obtain a medical degree in the United States, after having been turned down by 39 medical schools. The faculty of Geneva Medical School, New York, assumed that the all-male student body would never agree to a woman joining their ranks, so put her admission to a vote. The students voted "yes" as a joke, and Blackwell gained admittance: She graduated in 1849. Barred from working in New York City's hospitals, in 1857 Blackwell decided to open her own—the New York Infirmary for Women and Children. She was helped by her younger sister Emily, also a doctor, and Marie Zakrzewska.

Blackwell appointed Cole an assistant physician and sanitary visitor, with the duty of visiting poor households and instructing mothers on hygiene and infant care. In her autobiography Blackwell later stated that Cole had the ideal intelligence and character for such a role, and that she had "carried on this work with tact and care."

KEY DATES

1846	Born in Philadelphia, Pennsylvania, on March 16
1863	Graduates from Institute for Colored Youth.
1867	Graduates with a medical degree from the Woman's Medical College.
1873	Sets up Women's Directory Center in Philadelphia.
1899	Becomes superintendent of the Association for the Relief of Destitute Colored Women and Children.
1922	Dies in Philadelphia on August 14.

Women's Directory Center
Cole later worked for a time in Columbia, South Carolina, before returning to set up an office in South Philadelphia. In 1873 Cole and Charlotte Abbey started the Women's Directory Center to provide medical and legal assistance to destitute women. According to some sources, Cole was also involved in the establishment of the National Association of Colored Women (NACW) in 1896, but this is not certain. In 1899 she was appointed superintendent of the Association for the Relief of Destitute Colored Women and Children in Washington, D.C.

Cole died in Philadelphia on August 14, 1922. The 1899 annual report of the Association for the Relief of Destitute Colored Women and Children declared that she accomplished much with "good sense and vigor... while her cheerful optimism, her determination to see the best in every situation and in every individual, have created around her an atmosphere of sunshine that adds to the happiness and well being of every member of the large family."

Further reading: Galloway-Wright, Brenda. "Cole, Rebecca J. (1846–1922)." Article in Darlene Clark Hine (ed.) *Black Women in America: An Historical Perspective*. New York, NY: Oxford University Press, 2005.
http://www.nlm.nih.gov/changingthefaceofmedicine/physicians/biography_66.html (Educational resource site at the National Library of Medicine).
http://www.aaregistry.com/african_american_history/1453/Rebecca_Cole_pioneering_doctor (African American Registry page on Cole).

COLEMAN, Bessie
Aviator

Bessie Coleman is an important figure in aviation history. She was the first African American woman to become a licensed pilot.

Born in Atlanta, Texas, on January 26, 1892, Coleman was one of 13 children. Her parents, George and Susan Coleman, were poor farmers, or sharecroppers. Her father was part African American and part Cherokee. When Coleman was young, her family moved to Waxahachie, Texas, where her father bought a plot of land in the black section of town, but he found Texas too racist and eventually left the family. Coleman's elder brothers left home soon afterward, leaving their mother to support Coleman and her sisters. Coleman had to look after her sisters while her mother worked as a housekeeper for a local family. Coleman attended the local school, however, and was an enthusiastic reader who liked the works of Booker T. Washington and Paul Laurence Dunbar.

Between 1912 and 1917 Coleman lived in Chicago with two of her brothers, taking beauty classes. Coleman's brother John told her about the women who flew planes in France during World War I (1914–1918). Coleman was fascinated by the idea and decided to become a pilot.

Following a dream

In 1920 Coleman moved to France to study aviation after failing to get a place in a U.S. school. Robert Sengstacke Abbott, founder of the *Chicago Defender* newspaper, and the banker Jesse Binga funded Coleman's training. In 1921 Coleman received her pilot's license, the first awarded to an American woman by the Fédération Aéronautique Internationale (FAI) and the first to an African American woman anywhere.

In 1922 Coleman returned to the United States, appearing just a few months later in her first air show, held at Curtiss Field on Long Island, New York; Abbott and Binga sponsored the show. Coleman later performed in

▲ *Aviator Bessie Coleman, photographed in 1923, near the height of her fame.*

shows in Chicago and Indiana but refused to perform for segregated audiences. David Behncke, founder of the International Airline Pilot Association, became her manager. Coleman was very popular with American audiences; she was widely photographed and asked to advertise products for companies such as the California Coast Firestone Rubber Company.

On April 30, 1926, Coleman's career was cut tragically short when her plane failed to recover from a dive. She was not wearing a parachute and fell to her death. Around 5,000 people attended her memorial service, while the Illinois National Guard served as pall bearers. In 1995 the U.S. Postal Service issued a Bessie Coleman stamp commemorating her achievement as the world's first African American woman pilot.

See also: Abbott, Robert Sengstacke; Dunbar, Paul Lawrence; Washington, Booker T.

Further reading: http://www.bessiecoleman.com (Site dedicated to Coleman; features biography).

KEY DATES	
1892	Born in Atlanta, Texas, on January 26.
1921	Receives pilot's license in France.
1922	Returns to United States and puts on first air show.
1926	Dies in an accident on April 30.

COLEMAN, Ornette
Musician, Composer

Ornette Coleman is a revolutionary saxophonist and the creator of free jazz, a musical style introduced in the late 1950s. He created the concept of "harmolodics," in which musicians improvise together while staying in the flow and direction of their fellow players. Through innovation and creativity Coleman taught and continues to teach the world new ways of listening to music.

Controversial style

Born in Fort Worth, Texas, on March 9, 1930, Coleman received his first saxophone at age 14. Teaching himself to read and play music, he joined local rhythm and blues (R&B) bands before forming his first band in 1945. While living in Los Angeles, California, in the early 1950s, Coleman developed his own style. He managed to enlist musicians to play his compositions, including trumpeter Don Cherry, bassist Charlie Haden, and drummers Ed Blackwell and Billy Higgins. In 1954 Coleman married poet Jayne Cortez. In 1956 they had a son, Denardo, who from age 10 played drums in Coleman's bands.

In 1958 Coleman released his debut album, *Something Else*. The following year he played a legendary residency at the Five Spot Jazz Club in New York City, going on to record the albums *The Shape of Jazz to Come* (1959) and *Free Jazz* (1960). Coleman then began to play the trumpet and violin and composed string quartets and symphonic works. In 1972 his symphonic piece *Skies of America* was recorded on Columbia Records performed by the London Philharmonic Orchestra.

In 1975 Coleman formed his band Prime Time, which combined elements of jazz, funk, R&B, and rock. In 1976 Coleman's interest in African music led him to make the album *Dancing in Your Head*, which featured him playing with Moroccan musicians. Broadening his audiences in the

▲ *Ornette Coleman is shown here playing trumpet, an instrument he played occasionally, in 1987.*

1980s, Coleman collaborated with jazz guitarist Pat Metheny on *Song X* (1985) and rock guitarist Jerry Garcia on *Virgin Beauty* (1987).

Coleman composed and performed throughout the 1990s, including a ballet, *Architecture in Motion*, and soundtracks for the movies *Naked Lunch* (1991) and *Philadelphia* (1993). He has received numerous honors, including the MacArthur Foundation Award (1994) and the American Music Center Letter of Distinction (2004).

See also: Cherry, Don; Cortez, Jayne

Further reading: Wilson, Peter Niklas. *Ornette Coleman: His Life and Music.* Berkeley, CA: Berkeley Hills Books, 1999. www.harmolodic.com (Coleman's personal site).

KEY DATES	
1930	Born in Fort Worth, Texas, on March 9.
1958	Releases debut album, *Something Else.*
1960	Records the album *Free Jazz.*
1975	Forms the band Prime Time.
1994	Receives MacArthur Foundation Award.

COLLINS, Marva
Educator

Through her teaching methods Marva Collins has had a profound effect on disadvantaged children nationwide. Marva Delores Knight was born in Monroeville in the segregated state of Alabama on August 31, 1936. Her family and teachers at the Bethlehem Academy school helped give Knight a good education. She went on to study secretarial sciences at Clark College in Atlanta, Georgia, before teaching secretarial skills and business law at Monroe County Training School.

Successful methods

In 1959 Knight moved to Chicago and married Clarence Collins. They had two children, Patrick and Cynthia. Two years later she began teaching. She was appalled by the public education system, which she believed was failing children, leaving thousands of young African Americans few prospects other than a life of crime or dependence on welfare. Collins responded by implementing her own teaching standards, which included improving traditional reading skills and advanced subjects and materials that children are not usually taught. She also encouraged children to believe in themselves.

Collins's methods were a great success, and in 1975 she established the Daniel Hale Williams Westside Preparatory School on the second floor of her home. By the end of the year her class had expanded from four children, including her own son and daughter, to 20. Collins accepted students rejected by other schools because of their severe behavioral and learning problems; after only a year in her school students usually showed test results five points higher than the national average.

▲ Marva Collins's teaching methods, centered on the development of the individual child, have had an enormous influence on teaching in the United States.

Recognition

In 1979 Westside School was featured on *60 Minutes*, and Collins became the focus of national interest. *Time*, *Newsweek*, *Jet*, and *Black Enterprise* magazines all ran features on her, and in 1981 CBS aired a dramatization of Collins's life, *The Marva Collins Story*, starring Morgan Freeman and Cicely Tyson. Rejecting an offer from President Ronald Reagan in 1981 to become secretary of education, Collins remained in teaching and has helped turn around some of America's worst-performing inner-city schools. Although she has been criticized by educators who believe her methods do not produce lasting effects, hundreds of schools in the United States apply her principles. Collins has received 42 honorary doctorates for her work, and her numerous awards include the Jefferson Award for the Greatest Public Service Benefiting the Disadvantaged and the Lincoln Award of Illinois. She was a director of the Points of Light Foundation, has published several books, and lectures around the world. Her children now run Westside School. In 2004 President George W. Bush awarded Collins the National Humanities Medal.

See also: Freeman, Morgan; Tyson, Cicely

Further reading: Collins, Marva. *Marva Collins' Way*. New York, NY: Jeremy P. Tarcher, 1990.
www.marvacollins.com (Official site).

KEY DATES

1936	Born in Monroeville, Alabama, on August 31.
1961	Begins teaching in Chicago public schools.
1975	Establishes the Daniel Hale Williams Westside Preparatory School to teach underachieving students.
1979	Features in a *60 Minutes* documentary about Westside School and her teaching methods.
1981	CBS broadcasts *The Marva Collins Story*; receives the prestigious Jefferson award.
2004	Receives the National Humanities Medal.

THE COLOR BAR AND PROFESSIONAL SPORTS

During the first half of the 20th century an unwritten color bar meant that African American athletes were forced to endure segregation on the playing field, just as they did in so many other areas of life.

After World War II (1939–1945), as the nation began to make halting progress toward integration (*see box on p. 26*), a talented group of African American athletes, aided by the larger black community and sympathetic whites, broke down the barriers of segregation. By the 1970s the black talent on the field had raised the level of competition and proved that African Americans had always belonged among the sporting elite.

Early years

In the late 19th century professional sports began to gain importance in American life. African Americans played a limited but sometimes significant role in several early professional sports. In horse racing riders such as Isaac Murphy and Jimmy Winkfield were at the pinnacle of the sport; 15 of the first 28 Kentucky Derby winners were ridden by African Americans. On the baseball diamond a few blacks played at the major league level, and in the boxing ring some of the top fighters of the era were black.

As professional sports began to be accepted by mainstream America, however, they also began to incorporate white racist attitudes. In the early 20th century black athletes found that the limited opportunities they had once enjoyed were increasingly closed to them.

A key turning point came in 1910, when black heavyweight champion Jack Johnson defeated the white former champion Jim Jeffries in a highly publicized title bout. White Americans instigated some of the worst race rioting in American history and deepened their resolve to bar blacks from competitive sports.

Baseball

Excluded from mainstream sports, African Americans developed a thriving sports culture of their own. All-black teams had been a part of baseball since the end of the Civil War (1861–1865), but it was not until 1920, under the guidance of Andrew "Rube" Foster, a black former pitching star, that these teams were organized into the Negro National Baseball League.

The Eastern Colored League, eventually renamed the Negro American League, was formed in 1923. Despite financial struggles and several organizational realignments, the Negro Leagues thrived for almost three decades, producing some of the game's most talented players and legendary teams. William "Judy" Johnson, John Henry "Pop" Lloyd, Leroy "Satchel" Paige, Walter F. "Buck" Leonard, Josh Gibson, and James "Cool Papa" Bell all excelled on teams such as the Pittsburgh Crawfords, Kansas City Monarchs, and Homestead Grays. In the 1970s, when racial attitudes had improved, such men and others from the Negro Leagues achieved the recognition denied them in the prime of their playing careers when they were enshrined in baseball's Hall of Fame.

Football

In the first half of the 20th century professional football was not nearly as popular as baseball and, as a result, the color bar was not as strictly enforced. Until 1933 a handful of African Americans were able to play on the white-dominated professional teams of the era. Two of the early game's

---

KEY DATES

1910   Boxer Jack Johnson defeats Jim Jeffries in Reno, Nevada, on July 4; race riots erupt throughout the nation.

1923   Debut of the New York Renaissance basketball team at Harlem's Renaissance Ballroom on November 30.

1947   Jackie Robinson breaks baseball's color barrier on April 15.

1950   Chuck Cooper becomes the first African American player drafted by an NBA team on April 25.

1980   Arthur Ashe is named captain of the U.S. Davis Cup tennis team on September 7.

Members of the famed Harlem Globetrotters pose for the press before leaving on a four-month, 76-game tour of Europe and North Africa in 1951.

1926 by white promoter Abe Saperstein, the Globetrotters started out in Chicago but were soon traveling the country like the Rens. Saperstein added Harlem to the club's name so people would identify them as a black team. They began to use clowning, trick shots, and other antics to keep their games close, entertain the fans, and avoid embarrassing opponents. For stars like Al "Run" Pullins, Reese "Goose" Tatum, and Marques Haynes, playing for the Globetrotters was the best opportunity available before integration came to professional basketball in the 1950s. Their style of basketball proved so popular that the team began to travel the world and remains a popular attraction today.

greatest African American stars, Fritz Pollard and Paul Robeson, played on the NFL's first championship team, the 1920 Akron Pros. Other black stars of early pro football included Henry McDonald, Fred "Duke" Slater, and Joe Lillard.

In 1933 the NFL's owners, led by George Preston Marshall of the Washington Redskins, enforced a "gentlemen's agreement" barring blacks from league rosters. For the next 12 seasons the most talented African Americans in the game were limited to competing on segregated teams and in minor leagues in the western part of the country where black participation was still tolerated.

Basketball

Early professional basketball teams were unwilling to add blacks to their rosters, fearing that doing so would limit paid attendance. As a result, the best African American players were forced to compete on traveling teams that barnstormed the nation. Two of these squads, the New York Renaissance (the Rens) and the Harlem Globetrotters, rank among the most talented teams ever to have played the game.

The Rens, founded in 1923 by Robert Douglas, spent nearly 30 years traveling the country competing against, and usually defeating, the best teams that would play against them. Led by stars Charles "Tarzan" Cooper, Clarence "Fats" Jenkins, and Clarence "Pudgy" Bell, the team went to Chicago in 1939 and won the first ever professional basketball championship of the world, an event open to both white and black teams.

The Globetrotters won the same championship tournament the following year. Founded in

Change

When the color barrier began to crumble in professional sports after World War II, change came first to football, where the participation of African Americans was less controversial than in baseball, which was seen as the national pastime. In 1946 the Los Angeles Rams, bowing to pressure from the city's municipal authorities who controlled their stadium, signed former UCLA standouts Kenny Washington and Woody Strode. That same year the Cleveland Browns of the new All-America Football Conference featured running back Marion Motley and guard Bill Willis, who would later be enshrined in the Pro Football Hall of Fame.

International political events played a significant role in breaking down the color bar in professional sports. During World War II (1939–1945) the United States faced an enemy, Nazi Germany, that explicitly embraced racist doctrines and persecuted those it considered to be of impure racial origin. In opposing the Nazi philosophy, many Americans were forced to make a more honest assessment of their own nation's race relations. Two sports events in the 1930s helped crystallize American feelings. The 1936 Olympic Games were held in Berlin, Germany. When Jesse Owens won four gold medals, he was seen as a hero who had crushed the Nazi belief in white supremacy. Nazi leader Adolf Hitler refused to present medals to African American winners. Owens later recalled, "I wasn't invited to shake hands with Hitler, but I wasn't invited to the White House to shake hands with the President, either."

In 1936 German boxer Max Schmeling defeated Joe Louis in a fight. In 1937 Louis won the heavyweight championship. Before the two men fought for the title on June 22, 1938, President Franklin D. Roosevelt expressed the feelings of the nation when he gripped Louis's arm and said "Joe, we're depending on those muscles for America." When Louis knocked Schmeling out in the first round he became a hero who had defeated the Nazi white hope.

The following year, amid a great deal more controversy, Jackie Robinson integrated Major League Baseball. In the National Basketball Association the color bar fell in 1950, when Chuck Cooper, Earl Lloyd, and Nat Clifton entered the league.

Golf and tennis

Tennis and golf developed as forms of recreation enjoyed by those who could afford memberships to private clubs where the games were usually played. Many black golfers were introduced to the game when working as caddies at country clubs. Using their free time after work to practice and play, some of them became top-flight golfers. Barred from competing in the nation's most prestigious events, the best black players began to compete in tournaments sponsored by the United Golf Association, a black professional tour founded during the 1920s.

In 1947 Bill Spiller and Ted Rhodes became the first African Americans to play in a Professional Golfers Association (PGA) tournament, the Los Angeles Open. The following year a court case in Baltimore declared the segregation of public golf courses illegal. Charles Sifford became the first African American to play in a PGA tournament in the South when he competed in the Greater Greensboro (North Carolina) Open in April 1961. In 1975 Lee Elder broke the color barrier at golf's most prestigious event, the Masters, in Augusta, Georgia.

African Americans were excluded from events sponsored by the United States Lawn Tennis Association (USLTA), but the game was popular at black colleges and in 1916 the American Tennis Association (ATA) was founded to promote competition among the most talented black players. Integration came slowly to tennis and, when it did, it was a woman, Althea Gibson, who broke the color barrier when she successfully applied for entrance to the U.S. Open at Forest Hills in 1950. In 1956 Gibson became the first person of African descent to win the French Open and the following year she won both the Wimbledon and U.S. Open titles.

By the time Arthur Ashe reached adulthood in the early 1960s, the USLTA had opened its doors to African Americans. Ashe became the first black to represent the nation as a member of the Davis Cup team in 1963 and the first African American male to win the U.S. Open in 1968. In 1975 he won Wimbledon, becoming the first African American man to win tennis's most prestigious title.

See also: Ashe, Arthur; Bell, James "Cool Papa"; Elder, Lee; Foster, Andrew "Rube"; Gibson, Althea; Gibson, Josh; Johnson, Jack; Leonard, Buck; Louis, Joe; Motley, Marion; Murphy, Isaac; Owens, Jesse; Paige, Satchel; Pollard, Fritz; Robeson, Paul; Robinson, Jackie; Sifford, Charlie; Strode, Woody; Winkfield, Jimmy

---

Further reading: Porter, David L. *African-American Sports Greats.* Westport, CT: Greenwood Press, 1995. www.liu.edu/cwis/cwp/library/aaitsa.htm (African Americans in sports).

COLTRANE, John
Musician

One of the finest saxophone players and bandleaders of the 20th century, John Coltrane was a central figure in jazz from 1956 until his death in 1967. His expressive, intensely emotional music was different from traditional jazz and gave a new, unrestrained role to improvisation. Even in the early 21st century, his style of playing the tenor saxophone is dominant in jazz.

Early life

John William Coltrane was born in Hamlet, North Carolina, on September 23, 1926, but his family soon moved to High Point in the north of the state. His parents were passionate about music: His father, the tailor John Robert Coltrane, played the violin and ukulele, while his mother, Alice Blair Coltrane, sang and played piano in the local church. Religion played an important role in family life and was influential in shaping Coltrane's music and career.

Coltrane learned to play alto horn and clarinet in High Point's community band but later took up the saxophone after joining his high school ensemble. In 1939 Coltrane's father died, and his mother moved to Philadelphia to find work. Coltrane followed her after graduating from high school in 1942 and quickly became involved in Philadelphia's vibrant jazz scene, playing gigs and studying under local musicians. During a brief stint in the Navy (1945–1946) Coltrane played for a military band in Hawaii.

Apprenticeship and renewal

In the 1940s and early 1950s Coltrane was influenced by and took advice from the many musicians he met. He worked with some of the greatest jazz artists of the time, performing and recording with groups led by Dizzy Gillespie, Earl Bostic (1913–1965), and Johnny Hodges.

Coltrane had an insatiable appetite for learning and was curious about all kinds of music. In 1951 he underwent a period of intensive study at Granoff Studios in Philadelphia, perfecting his technique on the saxophone and immersing himself in musical theory and in the works of avant-garde concert composers such as the German-born American Paul Hindemith (1895–1963). Throughout his life Coltrane learned new instruments, including the soprano saxophone, flute, and clarinet.

Coltrane's commitment to his music and career put him under immense pressure, and to cope he drank heavily and took drugs. By 1948 he was suffering from chronic heroin addiction, which took a heavy toll on his health and professional life. In 1955 Coltrane married Juanita Naima Grubb, who helped him beat his addiction and eventually recover. They settled in New York City, at the time the center of the avant-garde jazz scene in the United States.

Ambition

That same year Coltrane joined the Miles Davis group, where his intense playing was recognized as the leading edge of jazz. He contributed to some of the greatest jazz albums, including *Kind of Blue* (1959), before leaving Davis in 1960.

Coltrane went on to form his own quartet, comprising Alfred McCoy Tyner (1938–) on piano, Elvin Jones (1927–2004) on drums, and Jimmy Garrison (1933–1976)

▼ *Legendary saxophonist John Coltrane, pictured here in 1962, was heavily influenced by the religious music that he listened to and played as a child.*

COLTRANE, John

INFLUENCES AND INSPIRATION

Throughout his career Coltrane was open to the influence of his fellow musicians, absorbing their ideas and innovations to create his own original sound. His career brought him into contact with some of the finest musicians of the 20th century, such as Miles Davis and the Indian sitar player and composer Ravi Shankar (1920–). Coltrane enjoyed a particularly close and fruitful relationship with the jazz pianist Thelonious Monk, who was also born and grew up in North Carolina.

During the 1940s Monk's playful, inventive style, featuring unusual harmonies and rhythms, influenced many younger musicians, including Coltrane, but his inspirational, freewheeling approach became especially crucial for Coltrane in 1957, when the two musicians performed together at the Five Spot Cafe in New York City. The exciting, groundbreaking collaboration was a high point in Coltrane's career and marked the beginning of his most fruitful work.

While the two friends hardly ever recorded together because they were on different music labels, they frequently discussed their ideas. One of their last conversations took place at Monk's Manhattan apartment in April 1967, a few months before Coltrane's death. At the time Coltrane was experimenting with new possibilities in his music.

on bass. He himself played not only tenor but also soprano saxophone, an instrument he brought into the jazz mainstream. With the quartet—considered by many critics to be the greatest jazz ensemble of all time—Coltrane was able to explore his musical ideas and create his most adventurous and groundbreaking work.

The John Coltrane quartet recorded numerous albums. In *A Love Supreme* (1964) Coltrane hoped to reflect through music his own spiritual awakening after recovering from his addiction to heroin. Instead, he had begun to use LSD; its influence was reflected in his 1965 album, *Ascension*, where he broke free from the conventions of jazz music, exploring simultaneous contrasting rhythms called polyrhythms and "stacked" chords. Coltrane's free style and the freedom he allowed his band members was even more apparent in the quartet's live performances, many of which survive in tape recordings. In signature pieces like "Favorite Things" (1960) the quartet's improvised solos are notable for their freedom of expression.

For listeners of the time the strange, wild cries that Coltrane created with his saxophone were something totally new. Because of its free form and disregard for conventional jazz harmonies and rhythms, some critics dubbed Coltrane's music "antijazz"; for his admirers it was simply the next step forward for jazz.

New direction
By 1966 Coltrane's uninhibited and restless search for new directions in his music had led to the departure of two of his band members, Tyner and Jones. The group was joined instead by the drummer Rashied Ali (1935–) and the pianist

KEY DATES

1926	Born in Hamlet, North Carolina, on September 23.
1942	Moves to Philadelphia, Pennsylvania.
1951	Studies at Granoff Studios in Philadelphia.
1955	Marries Juanita Naima Grubb; joins Miles Davis group.
1960	Leaves Miles Davis; forms first quartet.
1964	Records the album *A Love Supreme*.
1965	Records the album *Ascension*.
1967	Dies in Huntington, New York, on July 17.

Alice McLeod (1937–), whom Coltrane met in 1960. In 1963 Coltrane had left Juanita for McLeod, whom he married in 1966. They had three sons, John Coltrane, Jr., Ravi, and Oran.

The new ensemble did not have much chance to play, however. In the summer of 1967 Coltrane became sick. He died of liver cancer in New York on July 17, 1967, at age 40.

See also: Davis, Miles; Gillespie, Dizzy; Hodges, Johnny; Monk, Thelonious

Further reading: Fraim, John. *Spirit Catcher: The Life and Art of John Coltrane.* West Liberty, OH: Great House Co., 1996.
www.galegroup.com/free_resources/bhm/bio/coltrane_j.htm (Biography).
http://www.johncoltrane.com (Official site).

COMBS, Sean

Entrepreneur, Musician, Rapper,

One of the biggest hip-hop producers, songwriters, and entertainers of the mid- to late 1990s, Sean Combs—also known as Sean "Puffy" Combs, Puff Daddy, P. Diddy, and Diddy—built up a multimillion-dollar industry centered on his urban entertainment company, Bad Boy Worldwide Entertainment Group, and its flagship company, Bad Boy Records. Although his own music has won awards, Combs has been criticized for relying on samples from other records. Combs often appears in the news—more for his involvement in violence and legal controversy than for his talent.

Born in Harlem, New York, on November 4, 1969, Sean John Combs was three years old when his father, Melvin, was shot dead in the street. He continued to live with his

▼ *Hip-hop star P. Diddy (Sean Combs) speaks at a protest in New York City in 2002 against proposed budget cuts for education.*

mother, Janice, but spent much of his childhood in the middle-class suburb of Mount Vernon, New York. After attending a private school, Combs went to Howard University, Washington, D.C., but dropped out after convincing childhood friend and rapper Heavy D. to hire him as an intern for Uptown Records, the label for which Heavy D. recorded. At age 19 Combs became an artist and repertoire (A&R) executive, and in the following years he produced successful albums such as *Father's Day* (1990) for Father MC and *What's the 411?* (1992) for Mary J. Blige.

In 1993 Combs was dismissed from Uptown Records (*see box on p. 30*) and set up his own label, Bad Boy Records. He signed a string of artists such as Craig Mack, friend and former drug dealer Biggie Smalls (also known as the Notorious B.I.G.), Faith Evans, and the girl group Total. The label soon earned enough hits to secure a deal to distribute its releases with Arista Records. Widely known by now as Puff Daddy, Combs also turned his hand to producing such musicians as the girl group TLC, Mariah Carey, and Aretha Franklin.

Controversial rivalry

As Bad Boy Records became more successful, it developed a rivalry with Death Row Records, based in California. Combs and Smalls formed an alliance against Death Row head Suge Knight and one of its stars, Tupac Shakur. When Shakur was shot and wounded in 1994, Combs and his

KEY DATES	
1969	Born in Harlem, New York City, on November 4.
1993	Sets up Bad Boy Records.
1994	Highly publicized dispute breaks out between Bad Boy Records and Death Row Records, and ends in the deaths of Tupac Shakur and the Notorious B.I.G.
1997	Singles "Can't Nobody Hold Me Down" and "I'll Be Missing You" mark beginning of Combs's own music career.
1998	First album, *No Way Out*, wins Grammy for Best Rap Album.
1999	Arrested for weapons violations after he was present at a shooting in a New York nightclub.
2004	Wins the Council of Fashion Designers in America (CFDA) menswear designer of the year.

entourage were the main suspects. The two sides traded insults in interviews and songs over the next two years, but the feud finally escalated out of control. Shakur was killed in a drive-by shooting in 1996, and Smalls was shot dead while out with Combs six months later in March 1997. Both murders remain unsolved.

Although he lost a friend, Combs was successful during this period. His own music career took off with the singles "Can't Nobody Hold Me Down" and a tribute to Smalls "I'll Be Missing You," which sampled "Every Breath You Take" by the Police. The tribute song earned $3 million, which Combs donated to Smalls's family. In 1998 Combs released his first album, *No Way Out*, which featured artists on his label and went on to win a Grammy for Best Rap Album.

Mixed fortunes

In the late 1990s Combs had mixed fortunes. In 1997 he diversified his business by opening the first in a chain of restaurants called Justin's, named for his oldest son. In 1998 he established his own line of urban clothing, Sean John. The label was nominated for the Council of Fashion Designers of America (CFDA) award for menswear designer of the year four times in a row, winning the prestigious accolade in 2004. However, Combs has been criticized because the Honduras-based factories in which the clothes are manufactured are reported to violate local labor laws.

Combs's 1999 album *Forever* was a failure. He was also involved frequently in violent incidents. In April 1999 Combs was accused of assaulting Steve Stoute, vice president of Interscope Records. Later that year Combs and his then girlfriend Jennifer Lopez were present at a shooting at Club New York, a Manhattan nightclub. They were questioned by police, and in a subsequent investigation Combs was arrested for weapons violations. Matters were further complicated when it emerged that Combs tried to bribe his driver to take the blame.

Although Combs was later acquitted of all charges, Lopez ended their relationship. Combs became involved in several lawsuits and was the subject of daily tabloid attacks. Combs attempted to clean up his image: He changed his name to P. Diddy, released two albums (*Thank You* and *The Saga Continues*) in 2001, and collaborated with more mainstream artists such as David Bowie. The damage was already done, however, and Arista Records canceled its distribution deal with Bad Boy Records.

Branching out

In later years Combs pursued a career in acting, playing a role in the film *Monster's Ball* (2001) and appearing as Walter Lee Younger in the 2004 Broadway revival of *A Raisin in the Sun*. In 2002 Combs made his own reality show for MTV, *Making the Band 2*, in which contestants competed to become a new group on Bad Boy Records. Combs's company has branched out to include such diversified interests as music publishing, television and film production, clothing, and restaurants. In 2003 the company's sales approached $300 million, with Bad Boy Records—which agreed on a 50–50 joint venture with the Warner Music Group in 2005—accounting for a third of the revenue.

Combs was named 12th in *Fortune* magazine's "Richest People under 40" in 2002 and remains one of the most entrepreneurial talents in the music industry.

See also: Franklin, Aretha; Harrell, Andre; Knight, Suge; Notorious B.I.G.; Shakur, Tupac

Further reading: Bowman, Elizabeth Atkins. *Sean "Puffy" Combs (Black Americans of Achievement).* New York, NY: Chelsea House Publications, 2003.
www.p-diddy.com/pd/index.html (Official site for P. Diddy and Bad Boy Records).

CONE, James H.
Minister, Theologian

James Hal Cone was the first theologian to articulate and popularize "black theology." He is the author of over 100 articles and several books. Since 1977 he has been a professor at Union Theological Seminary, where he teaches 20th-century Christianity and liberation theology.

Early life

Cone was born in 1938 in Arkansas and raised in the segregated South. He graduated in 1958 from Philander Smith College, a historically black liberal arts school in Little Rock, Arkansas. He received his bachelor of divinity from Garrett Theological Seminary in 1961 and his MA and PhD from Northwestern University in 1963 and 1965 respectively.

Cone was ordained a minister in the African Methodist Episcopal Church. In 1977 he was named the Charles A. Briggs Distinguished Professor of Systematic Theology at Union Theological Seminary in New York City.

Liberation theology

Theology is the study of religious faith and practice. Cone is considered by many to be the father of the contemporary black theology movement. It began in the late 1960s as a response to what many African Americans believed was the failing civil rights movement led by Martin Luther King, Jr.

Militant civil rights leaders, such as Stokely Carmichael, Malcolm X, and Elijah Muhammad, had become critical of the nonviolent approach advocated by King and others. They argued that American Christianity served an oppressive white society that was determined to keep black Americans socially and economically subservient. These younger leaders championed the phrase "black power" and called for African Americans to achieve equality by any means necessary, violent or nonviolent.

Many black Americans were losing faith in the black churches, which they thought catered too much to the "white man's religion." In order to make Christianity relevant to an emerging generation of African Americans, Cone and other black theologians developed a system of beliefs that emphasized liberation and black power instead of integration and nonviolence.

In his two most influential books, *Black Theology and Black Power* (1969) and *A Black Theology of Liberation* (1970), Cone argued "that Christianity is essentially a religion of liberation" for the poor and oppressed in any society. In the American context that meant black people. African Americans, Cone maintained, had to "liberate themselves from white oppressors" by taking control of the social, political, and economic institutions in society and making them responsive to the needs of poor blacks. Cone believed that it was futile to wait for the nonviolent civil rights protests to shame white Americans into giving blacks equality. Instead, he developed a Christian theology that allowed African Americans to take the initiative in creating a society that responded to their needs.

Cone continued to champion liberation theology into the 21st century, working on behalf of other oppressed groups in North America, Latin America, and Africa. He was especially critical of mainline African American churches for their oppression of black women, and he actively supported the women who in the 1970s developed a black feminist theology called Womanism.

Honors

Cone has received many awards and honors, including the American Black Achievement Award in the category of Religion from *Ebony* magazine (1992), the Theological Scholarship and Research Award from the association of Theological Schools (1994), and the Fund for Theological Education Award from the American Academy of Religion/Society of Biblical Literature for contributions to theological education (1999).

KEY DATES	
1938	Born in Fordyce, Arkansas, on August 5.
1969	Publishes *Black Theology and Black Power*.
1970	Publishes *Black Theology of Liberation*; joins the faculty at Union Theological Seminary.
1977	Named Charles A. Briggs Distinguished Professor of Systematic Theology.

See also: Carmichael, Stokely; King, Martin Luther, Jr.; Malcolm X; Muhammad, Elijah; Religion and African Americans

Further reading: Cone, James H. *Black Theology and Black Power*. Maryknoll, NY: Orbis Books, 1997.
http://www.uts.columbia.edu/index.php?id=315 (Cone's page at Union Theological Seminary).

CONNERLY, Ward
Activist

Ward Connerly is a controversial opponent of affirmative action—the attempt to counteract prejudice against women and racial minorities by giving them preferential treatment in educational institutions and the workplace. Connerley argues that making a special case of previously oppressed groups is insulting to them and is thus another form of prejudice—slavery by a different name. He believes that racial quotas are reverse discrimination against whites.

Born in Louisiana in 1939, Connerley was raised by relatives, first in Washington and then in California after his father left home and his mother died when he was just a small boy. In 1959, while a student of political science at Sacramento State College, Connerley organized a protest against housing discrimination and was invited to testify during debates on a fair-housing bill, which was later passed. He graduated from Sacramento in 1962.

While working as a civil servant for state housing agencies (1962–1969), Connerly became friendly with rising Republican politician Pete Wilson. Connerly was later chief consultant to the California State Assembly Committee on Urban Affairs (1969–1970). From 1971 to 1973 he was deputy director of California's Department of Housing and Urban Development. In 1973 he founded Connerly & Associates, a housing and association management consultancy firm.

After a long period out of the public eye Connerly reemerged in 1993 when Wilson—now state governor—appointed him to the University of California Board of Regents. In 1995 Connerly became chair of the California Civil Rights Initiative (CCRI), a group of academics who were trying to stop affirmative action in education on grounds of race. Guided by Connerly in 1996, the CCRI persuaded the board to adopt its proposals.

Connerly then worked to end all affirmative action in California. Despite opposition from both the American Civil Liberties Union (ACLU) and the Clinton administration, preferential treatment based on race, gender, or national origin was made illegal in the state in 1997. That same year Connerly founded the American Civil Rights Initiative (ACRI) to spread his beliefs to other states. When he supported the University of California's proposal to offer health benefits to the partners of gay employees, people said that this contradicted his views on affirmative action. He maintained that it was consistent with his view that government should not infringe on personal liberties.

▼ *Ward Connerly at a briefing on Proposition 54, which called for a ban on official collection of information about race; it failed in 2003.*

KEY DATES	
1939	Born in Leesville, Louisiana, on June 15.
1962	Graduates from Sacramento State College, California.
1993	Appointed to University of California Board of Regents.
1996	Helps persuade California to end affirmative action.
1997	Founds American Civil Rights Initiative (ACRI).

See also: Affirmative Action

Further reading: Connerly, Ward. *Creating Equal: My Fight against Race Preferences*. San Francisco, CA: Encounter Books, 2000.
http://www.acri.org/people (American Civil Rights Institute site).

CONYERS, John, Jr.
Politician

John Conyers, Jr., has represented Michigan's 14th District as a Democrat since 1964. The *National Journal* has described him as one of the most liberal congressmen at the start of the 21st century.

Road to politics

Born in Detroit, Michigan, on May 16, 1929, Conyers attended Sampson Elementary School on the West Side, a public school for the wealthier families of the area. He studied at Wayne State University, Detroit, graduating with a BA in 1957 and a law degree in 1958.

After serving for a year with the Army Corps of Engineers in Korea, for which he received a citation, Conyers went to work as Senator John Dingell's assistant. In 1964, however, Conyers was elected to Congress. In 2005 he was the second most senior member in the House of Representatives and the longest-serving African American politician in the House's history.

Concerns

Conyers has always campaigned for equal rights and social justice. In 1969 he helped in the formation of the Congressional Black Caucus, which aimed to strengthen the ability of African American lawmakers to address the concerns of black and minority citizens.

Conyers is also the ranking member of the House Committee on the Judiciary, which in addition to overseeing the Department of Justice (including the FBI) and the federal courts, has jurisdiction over copyright, constitutional, consumer protection, and civil rights issues.

▲ **John Conyers, Jr., photographed in 1964 during his first electoral campaign. He has since been elected a further 18 times, in 2002 with 93 percent of the vote.**

In 1971 Conyers appeared in the top 20 on President Richard Nixon's "Enemies List," which featured about 600 people whom the Nixon administration considered to be its major political opponents. Conyers subsequently helped impeach Richard Nixon in 1974 and later was the only member of the House Committee on the Judiciary to have sat on both President Bill Clinton's 1999 impeachment and Nixon's.

Conyers sponsored several key acts, including the Alcohol Warning Label Act of 1988, the Violence against Women Act (VAWA), enacted in 1994 and reauthorized in 2001, and the Help America Vote Act of 2002. He was the primary instigator of the End Racial Profiling Act, legislation aimed at banning of racial profiling nationwide. Conyers also featured in Michael Moore's controversial film *Fahrenheit 9/11*, in which he discussed the aftermath of the Al Qaeda terrorist attacks carried out against America on September 11, 2001.

KEY DATES

1929	Born in Detroit, Michigan, on May 16.
1964	Elected to the House of Representatives.
1969	Helps form the Congressional Black Caucus.
1974	Sits on the Watergate impeachment panel.
1994	Introduces the successful Violence against Women Act (VAWA).
1999	Panel member for Bill Clinton's impeachment hearings.
2005	Campaigns for electoral reform.

Further reading: www.johnconyers.com (John Conyers, Jr.'s, official site).

COOKE, Sam
Musician

Songwriter and performer Sam Cooke was one of the most popular and influential African American singers to emerge in the late 1950s. According to *Rolling Stone* magazine, "Cooke invented soul music." His pure, clear vocals and suave, sophisticated image had wide cross-over appeal as Cooke scored a string of hit singles on both the rhythm and blues (R&B) and pop charts. Cooke's combination of gospel, R&B, and pop created a model that thousands of singers sought to copy.

Born in Clarksdale, Mississippi, on January 22, 1931, Samuel Cook (the "e" was added later) was one of the eight children (five sons and three daughters) of Reverend Charles and Annie Mae Cook. In 1933 the Cook family moved from the rural South to the northern city of Chicago, Illinois, in search of a better life. As a teenager Cooke was interested in music and sang gospel music with his brothers Charles and L. C. and sisters Hattie and Agnes in the Singing Children, after which he joined the nationally renowned gospel group the Highway QCs.

Crossing-over from gospel

Aged 19 Cooke hit the big time when he became the lead vocalist with the most popular gospel group of the day, the Soul Stirrers (*see box*). Cooke's smooth voice and good looks soon made him one of the best-known and most popular singers on the gospel circuit. Some music critics argue that Cooke's heyday as a singer was when he was performing gospel. The Soul Stirrers recorded with Aladdin Records and then were taken up by Specialty Records, which had originally been founded as an independent blues label by Art Rupe. The Soul Stirrers had hits with "Nearer to Thee" (1955), "Touch the Hem of His Garment" (1956), and "Jesus, Wash away My Troubles" (1956), among others. Cooke came under increasing pressure from Specialty to cross over into popular music. In 1956 he

▼ *Legendary musician Sam Cooke (right) produced his good friend boxer Muhammad Ali's 1963 recording of the "The Gang's All Here."*

INFLUENCES AND INSPIRATION

Sam Cooke's influence on modern pop music has been far-reaching. Musicians ranging from Rod Stewart, Al Green, and Michael Jackson to Smokey Robinson, Marvin Gaye, and Aretha Franklin have cited Cooke as key to their development as musicians.

Cooke himself was deeply inspired by gospel music. In particular the band the Soul Stirrers, with whom Cooke sang, had a tremendous impact on his career. The Soul Stirrers originally formed in the 1930s in Texas; the lineup included Rebert Harris, Jessie Farley, S. R. Crain, and T. L. Brewster. The band revolutionized gospel music; they used two lead singers, one crooning, the other shouting hoarse and low, a model later used by other gospel bands.

When Harris left the band in 1950, Cooke replaced him. Although Cooke initially based his style on Harris's, he gradually developed his own very distinctive way of singing that made him a gospel superstar. Cooke always remained grateful to the Soul Stirrers; he continued to write songs for them and recorded them on his label SAR.

released a pop song called "Lovable," singing under the name of Dale Cook so as not to alienate the gospel audience, but his voice was very recognizable.

Although "Lovable" sold about 25,000 copies, the costs for Cooke in the short term were huge—not only did he lose many of his gospel fans, but he was also released by the Soul Stirrers. Specialty Records gave Cooke's contract to Bumps Blackwell, the company's A&R (artist and repertoire) man, in lieu of payment that he was owed. He immediately signed Cooke to Bob Keane's new label Keen Records.

A phenomenal career

In 1957 Cooke released "You Send Me," which went to No. 1 on both the pop and R&B charts and sold 1.7 million copies. He signed with the William Morris Agency and hired Jess Rand as his manager, replacing Blackwell. Cooke's slick and sophisticated style made him popular with audiences, and he appeared on TV shows such as the *Ed Sullivan Show*. Such was his success that between 1957 and 1965 Cooke recorded 28 Top-40 pop hits and 30

Top-40 R&B hits, including "Chain Gang," "Only Sixteen," "Wonderful World," "Cupid," and "Twistin' the Night Away." Most of his hits were love songs with a rolling, medium tempo. By 1960 Cooke had begun to go back to his gospel roots and to the blues for his inspiration.

Cooke was also a good businessman: In 1959 he set up Kags Music (now ABKCO Records) with Roy Crains; later that year he established SAR Records (also ABKCO) with Crain and J. W. Alexander. Kags controlled all of Cooke's more than 150 compositions and also those recorded by SAR artists. In 1963 Cooke negotiated a special deal with RCA, which gave him a huge advance of $500,000 over three years and established his complete control over his own music—no mean feat for an African American star at this time. In the same year, however, Cooke experienced great personal tragedy when his 18-month-old son drowned in the family's backyard swimming pool. Further tragedy followed: On the night of December 11, 1964, Cooke was shot and killed by a Los Angeles motel manager, who claimed that she acted in self-defense after Cooke sexually assaulted a young woman. Almost 40 years later there are still questions about what happened that night. Almost 200,000 fans turned up for Cooke's memorial service, where Lou Rawls and Ray Charles performed. Cooke remains one of the influential figures in postwar popular music.

See also: Ali, Muhammad; Franklin, Aretha; Gaye, Marvin; Jackson, Michael; Robinson, Smokey

Further reading: Wolff, Daniel, with G. David Tenenbaum, Clifton White, and S. R. Crain. *You Send Me: The Life and Times of Sam Cooke.* New York, NY: Quill, 1996. http://www.samcooke.com/index.html (A comprehensive site on the artist, including a biography and discography).

KEY DATES

1931	Born in Clarksdale, Mississippi, on January 22.
1951	Becomes lead vocalist of the gospel group the Soul Stirrers.
1957	"You Send Me" reaches No. 1 on the pop singles chart.
1959	Sets up Kags Music and SAR Records.
1964	Shot and killed in Los Angeles on December 11.
1986	Inducted into the Rock and Roll Hall of Fame.

COOPER, Anna J.
Educator

Calling herself the "Black Woman of the South," Anna Julia Cooper championed the education of African American women as the salvation of African Americans from the curse of racism. She worked tirelessly throughout her life to educate and inform.

Early life

Cooper was probably born on August 10, 1858, although some biographies give the year as 1859, in Raleigh, North Carolina. She was the daughter of a slave. Her father was unknown and is thought to have been her mother's master. At the St. Augustine's Normal School and Collegiate Institute she became a teacher at age nine because of the lack of other African American teachers. Following her graduation in 1877, she married the Reverend George C. Cooper, another former student-teacher at her school. Since married women were not allowed to teach, Cooper had to give up her job. However, her husband died two years later.

Publication and teaching career

Cooper gained her BA (1884) and MA (1887) from Oberlin College, Ohio, a white college that allowed African Americans to attend. In 1892 she published *A Voice from the South by a Black Woman of the South*, a series of essays on feminism and race in which she argued that ability rather than race was the key to further education. Realizing that the South was becomingly increasingly segregated, she decided to devote the rest of her life to helping African Americans improve their chances in life by getting higher education.

In 1887 Cooper started as a teacher at the leading African American preparatory school in Washington, D.C., the M. Street Colored High School. In 1901 she became its principal. In 1906 she was forced to resign over a disagreement about the direction of the school. She insisted on preparing pupils for college, which upset many prominent Washingtonians. However, she returned as a teacher four years later and remained until she retired in 1930. The shock of being forced out convinced Cooper that she should study for a doctorate. While teaching Latin at M. Street, Cooper completed courses for her PhD in her spare time over the next few decades. In 1925, at age 65, she was awarded her doctorate from the Sorbonne, Paris, France, having written her thesis in French.

KEY DATES	
1858	Believed to have been born on August 10 in Raleigh, North Carolina.
1887	Awarded an MA from Oberlin College, Ohio.
1892	Publishes book of essays *A Voice from the South by a Black Woman of the South.*
1906	Dismissed as principal of M Street Colored High School.
1910	Returns to M Street.
1925	Receives a PhD from the Sorbonne, Paris.
1930	Retires from M Street; starts working at Frelinghuysen University.
1939	Death of her niece, Anna Cooper Haywood Beckwith.
1964	Dies in Washington, D.C., on February 27.

Retirement years

Following her retirement in 1930, Cooper devoted herself to the education of working adults; she became the second president of Frelinghuysen University, Washington, D.C., which had been founded in 1907 for working black Americans and was a forerunner of community colleges. Cooper spent the next decade working there and retired as its president in 1942. She was also active in a number of African American organizations, including the National Association for the Advancement of Colored People (NAACP). She was a founding member of the Colored Social Settlement in Washington, D.C.

With no children of her own, Cooper had adopted the five young orphaned children of her half-brother in 1915. Following the death of her beloved niece Anna, Cooper withdrew from public life in 1939, although she continued to write. She died at her home in Washington, D.C., on February 27, 1964, aged 105.

Further reading: Cooper, Anna J. *A Voice from the South by a Black Woman of the South.* New York, NY: Oxford University Press, 1988.
http://www.gwu.edu/~e73afram/be-nk-gbe.html (George Washington University page on Cooper).

COOPER, J. California
Writer

After nearly 20 years of writing plays that were well received by critics but failed to make a major impact, J. California Cooper turned to short stories and novels, and soon became recognized as one of the United States's premier storytellers.

Cooper is famously reclusive and releases only the sketchiest details about her background and current circumstances. She is particularly reticent about her date of birth, telling interviewers: "A woman who tells her age will tell anything." Cooper lives and works in California.

A writing career

Joan California Cooper began her writing career as a playwright and wrote 17 plays. In 1978 she was named Black Playwright of the Year for her play *Strangers*. The award brought her to the attention of poet and novelist Alice Walker, who encouraged her to try her hand at fiction. The result was *A Piece of Mine*, a book of short stories published in 1984. This was followed by *Homemade Love*, another collection of short stories, which won the 1986

▼ **J. California Cooper refuses to discuss details of her private life and will only talk about her writing.**

American Book Award (ABA). In 1988 Cooper received the James Baldwin Writing Award and the Literary Lion Award from the American Library Association. In 1991 she published her first novel, *Family*, a portrait of slavery seen through the eyes of the ghostlike narrator, Clora, during the Civil War. It sold half a million copies and established the author as one of the outstanding new voices in late-20th-century American fiction.

In the same year Cooper published another collection of short stories, *The Matter Is Life*, before returning to the novel with *In Search of Satisfaction* (1994). This was followed by *Some Love, Some Pain, Some Time* (stories;1995), *Wake of the Wind* (novel; 1998), *Future Has a Past* (stories; 2000), and *Some People, Some Other Place* (novel; 2004).

Cooper's short stories are not parables, but they have a clear moral purpose and explore universal themes, notably the struggles between good and evil, charity and greed, and hope and despair. Her novels are about families, a theme she says she chose "because everybody has one—either the one you were born into or one you find on your own." Her style has been summarized by Alice Walker as "deceptively simple and direct, and the vale of tears in which her characters reside is never so deep that a rich chuckle at a foolish person's foolishness cannot be heard."

KEY DATES	
1940s	Born in California at about this time.
1978	Named Black Playwright of the Year.
1984	Publishes *A Piece of Mine* (short stories).
1986	Publishes *Homemade Love* (short stories).
1991	Publishes *Family* (novel).
2004	Publishes *Some People, Some Other Place* (novel).

See also: Walker, Alice

Further reading: Carroll, Rebecca. *I Know What the Red Clay Looks Like: The Voice and Vision of Black Women Writers.* New York, NY: Clarkson Potter, 1994.
authors.aalbc.com/j.htm (African American Literature Book Club page on Cooper).

COPPIN, Frances Jackson
Educator

Frances "Fanny" Jackson Coppin was born a slave but rose to become one of the eminent leaders of African American education in the 19th century.

Coppin was born Frances Marion Jackson on March 23, 1837, to a slave mother and a white father. Some records give her birth date as 1835. She was freed at age 12, when her aunt Sarah bought her for $125.

At age 14 Coppin started working as domestic help in the house of author George Calvert. The value of education impressed her so much that from her meager salary, she paid to have private tutoring. She was admitted to the Rhode Island Normal School in 1859 and there discovered a love of teaching. In 1860 she joined Oberlin College, Ohio.

Coppin had a remarkable career at Oberlin, where she studied Greek, Latin, and mathematics, subjects that were generally considered suitable only for male students. Coppin became the first African American student tutor at the college. Oberlin had been concerned that white students might object to a black teacher, but Coppin's class became so popular that it had to be divided into two. She also started free evening classes for freed blacks.

The Institute of Colored Youth

When Coppin graduated from Oberlin with a BA in 1865, she was appointed principal of the Ladies Department of the Institute of Colored Youth (ICY) in Philadelphia, Pennsylvania. Within four years she became principal of the entire school; she worked there for 37 years.

Coppin recognized a need for educational institutions that taught industrial skills to blacks. By 1879 she had

▲ *Fannie Jackson Coppin played a key role in advancing education for African Americans.*

raised enough funds to begin an industrial department where skills such as carpentry, typing, cooking, dressmaking, and printing were taught.

A lasting influence

Coppin was a founding member and later vice president of the National Association for Colored Women (NACW). She married Reverend Levi Jackson in 1881 and in 1902 accompanied him to South Africa as a missionary. They returned to the United States in 1904 and settled in Philadelphia. Coppin had almost finished her autobiography when she died at home in 1913. Such was her popularity that thousands of people came to Coppin's funeral. Her autobiography, *Reminiscences of School Life and Hints on Teaching,* was published later that year.

Further reading: Perkins, Linda M. *Fanny Jackson Coppin and the Institute for Colored Youth, 1865–1902.* New York, NY: Garland Publishing, Inc., 1987.
http://docsouth.unc.edu/jacksonc/jackson.html (E-print of Coppin's autobiography).

KEY DATES	
1837	Born on March 23.
1865	Obtains BA; appointed principal of ICY Ladies Department.
1869	Appointed principal of ICY.
1881	Marries Reverend Levi Jackson.
1896	Founding member of the NACW.
1902	Leaves for South Africa.
1913	Dies in Philadelphia.

CORNISH, Samuel
Minister, Abolitionist

Samuel Cornish was an early Presbyterian minister and a prominent abolitionist. He was also an influential newspaper editor, cofounding *Freedom's Journal*, the first black newspaper.

Early life

Samuel Eli Cornish was born in Sussex County, Delaware, in 1795, the son of free parents. In 1815 he and his family moved to Philadelphia, Pennsylvania, and it was there that the young Cornish began his journey into the Presbyterian ministry. Trained by the founder of the first black Presbyterian Church, John Gloucester, Cornish became a licensed preacher in 1819. After a year in Maryland Cornish moved to New York City, where he was ordained a minister in 1822, leading the New Demeter Presbyterian Church.

Cornish worked as a minister in the New Demeter Church until 1828, when he left to become a traveling preacher. In 1824 he married Jane Livingston. The couple subsequently had four children. Although his ministry delivered a traditional Christian message, Cornish's conservatism did not prevent him from becoming involved with more radical political activity.

Abolitionist and editor

In his last year at New Demeter Cornish became a founding editor with John B. Russwurm (1799–1851) of *Freedom's Journal*, the United States's first African American owned and operated newspaper. The first issue came out on March 16, 1827. The newspaper provided international, national, and regional coverage, and its editorials denounced slavery, lynching, and other injustices. The newspaper circulated in 11 states. Cornish took sole control of *Freedom's Journal* in 1829, when Russwurm resigned and went to Liberia, West Africa. Cornish changed the newspaper's name to *The Rights of All*, but the publication lasted for less than a year. As the titles of his newspapers suggest, Cornish was a determined opponent of slavery in the United States and abroad.

In 1833 Cornish helped found the American Anti-Slavery Society. However, Cornish, like other conservative thinkers, was increasingly criticized by the organization's more radical members, particularly those who advocated women's rights. Cornish had a very traditional view of women's place in society. In 1840 the election of three women to the society's executive committee led Cornish

to leave with a group of likeminded men. Cornish formed the American and Foreign Anti-Slavery Society, serving for about nine years on its executive committee. The new organization concentrated on abolishing slavery and refused to support the women's rights movement.

Marginalization

The 1830s were a busy time for Cornish. As well as his antislavery work, he was an executive member of the American Missionary Society and vice president of the American Moral Reform Society. He also worked as a newspaper editor on the *Colored American*, which he had helped launch in 1836. The paper's mission was "the moral, social, and political elevation of the free colored people; and the peaceful emancipation of the slaves." Its pages focused on abolitionist activity and civil rights issues in the North. By 1838 the paper was in trouble financially, and Cornish resigned, moving with his family to New Jersey, where he became an increasingly marginal figure in the context of radical African American politics.

Around 1840 Cornish moved to Newark, New Jersey. When his wife died in 1844, Cornish moved his family back to New York City, where he led the Emmanuel Church until 1847. Three of his children died, and in 1855, in poor health, Cornish moved to Brooklyn. He died in 1858.

See also: Russwurm, John

Further reading: Sterling, Dorothy. *Speak Out in Thunder Tones*. Garden City, New York, NY: Di Capo Press, 1998. http://www.spartacus.schoolnet.co.uk/USAScornish.htm (Biography of Cornish with links to related topics).

CORTEZ, Jayne
Poet

A poet originally associated with the black arts movement of the 1960s and 1970s, Jayne Cortez uses her work to protest issues such as racism, rape, war, and world poverty. Her tough, vigorous style is deeply rooted in the jazz and blues music that she loves.

Early life

Cortez was born in Fort Huachuca, Arizona, on May 10, 1936, but was raised in Los Angeles. As a young adult she became deeply involved in the city's vibrant jazz scene, and in 1954, at age 18, she married the jazz saxophonist Ornette Coleman. The couple had a son, Denardo, but were divorced soon after. In the 1960s Cortez took an active part in the civil rights movement, and in 1967 she went to live in New York City, which has been her home ever since.

Cortez published her first book of poems, *Pisstained Stairs and the Monkey Man's Wares*, in 1969. Other volumes followed, including *Scarifications* (1973), *Firespitter* (1982), *Coagulations* (1984; a collected edition of her work), and *Jazz Fan Looks Back* (2002). Bristling with political anger and fiery, violent language, Cortez's poetry is primarily meant for public performance.

Cortez has made numerous sound recordings of her work, usually with a jazz accompaniment provided by her band, the Firespitters, which features her son Denardo as drummer. Her albums include *Celebrations and Solitudes* (1975) and *Maintain Control* (1986).

Tough poetry

Cortez deals with her subject matter in a direct, even brutal way. Her 1982 poem "Rape," for example, is about Inez Garcia and Joanne Litte, who in the 1970s killed the men

▲ *Award-winning poet and civil rights activist Jayne Cortez uses her work to highlight important issues.*

who raped them. "What was Inez supposed to do/for the man who declared war on her body," asks Cortez at the beginning of the poem. Other subjects have included the Vietnam War and apartheid in South Africa. More recently the poet has attacked a mainstream American culture that wants citizens simply to conform, summing up its ethos as "Just enter/emulate & exit."

Cortez has performed her poetry around the world and has received many awards, including the Langston Hughes Award and the American Book Award. She also set up the Watts Repertory Theater in 1964 and established Bola Press, a publishing company, in 1972.

Cortez is active in politics and is president of the Organization of Women Writers of Africa, which she helped found in 1991.

See also: Coleman, Ornette

Further reading: Nielsen, Aldon Lynn, et al. (eds.). *Black Chant: Languages of African-American Postmodernism*. New York, NY: Cambridge University Press, 1997.
www.jaynecortez.com (Cortez's official site).

KEY DATES	
1936	Born in Fort Huachuca, Arizona, on May 10.
1954	Marries jazz musician Ornette Coleman.
1969	Publishes *Pisstained Stairs and the Monkey Man's Wares*.
1975	Makes first sound recording, *Celebrations and Solitudes*.
1984	Publication of *Coagulations* (collected verse).

COSBY, Bill
Actor, Comedian

▲ *Bill Cosby's hugely successful comedy style mixes his gentle sense of humor with a serious message.*

Bill Cosby is one of the nation's most successful actors and comedians. He is also a writer, television and radio host, producer, and composer.

William Henry Cosby, Jr., was born in Philadelphia, Pennsylvania, on July 12, 1937. He was the eldest of four sons born to William Cosby, Sr., a ship welder and steward, and Anna, a domestic servant. His youngest brother, James, was born in 1941 but died at age six of rheumatic fever.

Path to fame

Bill Cosby attended Wister Elementary School in the Germantown district of Philadelphia. Although intelligent, he did not distinguish himself academically, and after being asked to retake 10th grade, he joined the Navy. He did not abandon his formal education, however, completing high school by correspondence course.

On his return to civilian life in 1961, Cosby went to Temple University in Philadelphia on a track and field scholarship. Cosby could have become a professional football player, but he wanted to be a physical education teacher. His life soon took a different turn, however. In order to pay tuition fees, he worked as a bartender. Before long he started doing stand-up comedy at a Philadelphia coffeehouse called the Cellar. He got his first professional booking as a comedian at another local club, the Underground. In 1962 he moved to New York City, where he became a regular comedian at the Gaslight Cafe in Greenwich Village, earning $60 a week with free board. The Gaslight soon tripled his salary, and he was offered a contract by the William Morris Agency. He recorded a comedy album and performed nationwide.

Television and film

In 1965 Cosby appeared on the *Tonight Show Starring Johnny Carson*. He was spotted by producer Sheldon Leonard, who offered him a part in his new weekly television series *I Spy*. It was the first time an American TV series had given equal top billing to black and white performers. Cosby and Robert Culp starred as Pentagon agents who traveled the world righting wrongs. The series made Cosby an international star; it was a huge hit, lasting three seasons until 1968.

In 1969 Cosby was given his own program, *The Bill Cosby Show*, a television situation comedy in which he played Chet Kincaid, a physical education teacher helping disadvantaged children in a fictional Los Angeles neighborhood. The show ran from 1969 to 1971. It was followed by *The New Bill Cosby Show* (1972–1973), *The Cosby Show* (1984–1992), and *Cosby* (1996–2000).

It seemed that Cosby could do no wrong: At a live show in 1986 he broke Radio City's 53-year-old attendance record. Between 1994 and 1995 he appeared in the *Cosby Mystery Series*; he also hosted two popular entertainment programs: *You Bet Your Life* (1992–1993) and *Kids Say the Darndest Things* (1998–2000). Cosby has also appeared in several films, the most successful of which was *Uptown Saturday Night* (1974), in which he costarred with Sidney Poitier. The others—including *Hickey and Boggs* (1972), and *Mother, Jugs & Speed* (1976)—did not do as well. As well as acting in his shows, Cosby composed music for them, working with the producer Quincy Jones on the score for *The Bill Cosby Show*.

Cosby has always been interested in education. From 1972 to 1984 he produced and hosted *Fat Albert and the Cosby Kids*, a Saturday morning cartoon show that was humorous but always had an underlying moral, which Cosby himself would point out at the end of the program.

INFLUENCES AND INSPIRATION

As a child Bill Cosby listened to the radio shows of Jack Benny, Burns and Allen, Jimmy Durante, and Fred Allen. As a performer during the early part of his career, the underlying gentleness of his humor owed a great deal to the comedy of Charlie Chaplin and Will Rogers.

At the height of his success Cosby had considerable influence in the television industry. He was able to name the price for his work, demanding and getting 50 percent of the profit from *The Cosby Show*. By 1992 Cosby had earned about $333 million from the series alone. He used much of the wealth philanthropically. In 1988, for example, he and his wife donated $20 million to Spelman College in Atlanta, the largest single contribution ever made to a black college. The Cosbys have also patronized aspiring artists and have one of the finest collections of African American art in the world.

Before Cosby became a popular entertainer, most companies were reluctant to use African Americans to endorse their products, but they awoke to the new possibilities after his success in advertisements for a range of products, including Jell-O, Kodak, Del Monte, and the Ford Motor Company.

Bill Cosby is an outspoken critic of unfavorable and stereotypical depictions of African Americans on television.

Meanwhile, in 1977 he completed a doctorate in education at the University of Massachusetts, Amherst: His dissertation was on "An Integration of the Visual Media via *Fat Albert and the Cosby Kids* into the Elementary School Curriculum as a Teaching Aid and Vehicle to Achieve Increased Learning."

Writing

Cosby has published several books. *Fatherhood* (1986), a humorous but serious look at parenting, became the fastest-selling hardcover ever. The follow-up, *Time Flies* (1987), had the largest first print run in publishing history: 1.75 million copies were produced. Both works topped the New York Times bestseller list. He is also the author of *Childhood* (1991), *Cosbyology: Essays and Observations from the Doctor of Comedy* (2001), and many books for children. Cosby received the Kennedy Center Honors in 1998 and has won four Emmy and eight Grammy awards. In 2002 Cosby received the Presidential Medal of Freedom, and in 2005 he featured in the top 50 of a poll to find the comedians' comedian, voted for by his peers. In the same year Cosby denied separate allegations made by two women that he had drugged and molested them.

Family life

Cosby and his wife, Camille Olivia, whom he married in 1964, had five children: four daughters and a son, Ennis William, who was murdered in an attempted robbery in 1997. Shortly after Cosby lost his son, a 22-year-old woman, Autumn Jackson, tried to extort $40 million from him by claiming that she was Cosby's illegitimate daughter. While Cosby admitted that he had had an affair with Jackson's mother, he denied he was the woman's father. Jackson received a 26-month jail sentence for extortion.

Cosby continues to make public appearances and is an outspoken critic of any part of black popular culture that fails to promote the value of having strong morals.

KEY DATES	
1937	Born in Philadelphia, Pennsylvania, on July 12.
1956	Drops out of school and joins the Navy.
1961	Enrolls at Temple University.
1962	Becomes a professional stand-up comedian.
1965	Stars in *I Spy* television series.
1969	Stars in *The Bill Cosby Show,* followed by *The New Bill Cosby Show* in 1972.
1977	Awarded PhD in education.
1986	Publishes *Fatherhood*.
1987	Publishes *Time Flies*.
1997	Son Ennis is murdered.
2002	Receives Presidential Medal of Freedom.

See also: Black Identity and Popular Culture; Historically Black Colleges and Universities; Jones, Quincy; Poitier, Sidney

Further reading: Cosby, Bill. *Cosbyology: Essays and Observations from the Doctor of Comedy.* New York, NY: Hyperion, 2001.
www.mp3.com/bill-cosby/artists/118/ biography.html (Biography).

COSE, Ellis
Journalist

Ellis Cose has combined a distinguished journalistic career writing for newspapers and magazines with publishing books that attempt to analyze the condition of different sections of the African American community in contemporary America.

Early writing

Ellis Jonathan Cose was born on February 20, 1951, in Chicago, Illinois. Growing up on the West Side of Chicago, in one of the city's public housing projects, he witnessed the riots of the late 1960s that followed the assassinations of Malcolm X and Martin Luther King, Jr. Cose started to write in response to the violence, which he saw as a result of people not understanding each other.

Since then his writing, whether journalism or books, has been an attempt to bridge that gap. Aged 19, he became the youngest-ever contributor to work for a Chicago newspaper when he began writing for the *Chicago Sun-Times* while studying psychology at the University of Illinois. Assigned to cover Jimmy Carter's 1976 presidential campaign, Cose was exposed to new issues, in particular the energy crisis of the 1970s, which he covered in a number of books.

A career in journalism

Following several years in print journalism, Cose moved to California to run the Institute for Journalism Education in 1983. He left in 1986 to concentrate on writing books and working in magazines. After a period at *Time* magazine he joined *Newsweek* in 1993 as contributing editor, a position he still held in 2005. He has also written on management and workplace issues for *USA Today* and served on the editorial board of the *Detroit Free Press*.

Cose married Lee Llambelis, general counsel for the Bronx Borough president, in 1992, and they have one daughter.

Race, class, and the African American community

Cose's later books have examined issues of race and class. *The Rage of a Privileged Class* (1994) looked at discrimination against middle-class African Americans who have struggled hard to succeed but feel that they are still not accepted by society because of their color. *Color-Blind: Seeing beyond Race in a Race-Obsessed World* (1997) explored the United States's obsession with race. Subsequent books examined the position of African Americans in contemporary America. *The Envy of the World* (2002) is a detailed look at the state of African American men. In *Bone to Pick: On Forgiveness, Reconciliation, Reparation, and Revenge* (2004) Cose widened his scope to examine societies beyond the United States, such as South Africa, and studied the ways in which they have dealt with atrocities.

Honors

Cose has received many awards in recognition of his work on race and class, including the University of Missouri medal for career excellence and distinguished service in journalism, four National Association of Black Journalists first place awards, and two Clarion awards. In 2002 Cose was given a lifetime achievement award by the New York Association of Black Journalists. In 2003 he won an award for best magazine feature from the National Association of Black Journalists. In 2004 the Maynard Institute for Journalism Education, renowned for its training of minority students, gave Cose its newly inaugurated Robert C. Maynard Vision Award for his work to further diversity in the United States.

KEY DATES	
1951	Born in Chicago, Illinois, on February 20.
1970	Becomes a columnist for the *Chicago Sun-Times*.
1972	Graduates from the University of Illinois.
1983	Heads up the Institute for Journalism Education.
1993	Joins *Newsweek* as contributing editor.
1994	Publishes *The Rage of a Privileged Class*.
2002	Winner of New York Association of Black Journalists lifetime achievement award.
2004	First recipient of Vision Award from the Maynard Institute.

See also: King, Martin Luther, Jr.; Malcolm X

Further reading: *Contemporary Authors*, New Revision Series. Vol. 99. Gale Group, Detroit, 2002.
www.elliscose.com (Cose's official site).

COX, Elbert F.
Mathematician, Educator

Elbert Frank Cox was the first African American to be awarded a PhD in mathematics. He became professor and chair of mathematics at Howard University, where he helped many students achieve their degrees.

Early life

Cox was born on December 5, 1895, in Evansville, Indiana, the first of three children. Unlike many African Americans of his time, Cox was surrounded by educational opportunities—his father, Johnson D. Cox, was a school principal, and his family held a great respect for learning. Cox showed exceptional talent in the sciences at high school, particularly math and physics. Such was his ability that he went on to Indiana University, graduating with a mathematics degree in 1917. Cox's academic career was interrupted by the United State's involvement in World War I (1914–1918), however; he served in France, where he rose to the rank of staff sergeant. Following the end of the war in 1918, Cox became a mathematics teacher in Henderson, Kentucky.

A love of teaching

From 1920 to 1921 Cox taught physics, chemistry, and biology at Shaw University, Raleigh, North Carolina, before enrolling in a doctoral program in mathematics at Cornell University, New York, in September 1922.

In 1925 Cox received his PhD in mathematics, awarded for his thesis in polynomial solutions of difference equations. Cox was the first African American to receive a PhD in pure mathematics in the United States and indeed was the first black in the world to do so. To put his achievement into context, in the year he graduated only 28 PhDs were awarded in mathematics in the United States, and until then fewer than 50 African Americans had received doctorates of any kind. That same year Cox became the first African American to be inducted into the American Mathematical Society (AMS).

Cox's qualifications earned him a place teaching in the mathematics and physics department at West Virginia State College. In 1927 he married elementary school teacher Beulah P. Kaufmann. The couple subsequently had three sons.

In 1929 Cox took up a teaching post at Howard University, Washington, D.C., where he remained until his retirement in 1965. At Howard he became chair of the

KEY DATES

1895 Born in Evansville, Indiana, on December 5.

1917 Graduates with a BA in math from Indiana University.

1925 Completes a PhD in mathematics at Cornell University, becoming the first African American to receive such a qualification.

1929 Begins teaching mathematics at Howard University, Washington, D.C.; appointed chair of the department in 1957.

1965 Retires from teaching.

1969 Dies in Washington, D.C., on November 28.

mathematics department from 1957 to 1961. Although Cox did not live to see the inauguration of a PhD program at Howard, he did much to make it possible, building up the department and attracting a high standard of faculty and students. Cox taught thousands of students and supervised more masters degrees than any other member of the department.

Retirement and honors

Four years after his retirement, Cox died on November 28, 1969. Although he received little recognition during his lifetime, Cox has been widely commemorated since his death. In 1975 Howard University established the Elbert F. Cox Scholarship Fund for undergraduate mathematics majors to encourage black students to study math at the graduate level. Cox's achievements were also honored in 1980 by the National Association of Mathematicians, which inaugurated the Cox–Talbot Address, a speech given at every annual conference. It is named jointly for Walter Richard Talbot (1909–1977), the fourth African American to earn his PhD in mathematics, from the University of Pittsburgh in 1934. Talbot became department chair at Morgan State University, Maryland.

See also: Historically Black Colleges and Universities

Further reading: Sammons, Vivian O. *Blacks in Science and Education.* Washington, D.C.: Hemisphere Publishers, 1989.
http://www.math.buffalo.edu/mad/madhist.html (A history of African Americans in mathematics).

CREW, Spencer R.
Historian, Museum Director

Spencer R. Crew is the executive director of the National Underground Railroad Freedom Center in Cincinnati, Ohio. He has had a distinguished career as a historian and curator. His driving ambition is to make history, in particular African American history, accessible to as many people as possible.

Early life

Spencer R. Crew was born in Poughkeepsie, New York, in 1950, and was raised in Cleveland, Ohio. His mother was a psychiatric nurse and his father, a chemist. In 1971 Crew graduated from Brown University, Rhode Island, and went on to earn an MA (1973) and a PhD (1979) from Rutgers University, New Jersey. He began his career as an academic, working as an assistant professor of African American history and American history at the University of Maryland, Baltimore County.

In 1981 Crew became a curator at the Smithsonian National Museum of American History (NMAH) in

▼ *Crew applauds First Lady Laura Bush at a 2004 dedication ceremony in the National Underground Railroad Freedom Center, which he helped establish.*

Washington, D.C. His goal was to create vibrant interactive exhibitions that brought historical events, personalities, and issues to life. One of his most successful exhibitions was "Field to Factory" (1987), which documented the Great Migration in which thousands of southern African Americans moved to the industrial cities of the North in the early 20th century. It was a subject close to Crew's heart—his own grandfather had migrated from South Carolina to Cleveland in the early 1920s.

In 1994 Crew was appointed director of the NMAH—the first African American director of a major Smithsonian museum. During his tenure the museum flourished; donations soared, and the number of visitors rose from 5.6 million in 1992 to almost 6.5 million in 2000. A major attraction was the early 19th-century "Star-Spangled Banner," which had been freshly restored and preserved under Crew's direction.

Celebrating freedom

In 2001 Crew left the NMAH to help set up and direct the National Underground Railroad Freedom Center. A $110 million facility, the museum was opened to the public in September 2004. It documents the history and heroes of the Underground Railway, the secret network of routes and safe houses set up during the 19th century by people in the North to help runaway slaves reach freedom in Canada, the Caribbean, and Mexico. The museum's goal is to celebrate and record the ways in which African Americans and other people around the world have struggled for freedom.

KEY DATES	
1950	Born in Poughkeepsie, New York.
1994	Appointed director of the National Museum of American History, Washington, D.C.
2001	Becomes director of the National Underground Railroad Freedom Center, Cincinnati.

See also: Great Migration and Urbanization; Slavery

Further reading: Crew, Spencer R. *Field to Factory: Afro-American Migration, 1915–1940.* Washington, D.C.: Smithsonian Institution, 1987
www.historians.org/pubs/careers/crew.htm (Biography).

CROCKETT, George W., Jr.
Lawyer, Civil Rights Activist

George William Crockett, Jr., was an outspoken attorney, civil rights leader, and congressman who earned a reputation for fighting for social justice. He was the first African American judge to sit in a recorder's court and one of the founders of the first interracial law firm in the United States. He entered the House of Representatives at age 71, representing Michigan. During his four terms in office he was at the forefront of controversial issues: He introduced the Mandela Freedom Act in Congress requesting that the South African government release Nelson Mandela from prison, and he brought a lawsuit against President Ronald Reagan for his use of military forces in El Salvador in the 1980s.

Legal career

Crockett was born in Jacksonville, Florida, on August 10, 1909. He graduated from Morehouse College, Atlanta, in 1931. He earned a degree from the University of Michigan Law School in 1934 and was admitted to the Florida Bar

KEY DATES

1909 Born in Jacksonville, Florida, on August 10.

1934 Receives JD from Michigan Law School; admitted to Florida Bar.

1950 Founds first interracial law firm in Detroit; jailed for contempt of court at the end of the Smith Act Trial.

1966 Elected as judge in recorder's court.

1980 Elected as a Democrat to the 96th Congress and 97th Congress following Charles C. Diggs's resignation.

1991 Retires from Congress.

1997 Dies in Washington, D.C, on September 7.

▼ *George W. Crockett in 1969 on his way to police headquarters to seek the release of people being held for questioning following a meeting of a black separatist group, the Republic of New Africa.*

that same year. In 1939 Crockett became the first black lawyer to work for the Department of Labor. In 1943 he was a hearing officer at the Federal Fair Employment Practices Commission and acted as counsel to the United Auto Workers Union. In 1949 Crockett defended one of the 11 Communist leaders charged with conspiring against the U.S. government in the Smith Act Trial. At the end of the trial in 1950 the judge sentenced all five defense attorneys, including Crockett, to four months in prison for contempt of court. In 1969, a year after race riots in Detroit, he was involved in the New Bethel Church murder case, in which a police officer was shot dead outside a Detroit church, and the entire congregation was arrested. Crockett freed many of them, arguing that they would not have received a fair trial were it not for his intervention.

Congressman Crockett

In 1980 Crockett won a special election to both the 96th and 97th Congress in order to fill the vacancy left by Charles C. Diggs's resignation. He became an authority on constitutional and foreign affairs. Crockett retired in 1991; he died of bone cancer on September 7, 1997 in Washington, D.C.

See also: Civil Rights

Further reading: http://www.aaregistry.com/
african_american_history/1067/
Lawyer_JudgeCongressman_George_Crockett (Biography).

CROSTHWAIT, David, Jr.
Engineer

David Crosthwait, Jr., was a mechanical and electrical engineer who became an inventor and pioneer in cooling and heating technology.

Early life

David Nelson Crosthwait, Jr., was born in Nashville, Tennessee, but his family moved to Kansas City, Missouri, where he received his elementary and high school education. Overcoming the prejudices of that time, he was able to gain entry to college and the comparatively liberal environment of Purdue University in Lafayette, Indiana, where he got his BS degree in 1913 and his MA in engineering in 1920.

Innovative engineering

Crosthwait's first commercial building engineering experience was with the heating installation and engineering firm C. A. Dunham Company (now Marshall Engineered Products Co.) of Marshall Town, Iowa, where he started work after graduating from Purdue in 1913. He was employed to design heating systems.

Crosthwait was promoted to director of the company's research department in 1925 in recognition of his growing reputation as an inventive engineering designer, responsible for more than 30 patented designs for heat transfer, ventilation, and cooling devices. His refrigeration units were widely adopted for the rapidly expanding air-conditioning market. It would have been impossible to build steel, concrete, and glass skyscrapers that were habitable in hot humid summers without temperature control and air-conditioning.

Crosthwait also pioneered improvements in the efficiency of steam heating through the invention of better boilers. Again, this work was vital in providing efficient, economic winter heating for the skyscrapers that were being built during the urban office-building boom of the mid-20th century. To maintain a comfortable office work environment while consuming energy efficiently, Crosthwait also designed and patented several temperature control devices, now universally known as thermostats, and a differential vacuum pump for moving water through heating systems.

These inventions made Crosthwait a sought-after design engineer for prestige building projects. His best-known engineering achievement was the design and

installation of the heating system for two of midtown Manhattan's landmark buildings, the world-famous Radio City Music Hall, which opened on December 27, 1932, and Rockefeller Center, built between 1929 and 1934.

Consultant

Crosthwait's manual on building heating and cooling systems became a standard reference text for building engineers, and he consulted on numerous projects throughout the United States. Over the course of his career Crosthwait received 39 U.S. and 80 foreign patents relating to the design, installing, testing, and service of HVAC (heating, ventilation, and air-conditioning) systems.

In 1956 the C. A. Dunham Company and the Bush Manufacturing Company merged to form Dunham-Bush Inc. Crosthwait served as the technical adviser until his retirement in 1971. In retirement he taught engineering courses in the theory of steam heating and control systems at Purdue University, which awarded him an honorary doctorate in 1975.

Crosthwait was a Fellow of the American Association for the Advancement of Science (AAAS) and a member of the American Society of Heating, Refrigerating, and Air Conditioning Engineers, the American Chemical Society, and the National Society of Professional Engineers. He died in 1976.

KEY DATES	
1891	Born in Nashville, Tennessee, on May 27.
1913	Earns BS from Purdue University, Indiana.
1925	Becomes director of research, Dunham Company, Iowa.
1931	Creates heating systems for Rockefeller Center and Radio City Music Hall.
1975	Awarded honorary PhD by Purdue University.
1976	Dies.

Further reading: Sammons, Vivian O. *Blacks in Science and Education*. Washington, D.C.: Hemisphere Publishers, 1989. http://inventors.about.com/library/inventors/blcrosthwait.htm (Includes link to patents and illustration).

CROUCH, Stanley
Writer

Stanley Crouch is an often controversial essayist, columnist, and novelist. His provocative statements about black icons, Afrocentrism, and gangsta rap music have led some black critics to condemn him as a conservative who has betrayed his race, while others agree with his outspoken comments.

Crouch was born in Los Angeles, California, in 1945. He began writing at age eight, encouraged by his mother, Emma Bea. Crouch did not meet his father until he was a teenager. He was educated during the civil rights period and became active in the movement while still at East Los Angeles Junior College; he taught literacy in a federal antipoverty program in a deprived area of Los Angeles.

Development of ideas

In August 1965 Crouch witnessed the Watts riots, during which 34 people were killed. The experience radicalized him, and he became a black nationalist. He joined a theater group, the Studio Watts Company, as an actor-playwright and remained there for the next two years. Extensive study of writers such as Ralph Ellison and Albert Murray convinced him that black nationalism was not radical enough to achieve its aims.

In 1968 Crouch began teaching at Claremont College in California. In 1975 he moved to New York to take a job as a drummer in a jazz band. Crouch and tenor saxophonist David Murray opened their own loft space, Studio Infinity, above the Tin Palace, a club in the East Village where they held avant-garde jazz evenings. From 1979 to 1988 Crouch worked as a staff writer on the *Village Voice*. Having established a reputation as a journalist, he became the spokesperson for jazz trumpeter Wynton Marsalis. Since 1987 Crouch has served as an artistic consultant at Lincoln Center and is cofounder with Marsalis of the department there known as Jazz.

Crouch has also written for the *New York Daily News*, the *New Yorker*, the *New Republic*, and *Esquire*. In 1990 he

▲ **Writer Stanley Crouch has both delighted and offended African Americans by his comments.**

published the book of essays *Notes of a Hanging Judge*. In 1993 Crouch won the Jean Stein Award from the American Academy of Arts and Letters and was awarded a MacArthur Foundation grant. Crouch brought out two more collections of occasional writings: *The All-American Skin Game, or, The Decoy of Race: The Long and Short of It, 1990–1994* (1995) and *Always in Pursuit: Fresh American Perspectives, 1995–1997* (1998). In 2000 he wrote *Don't the Moon Look Lonesome: A Novel in Blues and Swing*. From 2002 to 2003 Crouch was Louis Armstrong Visiting Professor of Jazz Studies at Columbia University.

See also: Ellison, Ralph; Marsalis, Wynton

Further reading: Crouch, Stanley. *Don't the Moon Look Lonesome: A Novel in Blues and Swing.* New York, NY: Vintage, 2004.
http://www.thehistorymakers.com/biography/biography.asp?bioindex=107&category=mediaMakers (Biography).

KEY DATES	
1945	Born in Los Angeles, California, on December 14.
1990	Publishes first book of essays.
2000	Publishes novel *Don't the Moon Look Lonesome.*

CRUMMELL, Alexander
Intellectual, Minister, Writer

American scholar and Episcopalian minister Alexander Crummell founded the American Negro Academy in 1897. He was committed to the establishment of independent black institutions, wrote frequently about the idea of authority and society, and encouraged scholarship and leadership among young black people.

Path forward

Born in New York in 1819, Crummell's father, Boston Crummell, was the son of a West African chief, a former slave, and owner of a small oyster house; his mother,

▲ *Alexander Crummell's ideas and writings influenced many young African Americans.*

Charity Hicks, was a freeborn woman. Crummell was educated at the African Free School in Manhattan. In 1835 he went to Canaan, New Hampshire, to study at the newly established Noyes Academy, an integrated school. However, the building was destroyed by local residents who objected to its policy of educating white and black students together. After finishing his schooling at the Oneida Institute in upstate New York, Crummell was rejected by the General Theological Seminary of the Protestant Episcopal Church in 1839 because of his color.

Undeterred, Crummell studied theology privately with sympathetic clergymen in Providence and Boston, and unofficially attended lectures at Yale University. His perseverance paid off, and he became an Episcopalian minister in 1844, but his fellow clergymen refused to accept him. Crummell had married in 1841, and he and his family lived in poverty and faced racism and discrimination on a daily basis.

During this time Crummell was also involved in the antislavery movement. He wrote for the *Colored American* newspaper in the early 1840s and identified himself with "race men"—people working for the specific interests of people of African descent.

In 1847 Crummell traveled with his family to England to raise funds for a new church for poor blacks after a fire destroyed the original building; he lectured against slavery and managed to raise money for the church and also to study at Queen's College, Cambridge, a lifelong dream. His studies were interrupted by his wife's illness and the death of one of his five children. Despite this, he gained his theology degree in 1853.

Liberia

Deciding that he wanted to raise his children among free black people, Crummell traveled to Liberia in West Africa to work as a missionary. He was criticized for his decision since many people knew that he was against colonization, and many African Americans viewed Liberia with mixed feelings. For the next 20 years Crummell lived and worked in Liberia as a parish rector and as professor of intellectual and moral science at Liberia College, but he still traveled back to the United States to lecture on behalf of the American Colonization Society and Liberia College. He became a well-known advocate of Liberian nationalism and promoted the adoption of Christianity and the

INFLUENCES AND INSPIRATION

While in Liberia Crummell was heavily influenced by President Edward James Roye (1870–1871). He supported Roye's policies of integrating with the local native population through marriage and and education.

Roye was born in Ohio in 1815 into a wealthy family. He gained a degree from Ohio University and emigrated to Liberia in 1846, one year before the colony's independence. He became the fifth president of the country in May 1869. Roye disagreed with the policies of J. J. Roberts, Liberia's first president, and he found in Crummell a friend and supporter. Crummell viewed Roberts's and the Republican Party's politics as designed to keep the native population in a permanently inferior status. He referred to them as the "venal mulatto elite." Roye was deposed on October 26, 1871, following a coup led by Roberts. When Roye died in mysterious circumstances in February 1871, Crummell fled from Liberia. The elections following Roye's death brought Roberts back into power.

education of Africans by skilled, educated blacks from all over the world. Crummell supported the ideas of President Edward James Roye, who believed in integration between the new black migrants to Liberia and the native Africans (*see box*). He despised Roye's political opponents, the Republican Party, whom he viewed as separatist and elitist. After Roye's death Crummell fled the country, returning to the United States.

While he was dedicated to his public life, Crummell was often alienated from his family: His marriage had never been a happy one, and at the time of his wife's death in 1878 the couple were living separately. In 1880 Crummell married Jennie Simpson, a member of his church and social network.

A life in America

After returning to the United States, Crummell worked as rector of St. Mary's Church in Washington, D.C. In 1880 he founded St. Luke's Episcopal Church there and served as its pastor until his retirement in 1894.

Crummell became a spokesperson for African Americans looking for greater recognition in the church, and he promoted a program of industrial and moral education for poor black women. In 1883 he led the Conference of Church Workers among Colored People. When some bishops proposed a separate missionary district for black parishes, Crummell organized a group, now known as the Union of Black Episcopalians, to fight the proposal.

Crummell lectured at Howard University after his retirement and in 1897 founded the American Negro Academy, which promoted the publication of scholarly work dealing with African American culture and history. Members included W. E. B. DuBois and Paul Laurence Dunbar. DuBois later wrote about Crummell in his book

KEY DATES

1819	Born in New York on May 3.
1844	Ordained as a priest.
1847	Travels to England.
1853	Is awarded a degree from Cambridge University; moves to Liberia.
1871	Returns to America following Roye's death.
1872	Becomes rector of St. Mary's Church, Washington, D.C.
1880	Establishes St. Luke's Episcopal Church.
1897	Founds the American Negro Academy.
1898	Dies in Red Bank, New Jersey, on September 10.

The Souls of Black Folk (1903). Crummell wrote and lectured widely against racism and appealed to educated blacks to provide leadership for their communities. He questioned the relationship of human nature to authority and how educated blacks fit into this area.

Crummell published three books: *The Future of Africa* (1862); *The Greatness of Christ and Other Sermons* (1882); and *Africa and America* (1891). He died in 1898.

See also: DuBois, W. E. B.; Dunbar, Paul Laurence

Further reading: Rigsby, George U. *Alexander Crummell: Pioneer in Nineteenth-Century Pan African Thought.* Westport, CT: Greenwood Press, 1987.
http://www.spartacus.schoolnet.co.uk/USAcrummellA.htm (Biography).
http://www.bartleby.com/114/12.html (Online chapter on Crummell from W. E. B DuBois's book).

CUFFE, Paul
Seaman, Merchant, Philanthropist

Paul Cuffe was the wealthiest African American of his time. Considered by some people to be the father of pan-Africanism almost a century before African American intellectuals W. E. B. DuBois and Marcus Garvey supported the idea of resettling African Americans in Africa, Cuffe organized the settlement of a group of freed blacks in the West African country of Sierra Leone.

Cuffe was one of 10 children born to Kofi (later Cuffe) Slocum, a former slave, and Ruthe Moses, a Wampanoag Native American, on Cuttyhunk Island off southern Massachusetts in 1759. Cuffe rejected his father's slave name, taking his given name instead.

Both Cuffe's parents lived their lives according to Quaker ideals, although their race excluded them from membership in the Society of Friends. When Cuffe was seven years old, his parents bought a 116-acre (47ha) farm in Dartmouth, Massachusetts. The Slocums taught their children that hard work, honesty, and frugality were important principles by which to live. They also taught them to respect their cultural heritages and to oppose discrimination.

Deciding that knowledge was the key to success, Cuffe educated himself. At age 16 he decided to go to sea to earn his living and for several years he worked as a seaman on whaling and fishing boats. He eventually built up a small coastal trading business with his brother. In later life he owned several ships that engaged in trading and whaling around the world and were crewed by blacks.

In 1780 Cuffe and his brother John petitioned the Massachusetts government to stop taxing African and Native Americans on the grounds that they were denied voting rights. Although they lost the petition, their efforts were recognized in the 1783 Massachusetts Constitution, which gave equal rights and privileges to every citizen of the state.

A wealthy man

Cuffe earned a fortune from trade and whaling. His Quaker ideals and his disgust with the slave trade and the way in which nonwhite groups were treated led him to donate much of his money to improving the lives of black and Native Americans.

Believing that black people would never really be equal in America, Cuffe looked to Africa. After learning about the Sierra Leone Colony, started by English philanthropists in 1787 for the resettlement of former slaves, Cuffe worked to send settlers there from America. In 1815 he sailed there with 38 settlers; but before he could establish a proper colony, he died in 1817.

▲ *Paul Cuffe became rich through trade and whaling, but donated much of his wealth to others.*

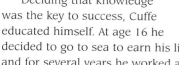

KEY DATES	
1759	Born on Cuttyhunk Island, Massachusetts.
1780	With brother John petitions Massachusetts government for voting rights for African and Native Americans.
1815	Sails to Sierra Leone with 38 migrants.
1817	Dies in Westport, Connecticut, on September 9.

See also: DuBois, W. E. B.; Garvey, Marcus

Further reading: Harris, Sheldon H. *Paul Cuffe: Black America and the African Return*. New York, NY: Simon & Schuster, 1972. http://college.hmco.com/history/readerscomp/rcah/html/ah_022300_cuffepaul.htm (Biography).

CULLEN, Countee
Poet

Although Countee Cullen remains one of the lesser-known writers of the Harlem Renaissance (the flowering of black writing in New York in the 1920s) he was considered by many to be one of the most talented African American literary figures of the period.

Road to success

There are few confirmed details of Cullen's early life, in part because the poet was rather secretive about his upbringing. Different sources list his birthplace in 1903 as Baltimore, New York, or Louisville, Kentucky. The last is more likely; Cullen once listed Louisville as his birthplace on a registration form for New York University.

Cullen was raised by Amanda Porter, who was generally assumed to be his paternal grandmother. After she died, Cullen moved in with Reverend Frederick Asbury Cullen, pastor of the Salem Methodist Episcopal Church in Harlem. Under Reverend Cullen's strict supervision Countee excelled in scholarly studies, emerging as a top student in the almost exclusively white DeWitt Clinton High School in Manhattan. While he was in high school, one of his poems won a citywide competition.

In 1921 Cullen enrolled in New York University (NYU) and was elected to the Phi Beta Kappa fraternity in his junior year. He completed his BA in 1925 and received an MA from Harvard University the following year.

Cullen's first collection of poems, *Color*, was published in 1925 during his final year of study at NYU and received immediate national acclaim. By the mid-1920s Cullen had won numerous literary awards and was considered the most significant black poet in the nation. In 1927 he published two poetry collections, *Copper Sun* and *The Ballad of the Brown Girl*, neither of which received as much praise as his first volume.

In 1928 Cullen was awarded the Guggenheim Fellowship to study in Paris, France, and he married Yolande DuBois, the only child of prominent intellectual and activist W. E. B. DuBois. They divorced in 1930.

Although Cullen continued to publish, none of his later works attracted the critical acclaim of his early poems. He published his only novel, *One Way to Heaven*, in 1932, and *The Medea and Some Poems* in 1935. He also wrote two books for young readers in 1940 and 1942. Cullen taught at Frederick Douglass Junior High School from 1934 until his death on January 9, 1946.

▲ *Countee Cullen received much critical acclaim for his work, winning several awards during his lifetime.*

KEY DATES	
1903	Born probably in Louisville, Kentucky, on March 30.
1925	Publishes *Color*.
1927	Publishes *Copper Sun* and *The Ballad of the Brown Girl*.
1928	Awarded Guggenheim Fellowship; marries.
1929	Publishes *The Black Christ and Other Poems*.
1940	Publishes *One Way to Heaven* and *The Lost Zoo*.
1942	Publishes *My Lives and How I Lost Them*.
1946	Dies in New York on January 9.

See also: DuBois, W. E. B.; Harlem Renaissance

Further reading: Shucard, Alan R. *Countee Cullen*. Boston, MA: Twayne Publishers, 1984.
www.english.uiuc.edu/maps/poets/a_f/cullen/life.htm (Modern American Poetry site page on Cullen).

DANDRIDGE, Dorothy
Actor

Renowned for her talent, beauty, and singing voice, Dorothy Dandridge was the first African American actor to receive an Academy Award nomination for best actress. An inspiration to generations of black women, including actor Halle Berry (*see box on p. 54*), Dandridge once said, "If I were white, I could capture the world."

Early life
Born in Cleveland, Ohio, on November 9, 1922, Dorothy Jean Dandridge was the daughter of Ruby Dandridge, an aspiring actor; her grandmother was the performer Madame Sul-Te-Wan. Ruby Dandridge walked out on her husband before Dandridge's birth. Both Dandridge and her sister Vivian displayed a talent for singing and reciting poetry from a young age. When Geneva Williams, Ruby's friend and lover, moved into the Dandridge household, she taught the girls singing and dance.

Williams moved with the Dandridges to Nashville, Tennessee, where Dorothy and Vivian performed under the name the Wonder Children. They were signed to tour the southern states with the National Baptist Convention, which they did for three years, although the sisters found performing tiring and demeaning.

In the 1930s Ruby Dandridge took her daughters to Hollywood. The girls were enrolled in the Hooper Street School, where they took dance lessons. They found work as the Dandridge Sisters, singing in clubs around California. Their break came when they got a spot at the Cotton Club in New York. Both girls were beautiful and talented, and they were very popular with audiences. In 1939 they went on tour in Europe, but returned home to New York and the Cotton Club after the outbreak of World War II (1939–1945).

An unhappy home life
In 1942 Dandridge married Harold Nicholas, part of the successful Nicholas Brothers dancing act, and the couple set up home in Hollywood. Although Dandridge tried to make the marriage work, Nicholas had affairs with other women. In 1943 Dandridge gave birth to a daughter, Lynn, and put all of her energy into raising her, especially after it became apparent that Lynn had learning difficulties. Nicholas provided them with little emotional support, and in 1949 Dandridge left him. Ruby and Vivian Dandridge helped look after Lynn while Dandridge reestablished her

▲ *Dorothy Dandridge performed at the Mocambo Club in Hollywood. She was one of the few black stars allowed to sing there.*

career. She collaborated with the arranger Phil Moore to create a new sexy image for herself. Dandridge sang in many Los Angeles clubs, but she hated the fact that she was often excluded from using the club's facilities because of her race.

Movies at last
Dandridge had always dreamed of becoming a big movie star, but she did not want to play the stereotypical "mammy" or servant roles usually given to black actors. In the 1930s and 1940s she had several often uncredited bit parts in movies such as *A Day at the Races* (1937) and *Since You Went Away* (1944). In 1951, however, Dandridge got a break when she appeared as Melmendi, the jungle

INFLUENCES AND INSPIRATION

Dorothy Dandridge has influenced many black American actors—including Halle Berry, who was also born in Cleveland, Ohio. Berry idolized Dandridge and fought hard to play the actor in the TV biographical movie *Introducing Dorothy Dandridge*. Berry, who was also executive producer of the program, won a Golden Globe award for her performance. Although Dandridge was the first black woman to be nominated for the Academy Award for Best Actress in 1954, Berry was the first African American woman to win the Oscar for her performance in *Monster's Ball* (2000). Berry's acceptance speech payed homage to Dandridge and other black actors. She said, "This moment is for Dorothy Dandridge, Lena Horne, Diahann Carroll. It's for the women that stand beside me ... and it's for every nameless, faceless woman of color that now has a chance because this door tonight has been opened."

queen, in *Tarzan's Peril*. She also had a small part in the low-budget but successful *Harlem Globetrotters*. Dandridge continued to sing in nightclubs, and her growing popularity resulted in her being asked to perform in Paris, France. She was also the first African American to play at the Waldorf Astoria in New York.

In 1953 she played a school teacher in the film *Bright Road*; her costar Harry Belafonte became a close friend and the couple starred in several films together, including Otto Preminger's movie version of Bizet's opera *Carmen*. There were very few good roles for black actors, and Dandridge worked hard to convince Preminger that she was right for the lead role; Belafonte was cast as Joe. However, both stars were disappointed when Preminger dubbed their voices. *Carmen Jones* (1954) was a huge success, and Dandridge received an Oscar nomination for best actress, making her the first African American woman to do so. She lost to Grace Kelly.

Dandridge became Preminger's lover during the shooting of *Carmen Jones*. Their turbulent relationship continued for many years, even though Dandridge found it a huge strain: Preminger was married, and their relationship had to be kept secret. She also followed Preminger's advice to turn down a part in the movie *The King and I* since it was not a lead role. Dandridge regretted her decision, especially after actor Rita Moreno took the part, and the movie was a huge success.

Dandridge acted with Belafonte again in Robert Rossen's movie *Island in the Sun* (1957), a film that was both successful and highly controversial because it portrayed an interracial relationship between Belafonte and white actor Joan Fontaine. Dandridge thought it unrealistic and preferred the 1957 Italian–French production of *Tamango*, in which she appeared with German actor Curt Jurgens, which explored themes similar to Rossen's movie.

In 1959 Dandridge starred with Sidney Poitier in *Porgy and Bess*. Preminger came on board as the director; and although his relationship with Dandridge was over, he made life particularly difficult for her. Dandridge won a Golden Globe Award for Best Actress in a Musical.

Dandridge married white restaurant owner Jack Denison in 1959. The marriage was not a success: Not only did Denison misuse Dandridge's money, but he also beat her, and Dandridge began to drink heavily. When Dandridge finally left Denison in 1961, her finances were depleted; she had to declare herself bankrupt in 1963.

Although her friend Earl Mills tried to help Dandridge get back on her feet, getting her work in nightclubs, she was drinking while taking the antidepressant drug Tofranil. On September 8, 1965, Dandridge was found dead in her apartment. Although initially thought to have died from a blood clot, Dandridge had taken a drug overdose.

See also: Belafonte, Harry; Berry, Halle; Poitier, Sidney

Further reading: Bogle, Donald. *Dorothy Dandridge*. New York, NY: Berkley Publishing Group, 1999.
http://home.hiwaay.net/~oliver/dandridge.html (Tribute site).

KEY DATES

1922	Born in Cleveland, Ohio, on November 9.
1942	Marries Harold Nicholas; the couple separate in 1949.
1951	Plays Melmendi, the jungle queen, in *Tarzan's Peril*.
1954	Stars in the lead role of *Carmen Jones*; receives Academy Award nomination for Best Actress.
1959	Marries Jack Denison; they separate in 1961.
1965	Dies in New York on September 8.

DASH, Damon
Record Producer, Business Executive

Former partner of and driving force behind the multiplatinum selling rapper Jay-Z (Shawn Corey Carter), Damon ("Dame") Dash is a highly respected producer, promoter, and entrepreneur in the hip-hop industry. Although in 2004 Dash sold Roc-A-Fella, the record company he helped found, he remains active in music production as well as earning millions of dollars from his clothing, magazine, and film ventures.

Young entrepreneur

Born in Harlem, New York, on May 3, 1971, and brought up by his mother Carol, Dash vowed to continue his education following her death when he was 15 years old. He won a scholarship to Dwight, a private preparatory school on Park Avenue in Manhattan, and despite being expelled was later awarded a place at Kent boarding school in Connecticut. By his late teens Dash was equally comfortable with hip-hop street culture and the lifestyle and attitudes of America's wealthy.

After hosting parties at the Cotton Club in Harlem as a teenager, Dash started out in the music business. He was helped into the industry by his cousin Darien Dash and worked as a manager. He soon set up his own label, Dash Entertainment. Although unsuccessful at first, Dash got a lucky break when a DJ friend Clark Kent (Rodolfo Franklin) introduced him to Shawn Corey Carter, a former drug dealer turned rapper.

Roc-A-Fella Records

Despite initial differences and difficulties such as the traditional rivalry between Harlem and Brooklyn, not having a record deal, and little money, Dash and Carter collaborated to press and release Carter's first single, "In My Lifetime" (1995), under the name Jay-Z. Dash later commented, "We were so broke we distributed it ourselves out of the back of a car." The record began to gain notice and sales; with the money they made from it, Dash and Jay-Z set up Roc-A-Fella Records in partnership with Dash's old friend Kareem "Biggs" Burke. The label initially secured a manufacturing and distribution deal with Priory Records, but Jay-Z's first album, *Reasonable Doubt* (1996), and a collaboration with female rap star Foxy Brown brought Roc-A-Fella to the notice of Brown's label, Island Def Jam. In 1997 Roc-A-Fella agreed to a lucrative 50–50 deal with Island Def Jam.

Two years later Dash was among the first people to notice the popularity of street styles and the free promotion that rap stars were lending to leading brand names. He worked with Jay-Z to establish Roc-A-Fella's legendary marketing of hip-hop and street culture as a lifestyle brand in itself. Associated businesses under the Roc imprint include RocaWear Clothing, a street fashion line; Roc-A-Fella Films (established 1999); Armadale Vodka (purchased in 2002); a nonprofit community outreach project sponsoring youth basketball teams, Team Roc; and in 2004 a collaboration with Smokey Fontaine, former

▲ *Damon Dash was voted 15th in a 2004 U.S. poll of the most powerful men under 40.*

editor of *Source* magazine, to create *America Magazine,* a publication combining fashion and hip-hop.

Meanwhile, Jay-Z went on to become one of the most successful, high-earning, and charismatic rappers of the late 1990s and early 2000s. Other Roc-A-Fella signings include Cam'ron, Beanie Sigel, N.E.R.D., and Kanye West, all of whom went on to become successful artists. In 2003 cracks in the partnership began to appear when Dash insisted on signing former Wu Tang Clan member Ol' Dirty Bastard (ODB; real name Russell Jones) against Jay-Z's advice. Problems worsened in the wake of Dash's untimely collaboration with fading British popstar Victoria Beckham. In late 2004 the pair decided to part company. Jay-Z announced his retirement as a rapper, and Roc-A-Fella Records was sold to Island Def Jam, then a part of Universal Music Group, for $10 million.

New projects

Dash has long been interested in movies; his early ventures include helping Jay-Z write and produce his autobiographical movie *Street Is Watching* (1998) and the 2000 release of the hip-hop documentary *Backstage* through Roc-A-Fella Films in conjunction with Dimension Records. He has since been involved in making films in the gangster genre such as *Paid in Full* (2002) and *Death of a*

Dynasty (2003), which have given way to more inspired, independent films. One of the most controversial films, *The Woodsman* (2004), stars actor Kevin Bacon as a reformed pedophile. Dash jumped at the opportunity to be involved in the film, which won awards at both the Cannes and Sundance film festivals in 2004.

Dash continues to produce music. While Jay-Z went on to become president of the record company Def Jam, Dash took former Roc-A-Fella artists and formed the Damon Dash Music Group with Biggs Burke. In March 2005 he found himself having to use his own name and marketing talents to promote albums for the first two artists on the new label, both of whom were absent: Beanie Sigel, in prison on a federal weapons charge, and ODB, who died in November 2004 of a drug overdose.

The future

Meanwhile, Dash's business empire continued to thrive as he diversified into nightclubs, such as NA in New York, and boxing promotion, with Lou Dibella. Dash also had plans to open a restaurant chain and branch out into television, producing a reality program showing the pressures of his work. In 2005 Dash's businesses were estimated to be worth over $500 million, and he is reported to have a fortune of around $200 million.

Following a number of relationships that included being engaged to R&B star Aaliyah at the time of her death in 2001, Dash married Rachel Roy in 2005.

See also: Aaliyah; Black Identity and Popular Culture; Jay-Z; West, Kanye

Further reading: Jay-Z and Dream Hampton. Jay-Z: *The Black Book.* New York, NY: MTV Books, 2006. www.contactmusic.com/new/artist.nsf/artistnames/ damon%20dash (Biography).

KEY DATES

1971   Born in Harlem, New York, on May 3.

1995   Forms Roc-A-Fella Records with Jay-Z and Kareem "Biggs" Burke.

1999   Diversifies into clothing and films with RocaWear and Roc-A-Fella Films.

2004   Parts company with Jay-Z and sells Roc-A-Fella Records; executive produces *The Woodsman*.

DASH, Julie
Film Director, Writer

One of the United States's most distinguished African American filmmakers, Julie Dash is best known for *Daughters of the Dust* (1992), the first feature film directed by a black woman to have a national theatrical release. In her work Dash is committed to portraying the intimate realities of black lives, particularly those of women, and going beyond the usual stereotypes that dominate mainstream white filmmaking.

Early life
Dash was born and raised in New York City, but her father's family had been raised in the Gullah community of the Sea Islands off the coast of South Carolina and Georgia that would form a central part of her groundbreaking film, *Daughters of the Dust*. West African slaves were brought to the islands to work in the indigo trade. Isolated in the remote swamps, the Gullah culture was based on ancient Yoruba traditions from the region of modern Nigeria and the people spoke in a dialect that combined English and West African languages.

Dash began studying film in 1969 at Harlem's Studio Museum. In 1974 she received a BA in film production from the Leonard Davis Center for the Performing Arts, David Picker Film Institute, and moved to Los Angeles, California, where she continued her studies, first at the Center for Advanced Film Studies at the American Film Institute (AFI) and then at the University of California, Los Angeles (UCLA). While at UCLA Dash directed *Diary of an African Nun*, adapted from a short story by Alice Walker. It was screened at the Los Angeles Film Exposition and earned her a Director's Guild Award for a student film. She obtained her MA in fine arts in 1986.

Daughters of the Dust
While at UCLA Dash also began work on what was originally planned as a short film but became her first

▼ *Julie Dash's work features strong, positive African American women characters who play a central role in the narrative.*

KEY DATES

1952	Born in New York City.
1992	Releases *Daughters of the Dust*.
2002	Broadcasts *The Rosa Parks Story*.

full-length feature, *Daughters of the Dust*. It is the story of three generations of the Peazants, a traditional African American family living on the Sea Islands, at the point in 1902 when some of them are planning to leave the islands to start a new life. Told in dreamlike fragments, narrated by an unborn child, and with characters speaking in the Gullah dialect, the motion picture received little interest from producers. It took Dash 10 years to attract the necessary funding to complete it.

The film was finally released to great acclaim in 1992, winning the prize for best cinematography at the Sundance Film Festival. *Filmmaker's Magazine* named *Daughters of the Dust* as one of the 50 most important independent films ever made. The film has been archived in New York at the Schomberg Center for the Study of Black Culture. In 1999, the 25th Annual Newark Black Film Festival honored *Daughters of the Dust* as one of the most important cinematic achievements in 20th-century black cinema.

Dash said about the film in an interview, "I wanted to take the African American experience and rephrase it in such a way that, whether or not you understood the film on the first screening, the visuals would be so haunting it would break through with a freshness about what we already know."

Return to the limelight

Despite the success of *Daughters of the Dust*, Dash found it difficult to find work directing motion pictures, especially in Hollywood. This was in part owing to what was perceived to be the uncompromising nature of her

filmmaking and in part because of the prejudice she faced as both a woman and an African American. Nonetheless, Dash managed to carve out a successful career directing television movies, such as *Funny Valentines* (1998) and *Incognito* (1999), as well as music videos.

Rosa Parks

In 2002 Dash returned to public attention with her TV movie *The Rosa Parks Story*, an intimate film biography of one of the outstanding figures of the civil rights movement. It was awarded Best Television Movie at the Fourth Family Television Awards, a Christopher Award in the TV/Cable Category, and a 2003 NAACP Image Award for outstanding television movie. Angela Bassett, who starred in the title role, won the 2003 NAACP Image Award for Outstanding Actor in a Television Movie, and Dash was nominated for the Director's Guild of America Award for Outstanding Television Movie.

Dash shot the movie in Montgomery, Alabama, the setting for Park's historic refusal in 1955 to give up her seat in the white section of a bus. It was the first time that Parks had agreed to cooperate with a film about her life. Dash did not want to make Parks into a noble civil rights icon; instead she wanted the audience to identify with Parks by adding "tiny specifics ... those moments of whimsy, pathos and certainly sexuality. You don't often see African Americans on television very intimate, caring or loving. It's always something violent or rough. Or the opposite: the 'I love you, Babe' kind of thing."

See also: Bassett, Angela; Black Identity and Popular Culture; Parks, Rosa; Walker, Alice

Further reading: Bobo, Jacqueline (ed.) *Black Women Film and Video Artists*. Los Angeles, CA: AFI, 1998.
geechee.tv (Dash's site, including full biography as well as clips from her work).
http://voices.cla.umn.edu/vg/ (Biography).

DAVIDSON, Olivia
Teacher, Activist

Olivia Davidson was the assistant principal of the Tuskegee Institute, Alabama, where she worked with her husband, Booker T. Washington. She played a key role in the institute's early development.

Early life
The daughter of an ex-slave and a free woman, Davidson was born on June 11, 1854, in Mercer County, Virginia. In 1857 her family moved to Ohio, eventually settling in Albany. There Davidson attended the Enterprise Academy, a newly founded school that was run by African Americans. She also mixed with liberals from Oberlin College, a nearby educational institute that had a reputation for encouraging black applicants. During her period at the Enterprise Academy Davidson began to develop an interest in women's rights.

Davidson started to teach at age 16, working first in Ohio and then in Mississippi. In 1874 she moved to Memphis, Tennessee, to continue teaching. She returned to Ohio for a summer break in 1878 but due to an outbreak of yellow fever did not return to Memphis. Instead, she enrolled for studies at the Hampton Normal and Agricultural Institute in Virginia, another historically black institution. There she met her future husband, the educator Booker T. Washington. Washington had attended Hampton between 1872 and 1875, before returning there to teach.

Tuskegee Institute
After a further period of studies at Framingham State Normal School Davidson left for Tuskegee, where she joined Washington to teach at the Tuskegee Negro Normal Institute. The Tuskegee Institute was founded in 1881 after the Alabama House of Representatives voted to appropriate $2,000 for the establishment of a "Negro Normal School" in the town. Washington was approached to teach at the school; but when he arrived in Tuskegee, he found that the school consisted of little more than the grant awarded by the local government. To begin with, Washington taught in a tiny shack provided by a local church that held only 30 students. Shortly after he arrived, Washington sent for Davidson to join him. She was appointed assistant principal. Together they cowrote the institute's curriculum. Davidson also played a key role in the administration of the school.

KEY DATES	
1854	Born in Mercer County, Virginia, on June 11.
1857	Moves with family to Ohio.
1870	Begins teaching.
1881	Assists Booker T. Washington in the establishment of the Tuskegee Institute.
1886	Marries Washington.
1889	Dies in Tuskegee, Alabama, on May 9.

The Tuskegee Institute specialized in vocational subjects such as farming, carpentry, and brickmaking. This was in keeping with Washington's belief that African Americans should develop manual skills to help them gain economic self-sufficiency before studying more academic subjects. Washington's pragmatic position later drew criticism from other African American commentators such as W .E. B. DuBois, but at the time it appealed to the white philanthropists whose donations allowed the institute to grow. By 1888 the school owned 540 acres (219ha) of land and was attended by over 400 students. Davidson was heavily involved in raising funds, and much of her work revolved around meeting with donors.

Washington's first wife, Fanny Smith, died in 1884. Two years later he married Davidson. The couple had two children, Booker T., Jr., and Ernest. However, in 1889, only a few months after giving birth to her second child, Davidson died of tuberculosis of the larynx. Her death was the culmination of several years of ill-health. However, the academy that she had helped create continued to grow under her husband's guidance. By the time of his death in 1915 the institute was attended by 1,500 students.

See also: Historically Black Colleges and Universities; DuBois, W. E. B.; Washington, Booker T.

Further reading: Washington, Booker T.: *Up from Slavery*. Mineola, NY: Dover Publications, 1995.
http://www.aaregistry.com/african_american_history/ 947/Olivia_Davidson_a_secret_no_more (Biography).

DAVIS, Angela
Educator, Civil Rights Activist, Writer

Scholar, civil rights activist, political philosopher, writer, feminist, and communist, Angela Yvonne Davis has long been associated with the often violent struggle for African American and women's rights.

Early life

Davis was born in Birmingham, Alabama, on January 26, 1944, to Frank and Sally Davis. Both of her parents were politically active and had links with the NAACP and the Communist Party. In 1948 the Davis family moved to a white neighborhood; the experience of being the only black child on the block gave Davis an early taste of discrimination, especially after more black families moved into the area, and racial tensions increased. Davis attended local segregated schools until she was 14, when she joined a program run by the American Friends Service Committee to study at the integrated Elizabeth Irwin High School in Greenwich Village, New York. Davis boarded with a liberal Episcopalian priest and his family, and quickly began to adapt to her new environment. She was an eager reader, and she began to flirt with communism. Davis read and was impressed by Karl Marx's *Communist Manifesto* (1848). She went to lectures given by left-wing

organizations and attended meetings run by Advance, a Marxist-Leninist student organization.

In 1961 Davis attended Brandeis University in Massachusetts, then essentially a middle-class white educational facility. Davis felt lonely and alienated during her time there, especially since she was one of only three black students in her class. She graduated with a BA in French literature in 1965. While at Brandeis she met and was influenced by the great German Marxist intellectual Herbert Marcuse (*see box*). Davis entered the doctoral program to study philosophy at the German University of Frankfurt. Although Davis took part in political discussions and protests in Germany, she eventually returned to America to work in the emerging civil rights movement. She went to study at the University of California, where Herbert Marcuse and Theodor Adorno were teaching. Davis became a member of the Student Non-Violent Coordinating Committee (SNCC) in 1967, and a year later joined the

▼ *Angela Davis in 1970 with Arnold Kaufman of the American Federation of Teachers, which was prepared to back her if she took the University of California to court for firing her.*

INFLUENCES AND INSPIRATION

While studying at Brandeis University, an already politicized Angela Davis became influenced by her teacher, Marxist Herbert Marcuse (1898–1979). Davis and Marcuse began a long intellectual relationship. After her return from Germany Davis went to study with Marcuse in California.

Born in Berlin, Germany, on July 19, 1898, Marcuse studied at the University of Freiburg. He became interested in existentialism and Marxism, and cofounded the Institute for Social Research in Frankfurt with Max Horkheimer and Theodore Adorno. A member of the Social Democratic Party, Marcuse left Germany when Hitler and the Nazis came to power in 1933, moving first to Geneva, Switzerland, and then to the United States in 1934. He set up an affiliated office of the Institute for Social Research at Columbia University, where he stayed for seven years. When World War II broke out in 1939, Marcuse, who became a U.S. citizen in 1940, advised the government on German culture and European affairs; but he eventually returned to teaching. In 1958 he was appointed professor of politics and philosophy at Brandeis University. A charismatic teacher, Marcuse met Davis in 1964. Impressed by her intellect, he remained friends with Davis and publicly supported her during her 1972 trial.

more revolutionary Black Panther Political Party (separate from the Black Panther Party for Self-Defense). In 1968, after becoming disillusioned with both groups, she became a member of the Communist Party.

Communism, prison, and freedom

In 1970 Davis made the national news for two events. She was fired from her position as assistant lecturer at the University of California at San Diego by the Board of Regents because of her membership of the Communist Party. However, the event that really changed her life was her involvement in the trial of the Soledad Brothers, three black inmates of Soledad Prison, California, accused of killing a prison guard. Davis led the Soledad Brothers Defense Committee. On August 7 of that year the trial was interrupted when Jonathan Jackson, the younger brother of one of the three men, took a judge and four others hostage in a courtroom in a bid to free his brother. In the ensuing gunfight the judge, two prisoners, and Jackson himself died. A warrant was issued for Davis's arrest on the grounds that two of the guns used were registered in her name. Davis went underground and was listed among the FBI's 10 most wanted criminals. Captured in August, Davis was sent to prison for 18 months, although in 1972 she was acquitted of all charges by an all-white jury. Soon afterward Davis founded the National Alliance against Racist and Political Repression, which is still active today.

In 1980 Davis ran for vice president of the United States on the Communist Party ticket. She has taught at various institutions, including the University of California, Santa Cruz, where she is a professor. Her studies focus on issues to do with racial oppression, minorities and women's rights, prison reform, and the culture of music. She is the author of several books, including *Women, Race, and Class* (1981), and is a vocal advocate of prison reform.

See also: Civil Rights; Political Movements

Further reading: Davis, Angela. *Angela Davis: An Autobiography.* New York, NY: International Publishers, 1989. http://voices.cla.umn.edu/vg/Bios/entries/davis_angela_yvonne.html (Biography).

KEY DATES

1944   Born in Birmingham, Alabama, on January 26.

1965   Graduates with BA from Brandeis University, Massachusetts; goes on to study for a PhD at the University of Frankfurt, Germany.

1968   Works with Black Panther Political Party in Los Angeles; becomes a member of the Communist Party.

1970   Arrested on one count of murder and five counts of kidnapping after Johnathan Jackson takes a judge and four people hostage on August 7.

1972   Released from prison.

1979   Receives the Lenin Peace Prize.

1981   Publishes *Women, Race, and Class.*

1991   Appointed professor of history of consciousness at the University of California, Santa Cruz; appointed presidential chair in 1995.

DAVIS, Benjamin J.
Attorney, Politician, Editor, Writer

Benjamin Jefferson Davis was born in Dawson, Georgia, on September 8, 1903. He was educated in a segregated school before moving with his family to Atlanta in 1909, where his father founded the *Atlanta Independent* newspaper. He then attended Summer Hill School, Morehouse Academy, and Morehouse College in Atlanta. In 1923 Davis was arrested for refusing to obey the law on segregated city bus seating. The same year he left the South for Amherst College in Massachusetts and in 1926 entered Harvard Law School. After graduating, Davis returned to Atlanta and opened a law office.

Angelo Herndon
In his first case Davis undertook the defense of Angelo Herndon, a young African American activist in the Communist Party who had organized a protest march of unemployed workers on Atlanta's City Hall. Herndon was arrested at the march and charged with violating an 1861 Georgia statute penalizing slave insurrections. The trial was a travesty, and the prosecution and judge showered racial insults on both Davis and Herndon. The all-white jury found Herndon guilty and sentenced him to 18 years. Davis joined the American Communist Party and went on to defend in several other high profile racially biased trials, notably the Scottsboro Case, in which a group of African American men were falsely accused of the rape of a white woman.

Harlem experience
In 1935 Davis moved to Harlem, New York, where he immersed himself in editing and writing, largely giving up his legal practice as he worked on papers such as the *Negro Liberator*, *Amsterdam News,* and the *Daily Worker*.

KEY DATES	
1903	Born in Dawson, Georgia, on September 8.
1932	Joins the Communist Party.
1943	Elected to New York City Council.
1949	Found guilty of violating the Alien Registration Act; serves three years in prison.
1964	Dies in New York on August 22.

▲ *Benjamin J. Davis argues for African American civil rights at the 1945 Negro Freedom Rally in New York City.*

He also assumed a larger role in the Communist Party and in 1943 was elected to New York City Council. He fought against segregated housing, police brutality, and the color bar in major league baseball. In 1948, along with other leaders of the Communist Party, he was arrested and charged under the Alien Registration Act, also known as the Smith Act. Davis served three years in prison, where he wrote his autobiography. Once free, he remained a prominent member of the Communist Party and was charged in 1962 with violations of the Internal Security Act. He died of cancer in 1964 before the case was heard. Only then did the prison authorities release his autobiography.

See also: Civil Rights; Color Bar and Professional Sports

Further reading: Horne, Gerald. *Black Liberation/Red Scare: Ben Davis and the Communist Party*. Newark, DE: University of Delaware Press, 1994.
www.spartacus.schoolnet.co.uk/USAdennis.htm (Cases Davis has worked on).

DAVIS, Benjamin O.
Army Officer

Benjamin O. Davis not only paved the way for his son Benjamin, Jr., to achieve high rank in the military, he also served as an inspiration to every African American soldier who wanted to be a military officer.

Davis was born on July 1, 1877, in Washington, D.C. His interest in a military career was shaped by his father, who was a servant to Civil War general John A. Logan and through cadet training at the M Street High School. In 1897, while studying at Howard University, Davis entered the African American unit of the National Guard. The following year he saw his first foreign service fighting in the Spanish-American War (1898) as part of the 8th United States Volunteer Infantry. For a year Davis held the rank of temporary first lieutenant. However, in 1899 he was discharged; and when he reenlisted in the regular Army, he did so as a private in the 9th Cavalry.

Rising through the ranks

Although he started at the bottom of the military ladder, Davis's powers of leadership soon pushed him up the ranks. In February 1901 he became an officer once again when he was given the rank of second lieutenant, in which capacity he served with the 9th Cavalry in the Philippines. In 1905 he stepped up to the rank of first lieutenant and became a professor of military science at Wilberforce University, Ohio. He then spent three years (1909–1912) as a military attaché in Monrovia, Liberia.

From the end of his service in Monrovia to the conclusion of World War II (1939–1945) Davis steadily climbed the ranks, from captain in 1915 to colonel in 1930 and finally to brigadier general in 1940. Davis thus

▲ **Benjamin O. Davis on the day that he was promoted to brigadier general in 1940.**

became the first African American to attain the rank of general in the regular Army. During World War II Davis was dispatched to the European Theater of Operations to act as a special adviser on "matters pertaining to Negro troops." In particular he was charged with boosting the morale of African American soldiers and improving relations between them and the broader Army. His efforts were rewarded with a Distinguished Service Medal, which was presented to him in February 1945.

As well as the DSM, Davis was awarded the Bronze Star and, from France, the Croix de Guerre with Palm. He retired in 1948, the year President Harry S. Truman desegregated the military. Davis had an active retirement, serving on the American Battle Monuments Commission. He died on November 26, 1970. The U.S. Postal Service issued a stamp in his honor in 1997.

See also: Davis, Benjamin, Jr; Military

Further reading: Fletcher, Marvin E. *America's First Black General: Benjamin O. Davis, Sr.* Lawrence, KS: University Press of Kansas, 1989.
http://www.army.mil/cmh-pg/topics/afam/davis.htm (Official Army biography).

KEY DATES	
1877	Born in Washington, D.C., on July 1.
1898	Serves in the Spanish-American War with the rank of temporary first lieutenant.
1899	Reenlists in the Army as a private soldier.
1940	Achieves the rank of brigadier general, becoming the first African American general in the Army.
1945	Awarded the Distinguished Service Medal.
1970	Dies in Chicago, Illinois, on November 26.

DAVIS, Benjamin O., Jr.
Air Force Officer

Benjamin O. Davis, Jr., was born on December 18, 1912. He was the son of Benjamin O. Davis, who would later become the first African American general in the Army. Davis's military upbringing inspired him to follow in his father's footsteps. After going through high school, the Western Reserve University, and finally the University of Chicago, he entered the U.S. Military Academy at West Point, New York, in July 1932.

Fighting prejudice

Davis entered a military world that was still deeply segregated, with much opposition to the idea of black officers. At West Point no one spoke to him for four years, except for official communications, and he lived and ate alone. However, the ostracism only fueled Davis's determination to succeed. He graduated in 1936, ranking 35th out of a class of 276.

Despite his requests to join the Air Corps, Davis's first posting was as the commander of a black infantry company at Fort Benning, Georgia. In 1940, however, President Franklin D. Roosevelt created an African American fighter unit, the 99th Pursuit Squadron—more popularly known as the Tuskegee Airmen—and Davis joined the first 12 flying cadets in 1941. Davis received his pilot's license in March 1942, becoming the first black pilot to fly an Army Air Corps aircraft solo.

In December 1941 the United States entered World War II (1939–1945), and Davis began an exemplary combat career. As a lieutenant colonel, Davis led the Tuskegee airmen into combat over Germany and the Mediterranean, often escorting USAAF bombers into some of the most heavily defended areas of enemy territory. In 200 escort

▲ *Benjamin Davis, Jr., climbs into an advanced trainer in January 1942.*

missions the Tuskegee airmen prevented the loss of even one bomber. Davis was awarded the Distinguished Flying Cross for bravery and command skills.

The military was desegregated in 1948, and Davis became commander of the 477th Composite Group and the 332nd Fighter Wing. He returned to combat in Korea in 1953, in charge of the 51st Fighter-Interceptor Wing. After the war he was promoted to the rank of brigadier general, becoming the first African American general in the Air Force. He retired in 1970.

For the next five years Davis served under the administration of President Richard M. Nixon (1969–1974) as assistant secretary at the Department of Transportation. A final honor came in 1998, when President Bill Clinton made Davis a full general. Davis died on July 4, 2002.

See also: Davis, Benjamin O.; Military

Further reading: Davis, Benjamin O, Jr. *Benjamin O. Davis Jr., American: An Autobiography*. New York, NY: Plume, 1992.
http://www.wpafb.af.mil/museum/afp/davisbio.htm (Official Army biography).
http://www.aviation-history.com/airmen/davis.htm (Article).

KEY DATES	
1912	Born in Washington, D.C, on December 18.
1936	Graduates from the U.S. Military Academy, West Point.
1941	Joins the 99th Pursuit Squadron and becomes its commander during World War II.
1970	Retires from military service with the rank of lieutenant general.
2002	Dies in Washington, D.C., on July 4.

DAVIS, Ernie
Football Player

The story of Ernie Davis is a tale of both triumph and tragedy. He was the first African American to win the Heisman Trophy, awarded by the Downtown Athletic Club of New York to the best college football player. A football and basketball star at Syracuse University, Davis appeared to be on his way to a successful career in professional football when his life was cut short by leukemia. Honored annually by the Leukemia Foundation, which presents the Ernie Davis Award to an athlete of exemplary character and integrity, Davis is an inspiring example of courage in the face of severe adversity.

Early success

Born in New Salem, Pennsylvania, on December 14, 1939, Davis was raised by his grandparents until the age of 12, when he joined his mother and stepfather in Elmira, New York. Davis quickly became the town's star athlete, and during his junior and senior years at Elmira Free Academy

▼ *College running back Ernie Davis receives the Heisman Trophy in 1961.*

KEY DATES	
1939	Born in New Salem, Pennsylvania, on December 14.
1960	Leads Syracuse to 23–14 Cotton Bowl victory over Texas on January 1.
1961	Becomes the first black American to win the Heisman Trophy.
1962	Diagnosed with acute monocytic leukemia.
1963	Dies in Cleveland, Ohio, on May 18.

he was named to the national high school All-American teams in both football and basketball. With more than 50 college scholarship offers to choose from, a remarkable number for an African American athlete in 1958, Davis decided to stay close to home and attend Syracuse University, a school noted for producing outstanding running backs. Davis became a legendary runner, and in 1960, during his first season, he led the Orangemen to an undefeated season and the school's only national football championship. In the final game, a 23–14 Cotton Bowl victory over Texas, Davis scored two touchdowns, including one 87-yard pass reception, and added two two-point conversions to compound the victory. When the team's two African Americans were not allowed to attend the evening's postgame awards dinner, the entire Syracuse team boycotted the event.

In both of the next two seasons Davis earned first-team All-American honors and, in addition to football, also starred on the Syracuse basketball team. Following his senior year, he became the first African American to win the Heisman Trophy in 1961, in what was at the time the closest balloting in the history of the award. The first player selected in the 1962 National Football League (NFL) draft, Davis was set to join fellow Syracuse alum Jim Brown in the Cleveland Browns backfield when tragedy struck. While preparing for a college all-star game, Davis became too weak to play; he was later diagnosed as having acute monocytic leukemia. To the end of his life Davis made the best of his situation: In March 1963 he said, "In these years I have had more than most people get in a lifetime." Less than two months later Davis, one of the greatest running backs in the history of college football, was dead at age 23.

Further reading: Gallagher, Robert C. *Ernie Davis: The Elmira Express: The Story of a Heisman Trophy Winner.* Silver Springs, MD: Bartleby Press, 1999.
http://www.stargazettesports.com/ErnieDavis (Links to newspaper articles about Davis).

DAVIS, Reverend Gary
Musician

Legendary musician Reverend Gary Davis was a leading blues guitarist. Davis's intricate finger work and gruff but powerful singing voice made him famous. He influenced many musicians, including Bob Dylan, Bob Weir of the Grateful Dead, and Taj Mahal.

Gary D. Davis was born in Laurens, South Carolina, on April 30, 1896. He lost his sight at an early age, according to some accounts as a result of a reaction to some eye drops given to him when he was a baby. By age seven Davis had taught himself to play the harmonica, the banjo, and the guitar. He sang at the Center Raven Baptist Church in Gray Court, South Carolina, and wrote his first songs when he was 10. Davis played with a string band in his early teens, performing at house parties in the Laurens area, before moving to Greenville, where he began to play the blues. Between 1914 and 1915 Davis attended the Cedar Springs School for Blind People in Spartanburg. He left to return to Greenville and married a much older woman; but the marriage did not last and Davis took to the road, traveling all over the Carolinas.

Reverend Davis

By 1926 Davis was working as a street singer in Durham, North Carolina, playing spirituals, ragtime, blues, and gospel music. In the early 1930s he turned to religion, and he was ordained a minister of the Free Baptist Connection Church in Washington, North Carolina, in 1933. He toured as a singing preacher, playing a mixture of blues and gospel at revivals and in lumber camps.

In 1935 Davis recorded on the American Record Company label with musicians Blind Boy Fuller and Bull City Red. He moved to New York in 1940 after marrying blues singer Annie Bell Wright, and was ordained a minister of the Missionary Baptist Connection Church.

▲ *Reverend Gary Davis plays the blues not long before his death in 1972.*

Throughout the 1940s and 1950s Davis worked as a singing preacher in Harlem. By the late 1950s he was a recognized figure in the folk scene and recorded for labels such as Riverside and Folk-Lyric. He was featured in short films and in documentaries such as *Black Roots* (1970). Davis continued to act as a singing preacher until his death in 1972. He was awarded the "Lifetime Achievement Award" of the North American Folk Alliance in 2003.

Further reading: Tilling, Robert (ed.). *Oh, What a Beautiful City: A Tribute to Rev. Gary Davis.* Jersey, UK: Paul Mill Press, 1992.
http://www.revgarydavis.com/ (Davis's site).

KEY DATES

1896 Born in Laurens County, South Carolina, on April 30.

1933 Ordained a minister of the Free Baptist Connection Church in Washington, North Carolina.

1935 Records with Blind Boy Fuller and Bull City Red for the American Record Company.

1972 Dies in Hammonton, New Jersey, on May 4.

DAVIS, John Preston
Journalist, Publisher

A forthright journalist, publisher, and orator, John Preston Davis was devoted to the advancement of African American civil rights.

Early life

Born in Washington, D.C., in 1905, Davis was the son of a federal government employee. In 1922 he enrolled at Bates College, Lewiston, Maine, where he was made president of an honorary debating fraternity, Delta Sigma, edited the student newspaper *The Bobcat*, and contributed short stories to the black arts magazine *Opportunity*. In 1926 Davis graduated with double honors in English and psychology.

Davis was one of a group of writers, including Langston Hughes and Gwendolyn Bennett, who came together in the fall of 1926 to establish the quarterly arts and literary journal *Fire!!* Davis acted as the business manager on the magazine, which published the work of young African American artists and writers.

Davis was awarded a fellowship at Harvard University to study for an MA in journalism, which he achieved in 1927. Later that year he was appointed director of publicity at Fisk University, Tennessee, a position he held until 1928. Resuming his studies at Harvard, Davis acquired a law (LLB) degree from Harvard Law School in 1933.

Activist and publisher

Between 1933 and 1936 Davis served as executive secretary of the Joint Committee on National Recovery, an organization that ensured the integration of African American families into the Homestead Subsistence Division

▲ **Martin Luther King, Jr., leads demonstrators on a civil rights march from Selma to Montgomery, Alabama, in 1965. John Davis is second from the left.**

program. The program aimed to relocate people from overpopulated industrial areas to subsistence homestead communities. National Recovery also blocked moves to pay workers different amounts according to their race.

Davis also acted as governmental lobbyist for 26 national groups, including the National Association for the Advancement of Colored People (NAACP). In 1936 he helped found the National Negro Congress (NNC). He was appointed executive secretary, a position he held until 1942. The NNC represented more than 40 civil rights associations and worked to advance the economic interests of African Americans.

Davis was chief of the Washington bureau of the *Pittsburgh Courier* from 1943 until 1945, when he became publisher and editor of *Our World* magazine, a direct competitor of *Ebony*. One of Davis's greatest achievements came in 1966, when he edited the first edition of the comprehensive encyclopedia on African Americans, *The American Negro Reference Book*. Davis died in New York on September 11, 1973.

See also: Bennett, Gwendolyn; Hughes, Langston; King, Martin Luther, Jr.

Further reading: http://digilib.nypl.org:80/dynaweb/ead/scm/scdavisj/@Generic__BookTextView/145 (New York Public Library Digital Library Collections biography).

KEY DATES	
1905	Born in Washington, D.C., on January 19.
1926	Helps establish the journal *Fire!!*
1933	Become executive secretary of the Joint Committee on National Recovery.
1936	Helps found and is appointed executive secretary of the National Negro Congress.
1966	Edits *American Negro Reference Book*.
1973	Dies in New York City on September 11.

DAVIS, Miles
Musician

A fearless and unapologetic musician, Miles Davis was known for his enthusiasm for creating exciting new forms of jazz and for successfully bringing his music to a wide audience. Through his innovative style Davis developed jazz through bebop into cool jazz, modal jazz, and fusion.

Miles Dewey Davis III was born on May 26, 1926, in Alton, Illinois. Unlike many black musicians of the time, Davis came from a middle-class background and grew up in the 1930s relatively unaffected by the Great Depression. His father was a dentist, and his mother was a pianist. Two years before the stock market crash of 1929, Davis's family moved to East St. Louis, Missouri. The young boy grew up in the aftermath of the 1917 East St. Louis race riots, in which white mobs killed black residents and destroyed their property. Following the riots, East St. Louis came under tight segregation laws. The experience of segregation remained with Davis all his life.

Music in the blood
Despite hard times, Davis's family prospered. His father had a thriving dental practice that even local white people respected. Davis enjoyed an active childhood, playing sports and spending summers fishing and riding horses on

▲ *Miles Davis plays trumpet during a famous 1949 session at the Birdland jazz club in New York City.*

his grandfather's farm in Arkansas. A local black physician, Dr. Eubanks, gave Davis his first trumpet, and music soon drew Davis away from sports. He began taking music lessons and carrying the trumpet wherever he went. Although Davis considered becoming a physician, he knew he wanted to be a musician. While in high school Davis played with Billy Eckstein's band. When he finished school in 1944, Davis left the Midwest for New York City and went to the Juilliard School of Music. At the time the city was the center of the jazz scene, and his idols Dizzy Gillespie and Charlie "Bird" Parker played there.

Gaining experience
When Davis had free time, he went to listen to and play jazz on 52nd Street, also known as "The Street" because of the number of jazz clubs located there and the amazing streetlife. In Harlem Davis visited clubs, including the Savoy Ballroom and Small's Paradise, and he also spent a lot of time uptown at Minton's. While at the clubs he saw great jazz musicians play, such as Coleman Hawkins and Dexter Gordon. Davis spent most of his time at Minton's and began to develop his own musical style. He learned

KEY DATES	
1926	Born in Alton, Illinois, on May 26.
1944	Moves to New York City and enrolls in the Juilliard School of Music.
1948	Recorded the sessions that became *Birth of the Cool.*
1955	Forms first classic quintet with John Coltrane.
1959	Releases *Kind of Blue.*
1963	Forms classic quintet with Herbie Hancock.
1966	Releases *Miles Smiles.*
1969	Releases *In a Silent Way.*
1987	Wins a Grammy for 1986 record *Tutu* on Warner Brothers label.
1991	Dies in Santa Monica, California, on September 28.

INFLUENCES AND INSPIRATION

In the 1940s and 1950s jazz musicians formed a close-knit community in which junior musicians learned from jazz greats. Davis both benefited from and contributed to the system, learning much from master musicians such as Thelonious Monk, Duke Ellington, Coleman Hawkins, Dizzy Gillespie, and Charlie Parker. He was also influenced by his contemporaries, including Charles Mingus, Ahmad Jamal, and John Coltrane. Davis did not restrict himself to purely instrumental influences, however. He learned about phrasing from the singer Nat King Cole and actor Orson Welles. During the period when Davis was addicted to heroin, he was inspired to become more disciplined by the example of world boxing champion Sugar Ray Robinson. In his later career Davis admired and was influenced by Jimi Hendrix, James Brown, Prince, and the group Cameo.

Davis has also inspired numerous musicians himself. Herbie Hancock, Wayne Shorter, Chick Corea, and George Duke all played with Davis in his bands or recorded with him as studio musicians. Contemporary performers, including Marcus Miller and Wynton Marsalis, have been influenced by him. Davis continually reinvented jazz and by his own example set precedents that other musicians still follow.

about the concept of space in music from Thelonius Monk and about chords from piano sessions with Dizzy Gillespie. Davis gained confidence and got a major break when Parker invited him to join his band after Gillespie quit. After a year at Juilliard Davis grew impatient and quit.

In 1948 Davis formed a nine-piece band that became an influential group, considered by critics as a pioneer of a subtle, moody, and restrained form of jazz called "cool jazz." In 1949, after recording the sessions that became known as the *Birth of the Cool* (released in 1957), Davis left the band to play in the Paris Jazz Festival. In 1955 he formed a quintet with saxophonist John Coltrane. Like many jazz musicians in the 1950s, Davis became addicted to drugs, in particular to heroin. Drugs took a heavy toll on the musical community and killed a number of musicians, including Charlie Parker and Fats Navarro. Davis managed to kick the habit in the mid-1950s.

Success

Davis's quintet released several albums before breaking up. In the late 1950s he collaborated with jazz arranger Gil Evans (1912–1979). Evans had helped Davis arrange *Birth of the Cool*, and the two reunited to make the albums *Porgy and Bess* (1958) and *Sketches of Spain* (1960). Between recording them Davis made *Kind of Blue* (1959), which became one of the most popular jazz albums ever.

In 1963 Davis formed a new quintet that included keyboardist Herbie Hancock and from 1967 this group experimented with electronic music. The period culminated in the albums *In a Silent Way* (1969) and *Bitches Brew* (1970). In the 1970s Davis played and recorded with studio bands, making synthesized music that delighted his fans but drew criticism from traditional jazz lovers. In 1975 Davis retired owing to poor health but returned in 1980, producing music that mixed jazz and funk, and became known as fusion.

Davis also wrote music scores for movies that brought him mainstream success, including *Frantic* (1956), *Ascenseur Pour L'Echafaud* (Lift to the Scaffold, 1958), *Siesta* (1988), and a 1980s television commercial for Honda scooters.

Recognition

In 1986 Davis was awarded an honorary music degree from the New England Conservatory. During his career he received eight Grammy awards. In later life his paintings were well received in several international shows.

Throughout his career Davis promoted black musicians. He saw jazz as black classical music, and was dismayed at the racism to which black musicians were subjected and the compromises they sometimes had to make for white audiences. Davis died of pneumonia in Santa Monica, California, on September 28, 1991.

See also: Cole, Nat King; Coltrane, John; Ellington, Duke; Gillespie, Dizzy; Gordon, Dexter; Hancock, Herbie; Hawkins, Coleman; Hendrix, Jimi; Marsalis, Wynton; Mingus, Charles; Monk, Thelonious; Parker, Charlie; Prince; Robinson, Sugar Ray;

Further reading: Szwed, John. *So What: The Life of Miles Davis.* New York, NY : Simon & Schuster, 2002. www.milesdavis.com (Official site). http://www.plosin.com/milesAhead/ (Discography

DAVIS, Ossie
Actor

The actor Ossie Davis made up one half of a famous dramatic partnership with actress Ruby Dee, although he was also well known for his solo work.

He was born Raiford Chatman Davis on December 18, 1917, in Cogdell, Georgia. The nickname "Ossie" derived from a mishearing of his initials, R. C. A childhood talent for acting was sharpened at Howard University, Washington, D.C., from which he graduated in 1938. The following year Davis moved to New York, where he began writing and performing for the Rose McClendon Players in Harlem.

Stage and screen career

A strong performance in the Broadway play *Jeb* (1946) earned Davis a high public profile, and he went on to star in many other Broadway productions including *The Wisteria Trees*, *Green Pastures*, and *Anna Lucasta*. The latter featured Ruby Dee in the title role, and she and Davis married in 1948. With Dee Davis took a noncredited part in the movie *No Way Out* (1950), which signaled the start of a long movie career. His film credits included *The Cardinal* (1963), *The Hill* (1965), and a number of collaborations with director Spike Lee in the 1980s and 1990s, including *Do the Right Thing* (1989) and *Jungle Fever* (1991), both of which also featured Dee. Davis also enjoyed a healthy television career and became a household name through his appearances in shows and series such as *Car 54, Where Are You?*, *Bonanza*, and *The Defenders*.

▲ **Ossie Davis stars as Gabriel in the play** **The Green Pastures** **in 1951.**

Davis's contributions to television and film extended behind the camera into scriptwriting, directing, and producing. A particular success was *Cotton Comes to Harlem* (1970), an adaptation of a Chester Himes novel; Davis both directed the film and wrote its screenplay.

Davis was a vigorous campaigner for civil rights, especially during the 1960s and 1970s, and delivered eulogies at the funerals of both Malcolm X in 1965 and Martin Luther King, Jr., in 1968. Over the course of Davis's 65-year career he gathered numerous honors and awards. In 1994 he and Dee both received the Theater Hall of Fame Award and the Academy of Television Arts and Sciences Silver Circle Award. In 1995 they received a National Medal of Arts from President Bill Clinton. Davis died in 2005.

See also: Dee, Ruby; Himes, Chester; King, Martin Luther, Jr., Lee, Spike; Malcolm X; Poitier, Sidney

Further reading: Davis, Ossie, and Ruby Dee. *With Ossie and Ruby: In This Life Together.* New York, NY: HarperCollins Publishers, 2000.
http://www.npr.org/templates/story/story.php?storyId=1119605 (Audio interview with Dee and Davis).

KEY DATES	
1917	Born in Cogdell, Georgia, on December 18.
1939	Begins an acting career with the Rose McClendon Players in Harlem.
1948	Marries Ruby Dee.
1950	Appears in the movie *No Way Out* with Ruby Dee and Sidney Poitier.
1965	Reads a eulogy at Malcolm X's funeral.
1995	Receives National Medal of Arts from President Bill Clinton.
2005	Dies in Miami, Florida, on February 4.

DAVIS, Sammy, Jr.
Entertainer

Singer, actor, dancer, and entertainer Sammy Davis, Jr., was a highly acclaimed performer. He recorded about 40 albums and made numerous film, TV, and theater appearances during his career. As part of the famous "Rat Pack," which included singers Frank Sinatra and Dean Martin, Davis epitomized 1960s cool in cult movies such as *Ocean's 11*(1960).

Early life
Born in Harlem, New York City, on December 8, 1925, Davis was the son of vaudeville star Sammy Davis, Sr., and the Puerto Rican dancer Elvera "Baby" Sanchez. After his parents divorced, Davis went to live with his maternal grandmother for a short time; but when he was three, his

▼ **Multitalented entertainer Sammy Davis, Jr., was revered by many of his showbiz peers.**

father took him on the road to work the "Chitlin Circuit," a group of clubs that hired African American acts to fill-in between white acts. Black artists were only given a few minutes in which to perform and were not allowed to speak to the white audiences. Davis later recalled that this was where he learned his art: In order to hold the audience's attention he developed an act featuring several different dancing and singing styles, which he later used as the basis of his live performances. Davis had great talent as a singer and dancer, and he began to perform with his father and adopted uncle Will Mastin under the stage name "Silent Sam, the Dancing Midget." He was very popular, and the act was soon renamed the Will Mastin Gang.

Davis was coached by legendary tap dancer Bill "Bojangles" Robinson, who remained a lifelong influence, as did comedian Redd Foxx and actor Stepin Fetchit. Davis appeared in his first film when he was seven; he was cast as the son of Ethel Waters in the movie *Rufus Jones for President*.

Growing success
Davis's luck began to change when the Will Mastin Gang opened for Frank Sinatra, who was extremely impressed by the young Davis. Sinatra later said that Davis was one of the greatest talents he had ever seen, an opinion that comedian Groucho Marx echoed when he saw Davis perform in the early 1940s. In 1943 Davis's career was interrupted by World War II (1939–1945). He was drafted into the Army, suffering racism in his integrated unit.

After his discharge from the Army Davis continued to play in the newly named Will Mastin Trio, but he also accepted solo gigs. Davis believed that he could make audiences love him when he was performing. In 1946 Davis recorded "The Way You Look Tonight" for Capitol Records. *Metronome* magazine named it record of the year and called Davis the most outstanding new personality. In 1947 Davis opened shows for actor and entertainer Mickey Rooney, who persuaded him to add comedy to his routine; Davis also opened for Sinatra in New York in 1948.

The comedian Jack Benny, who liked the Will Mastin Trio, helped them get a booking at Ciro's in Hollywood and TV appearances on the *Colgate Comedy Hour* and *Ed Sullivan Show*. In 1952 Sinatra also invited them to play at the newly integrated Copacabana in New York.

INFLUENCES AND INSPIRATION

In 1954 Sammy Davis, Jr., was involved in a car accident. The bones in his face were fractured, and he lost his left eye. During his long recovery he had time to have conversations with Max Nussbaum, a rabbi who headed Temple Israel in Hollywood. Davis read Paul Johnson's *A History of the Jews* while in the hospital; he later said that he found parallels between the problems that African Americans and Jews suffered both historically and in modern society—both were oppressed minorities who faced discrimination on a daily basis. After much reflection Davis converted to Judaism, a faith that he followed until the end of his life. His decision was a shock to his friends: Some criticized him for "playing" at being Jewish. His conversion also isolated him from many members of the black community, and he never fully fit into the mainstream Jewish community. Ever the performer, Davis used his situation in his act, often making jokes about being the only one-eyed, black Jewish entertainer in show business.

In 1954 Davis signed with Decca Records and released the successful albums *Starring Sammy Davis, Jr.* and *Just for Lovers*. He also made the headlines when he was involved in a serious car crash. Davis was badly injured and lost his left eye, but the publicity made him a bigger star than ever. During his recovery he converted to Judaism (*see box*). In 1956 he resumed his career, starring on Broadway with the Will Mastin Trio in the musical comedy *Mr. Wonderful*. Three years later he resumed his film career in a breakthrough role as Sportin' Life in *Porgy and Bess* (1959), starring Dorothy Dandridge and Sidney Poitier.

Davis's individualistic style and his preference for flashy suits and jewelery made him seem very cool and hip. But he also attracted a lot of criticism for his relationships with beautiful white women such as the actor Kim Novak. In 1968 Davis had a short-lived arranged marriage to Loray White, a black dancer. Two years later he managed to offend both African Americans and white supremacist organizations, such as the Ku Klux Klan, when he married the Swedish actor May Britt.

Davis was deeply committed to the civil rights movement, however, and he used his position to highlight discriminatory practices such as segregation in hotels. He also gave large contributions to black charities. In 1969 he was awarded the NAACP's Spingarn Award.

The "Rat Pack" and beyond

Davis's association with the "Rat Pack" is legendary. The group included singers Dean Martin and Frank Sinatra, the actor Peter Lawford, and comedian Joey Bishop, and was considered the epitome of cool, raffish charm, and sophistication. The "Rat Pack" also had a reputation for fast living, drinking, and drugs. Davis performed with them at Sands Casino in Las Vegas, made

KEY DATES	
1925	Born in Harlem, New York City, on December 8.
1932	Appears in first movie, *Rufus Jones for President*.
1954	Signs with Decca Records.
1960s	Involved in civil rights movement with Martin Luther King, Jr.; becomes part of the "Rat Pack."
1965	Writes his first autobiography, *Yes I Can; Life in a Suitcase* (1980) and *Why Me?* (1989) follow.
1988	Tours with Frank Sinatra and Dean Martin.
1990	Dies in Beverly Hills, California, on May 16.

several films with them, and partied with them; but he was criticized by many African Americans for allowing himself to be the butt of the group's often racist jokes.

In 1964 Davis returned to Broadway in a successful musical adaptation of Clifford Odets's drama *Golden Boy*, for which he received a Tony nomination. Davis also hosted his own TV show in 1966 and had a No. 1 hit in 1972 with "Candy Man." During the late 1970s and 1980s Davis mainly performed on the Las Vegas casino circuit, although he appeared in the hit film *Tap* in 1989. He also fought hard to overcome an addiction to cocaine and alcohol. On May 16, 1990, Davis died of throat cancer.

See also: Dandridge, Dorothy; Fetchit, Stepin; Foxx, Redd; Poitier, Sidney; Robinson, Bill

Further reading: Early, Gerald Lyn. *The Sammy Davis, Jr. Reader.* New York, NY: Farrar, Straus, Giroux, 2001.
http://www.sammydavisjunior.com/Biography.htm (Tribute site).

DAVIS, William Allison
Educator, Anthropologist

William Allison Davis led a life dedicated to academic excellence and to eradicating racial inequalities in the education system. He published several pioneering studies on education and was responsible for the creation of the Davis–Ellis Intelligence Test, which measured mental development.

Early life
Born in Washington, D.C., on October 14, 1902, Davis was the son of John and Gabrielle Davis. Initially raised on a farm in Virginia, Davis later moved with his parents and two siblings back to Washington, D.C. He attended Dunbar High School, where he showed a strong intellect; he was valedictorian of his class. Dunbar was a segregated school, and Allison developed an early awareness of racial injustice.

Inadequate education
Following high school Davis attended Williams College, Massachusetts, from which he graduated with a BA in 1924. The following year Davis went to Harvard University, where he received an MA in English before moving on to a teaching career at the Hampton Institute, a school for African Americans. Davis's experiences there reinforced his belief that young African Americans suffered from a lack of suitable educational facilities. He decided to work on his own teaching skills by returning to Harvard in 1932 to complete another master's degree, this time in anthropology.

Anthropology for the greater good
Davis continued his anthropological studies in England at the London School of Economics, but after a year he decided to go back to the United States, where he took up a position as a research assistant to the influential anthropologist William Lloyd Warner (1898–1970) at Harvard. Warner specialized in studies of class and came up with the theory that there are three divisions of social class—upper, middle, and lower—and that each division has upper and lower strata. His work with Warner helped Davis establish a reputation in anthropology.

In 1935 Davis began teaching social anthropology at Dillard University, Louisiana, where he taught for four years. During this time he became director of the American Youth Commission of the American Council on Education before leaving in 1939 to work at the University of Chicago. At Chicago he worked as assistant professor in the Center for Child Development. Davis also furthered his own academic credentials and was awarded his doctorate in 1942, becoming an assistant professor. He became a full professor in 1948.

Unhappy with IQ tests, which he thought had too many biases, Davis worked hard to develop an intelligence test that was not culturally biased—the Davis-Ellis Intelligence Test was the result. Davis also wrote several important books: *Deep South: A Social Anthropological Study of Caste and Class* (1941) was cited in the Supreme Court decision in the landmark desegregation case *Brown v. Board of Education* (1954).

Later years
In 1965 Davis became a member of the Conference to Insure Civil Rights, and two years later he was the first educationalist to be appointed to the American Academy of Arts and Sciences. In 1968 Davis served on the White House Task Force for the Gifted. During his career, which ended with his retirement in 1978, Davis published several important works on sociology. His last book, *Leadership, Love, and Aggression*, was published in November 1983, just before he died from a failed heart operation on November 21.

KEY DATES	
1902	Born in Washington, D.C., on October 14.
1924	Graduates with a BA degree from Williams College.
1932	Awarded an MA in anthropology from Harvard University.
1935	Teaches social anthropology at Dillard University.
1939	Moves to the University of Chicago.
1942	Receives his doctorate.
1983	Dies on November 21.

Further reading: Harrison, Ira. *African American Pioneers in Anthropology*. Chicago, IL: University of Illinois Press, 1999.
http://www.lib.uchicago.edu/e/spcl/centcat/fac/facch25_01.html (Biography with photos and manuscripts).

DAWSON, William
Composer, Conductor

One of the most celebrated African American orchestral composers, William Dawson is best known for his *Negro Folk Symphony* (1934; revised 1952) and his directorship of the renowned African American Tuskegee Institute Choir. His pioneering works were among the first to incorporate the traditions of African American folk music into classical compositions.

At Tuskegee

William Levi Dawson was born on September 25, 1899, in the mining town of Anniston in northeast Alabama. When still a boy, he ran away from home and, aged 13, enrolled at Alabama's Tuskegee Institute—an African American college founded by Booker T. Washington in 1881. Dawson graduated in 1921 and went on to study at the Chicago Musical College and the American Conservatory of Music, where he gained his MA. Meanwhile, he had already begun composing and for a time was the principal trombonist with the Chicago Civic Symphony Orchestra.

In 1931, after a period teaching at public schools in Kansas City, Dawson returned to the Tuskegee Institute as a professor of music. He also assumed directorship of the college's 100-voice choir, which he rapidly transformed into one of the leading a cappella (voice-only) singing groups in the United States. The choir was particularly renowned for Dawson's moving, beautifully crafted arrangements of traditional spirituals. In 1932 it performed to great acclaim during the opening week of New York City's Radio City Music Hall.

A black national music

Dawson's compositional work was deeply imbued with his pride in his African American heritage. He was inspired by the example of the Bohemian (Czech) composer Antonín

▲ *Under William Dawson's directorship the Tuskegee Institute Choir performed for Presidents Herbert Hoover and Franklin D. Roosevelt.*

Dvořák (1841–1904), who had created a new national music by drawing on his country's folk traditions. In this respect Dawson's masterpiece was undoubtedly the *Negro Folk Symphony*, which fused black and white, American and European, folk and classical traditions. The symphony received its premiere in 1934, played by the Philadelphia Orchestra.

Dawson remained at Tuskegee for 25 years, during which time he continued to direct the choir and compose. Among his works was a revised version of his *Negro Folk Symphony*, inspired by a visit to West Africa in 1952. He died on May 2, 1990, and was buried on the grounds of Tuskegee Institute.

See also: Washington, Booker T.

Further reading: Johnson, John Andrew. "William Dawson, 'The New Negro,' and His Folk Idiom." *Black Music Research Journal*, Vol. 19, 1999.
www.alamhof.org/dawsonwl.htm (Biography).

KEY DATES	
1899	Born in Anniston, Alabama, on September 25.
1921	Graduates from Tuskegee Institute.
1931	Becomes director of the Tuskegee Institute Choir.
1934	Premiere of the *Negro Folk Symphony*.
1990	Dies in Alabama on May 2.

DAY, William Howard
Editor, Minister

Called "the grandest and most refined man of this country, regardless of race" by the *Harrisburg Telegraph* in 1898, William Howard Day was an editor, civil rights advocate, and minister. He spent his life fighting to improve the status of African Americans.

A lucky start

William Howard Day was born on October 19, 1825, in New York. His parents were a sailmaker and a seamstress. Day excelled at school; when J. P. Williston, a white inkmaker, visited the school, he was so impressed with Day that he persuaded the boy's parents to let him adopt their son. Williston took Day back to Northampton, Massachusetts, where Day went to school while he apprenticed with the *Hampshire Herald* as a printer.

After being refused admission to Williams College because of his color, in 1843 Day went to study at Oberlin College, Ohio. He graduated from there four years later. Day worked as a printer on the *Northampton Gazette*, and in New York City before moving to Cleveland, Ohio. Inspired by the example of abolitionist and writer Frederick Douglass, Day got a job with the *Cleveland True Democrat*, working from 1851 to 1852 as a reporter and local editor. He later went on to publish and edit the *Aliened American* (1853–1954). The paper's stated aim was "to aid the educational development of Colored Americans and to assist in enforcing an appreciation of the benefit of trades and to aim at our Social Elevation."

Day was a leading figure in the Negro Convention Movement, which encouraged black emigration to Canada but also tried to improve the lives of those who stayed in the United States. Day used his newspaper as a vehicle to express the movement's views. From 1854 to 1856 he worked as librarian for the Cleveland Library Association, the most influential cultural organization in the city.

Canada and Britain

In 1856 frustration at the situation of black people in the United States led Day to take his wife, whom he had married in 1852, to Canada. In 1858 he set out on a tour of Europe, where he made speeches and raised funds for the antislavery cause. Day had helped in the preparations for white abolitionist John Brown's unsuccessful raid on Harpers Ferry, Virginia, in 1859, printing Brown's alternative version of the Constitution by hand. Day was

KEY DATES

1825 Born in New York City on October 19.

1851 Becomes editor of *Cleveland True Democrat* until 1852.

1853 Becomes editor of *Aliened American* until 1854.

1867 Ordained as a minister in African Methodist Episcopal Church.

1900 Dies in Harrisburg, Pennsylvania, on December 3.

in Europe when Brown was captured and executed. Meanwhile, Day became involved in the African Aid Society, formed in 1860 to help men such as black nationalists Martin R. Delaney and Henry Highland Garnet in their bid to promote black emigration to the west coast of Africa. However, Day's involvement with his work harmed his marriage, and on his return to America he got divorced.

After the Civil War

Day returned to the United States after the Civil War (1861–1865) and worked for the Freedmen's Bureau, established in 1865 to supervise relief and education for refugees and freedmen. He became an inspector of schools for the bureau in Maryland and Delaware, founding more than 100 schools and hiring a similar number of teachers.

In 1867 Day was ordained a minister of the African Methodist Episcopal church (AME). In 1872 he bought a small newspaper in Harrisburg, Pennsylvania, which he renamed *Our National Progress*: The paper examined issues of interest to the black community. From 1875 to 1880 Day was general secretary of the General Conference of AME. From 1878 to 1893 he was a member of the Harrisburg School Board, becoming its first African American president in 1891. Day died in Harrisburg on December 3, 1900, aged 75.

See also: Delaney, Martin R.; Douglass, Frederick; Garnet, Henry Highland

Further reading: Gates, Henry Louis, Jr., et al (eds.). *African Americans*. New York, NY: Oxford University Press, 2002. http://www.spartacus.schoolnet.co.uk/USASday.htm (Brief biography).

DEAN, Mark
Computer Scientist

Mark Dean is an inventor and a leading computer scientist with International Business Machines (IBM). During the last two decades of the 20th century he was primarily responsible for increasing the power of personal computers in inverse proportion to their physical size.

Early life

Born in Jefferson City, Tennessee, in 1957, Dean learned his love of engineering from his father, a supervisor at a Tennessee Valley Authority dam,who helped the boy build a tractor from scratch.

One of the few black students to attend Jefferson City High, Dean was a straight A student and a good athlete. He recalled being asked if he was really black by a white student who could not believe that someone so smart could be African American. Dean went on to the University of Tennessee, graduating at the top of his class in 1979. He stayed on to specialize in electrical engineering. After receiving a BS, he gained a master of science in electrical engineering (MSEE) from Florida Atlantic University in 1982, and a PhD from Stanford in 1992.

IBM

From 1980 Dean worked for IBM. He rose quickly through the ranks to lead a team, along with colleague Dennis Moeller, that developed a microcomputer system with a control bus for peripheral processing devices, such as modems and printers. The control bus carries signals that report the status of the devices and enable the personal computer (PC) to communicate with them. Before Dean's work most PCs were too big to be practical in the home; his invention is one of the key reasons why they are now nearly as common in the home as televisions.

▲ **Mark Dean is one of IBM's top ideas people. He has worked on many groundbreaking projects.**

In 1995 IBM recognized Dean's achievement by awarding him a fellowship: Dean is one of only 50 of the corporation's 300,000 staff and the first black American to have been so honored. Two years later he took charge of the IBM Austin Research Laboratory in Austin, Texas. In April 2000 Dean was also appointed vice president of systems in IBM Research.

In 1997 Dean was inducted into the National Inventors' Hall of Fame. In 1999 he led the team of electronic engineers that built the first one-gigahertz chip, which is capable of performing a billion calculations a second. Dean said, "With technology, if you can talk about it, that means it's possible." In the same way he argues that many children today are not told that they can achieve whatever they want to: "There are no limits," he says. In 2005 Dean held more than 20 U.S. patents, including three of IBM's original nine, and had a further 10 pending.

KEY DATES	
1957	Born in Jefferson City, Tennessee, on March 2.
1979	Graduates from the University of Tennessee.
1980	Joins IBM; develops ISA systems bus.
1992	Awarded PhD by Stanford University.
1997	Inducted into Inventors' Hall of Fame.
1999	Perfects the first one-gigahertz computer chip.

Further reading: Killen, Michael. *IBM, the Making of the Common View.* New York, NY: Harcourt Brace Jovanovich, 1988.
www.research.ibm.com/people/d/deanm (IBM biography).

DEBAPTISTE, George
Abolitionist, Businessman

A wealthy Detroit businessman, George DeBaptiste was an important figure in the Underground Railroad, the secret network of routes and safe houses operated by black and white abolitionists that enabled fugitive slaves from the South to reach safety in the North during the decades before the Civil War (1861–1865). His younger brother, Reverend Richard DeBaptiste, was similarly active in the antislavery movement in Chicago.

A president's valet

George DeBaptiste was born to free parents in 1815 in Fredericksburg, Virginia. He was the grandson of John DeBaptiste, who had given distinguished service as a sailor during the American Revolution (1775–1783). Apprenticed as a barber while a teenager, DeBaptiste went to work in Richmond, where he first began to help runaway slaves.

In 1838 DeBaptiste moved to Indiana and was hired as a valet by General William Henry Harrison, whom he accompanied on his 1840 campaign for the presidency. In 1841 Harrison became the ninth president of the United States, and DeBaptiste went to live in the White House.

A businessman with a secret

After Harrison's sudden death from pneumonia shortly after his inauguration DeBaptiste returned to Indiana and resumed his barber's business. He soon moved to Michigan, finally settling in Detroit. There he established himself as one of the city's most prominent black leaders and businessmen. He also secretly became a manager of the Underground Railroad, on which Detroit was an important stop. It was a risky undertaking. In 1850 a new Fugitive Slave Act imposed tough penalties on those caught helping runaway slaves. DeBaptiste often spent his nights meeting escaped slaves and taking them to their next refuge, walking up to 20 miles (32km) and then working the next day.

From the 1820s until the Civil War began in 1861, about 40,000 slaves escaped to freedom. Some went to Pennsylvania, New York, and Massachusetts, but many more ended up in Illinois, Indiana, and Ohio. Thousands fled to Canada, others to Mexico and the Caribbean.

During the 1850s DeBaptiste ran a steamer named the *Whitney*, which he used to smuggle slaves across the Great Lakes into Canada. He met and corresponded with fellow abolitionist John Brown (1800–1859); DeBaptiste felt, like Brown, that sometimes extreme measures were justified. In a meeting with Brown in 1858 DeBaptiste proposed "a gunpowder plot" in which 15 white churches in the South would be blown up in an attempt to force the southern states to end slavery.

During and after the war

When war broke out in 1861, DeBaptiste helped raise troops for Michigan's black regiment and served as its sutler (food provisioner) during its campaigns. When the war ended, DeBaptiste set up a catering business.

In 1965 the Thirteenth Amendment, which abolished slavery, was ratified, followed in 1969 by the Fifteenth Amendment, which prohibited federal or state governments from infringing on a citizen's right to vote "on account of race, color, or previous condition of servitude." During celebrations in Detroit to mark those events, DeBaptiste hung out a sign marked: "Notice to Stockholders—Office of the Underground Railway: This office is permanently closed." African Americans rejoiced too soon, however, as for almost a century the law had little practical effect on their ability to vote, particularly in the South.

DeBaptiste became president of the Detroit Urban League and worked hard to integrate the schools in Detroit. He died of cancer in 1875. DeBaptiste is commemorated in Detroit's Gateway to Freedom memorial on the banks of the Detroit River, which was dedicated on October 20, 2001.

KEY DATES	
1815	Born in Fredericksburg, Virginia, on March 26,
1846	Moves to Detroit, where he manages the local Underground Railroad.
1875	Dies in Detroit on February 22.

See also: Slavery

Further reading: Blockson, Charles L. *The Hippocrene Guide to the Underground Railroad.* New York, NY: Hippocrene Books, 1995.
clarke.cmich.edu/undergroundrailroad/georgedebaptiste.htm (A contemporary obituary from the *Detroit Daily Post*).

DEE, Ruby
Actor

Ruby Dee was the first African American woman to appear in major roles at the American Shakespeare Festival in Stratford, Connecticut. In 1971 she won an Obie for her performance in Athol Fugard's play *Boesman and Lena*.

She was born Ruby Ann Wallace on October 27, 1924, in Cleveland, Ohio. Her father was a railroad porter and her mother was a schoolteacher. Shortly after her birth, her family moved to Harlem, New York City. Dee (the theatrical name she later adopted) was heavily involved in drama both at high school and at Hunter College, from which she graduated in 1945. During her college years Dee acted for the American Negro Theater. She made her professional debut in 1943 in *South Pacific*.

Broadway years

Once she left college, Dee's career took off. In 1947 she received acclaim for her performance in the title role of the Broadway play *Anna Lucasta*. A year later she married fellow actor Ossie Davis, whom she had met during an earlier Broadway production, *Jeb*, in 1946. Davis and Dee would go on to become two of the most recognizable African American faces in theater and television. They made their first joint film appearance in 1950 in the movie *No Way Out* and continued to appear together in numerous films and television series, hosting their own TV show *Ossie and Ruby!* (1980) and starring in the Spike Lee movies *Do the Right Thing* (1989) and *Jungle Fever* (1991). Ossie Davis died on February 4, 2005, in Miami, Florida.

▲ *Ruby Dee and Ossie Davis in 1963; their marriage lasted 56 years.*

Dee also enjoyed considerable solo success. She made her name in the biographical movie *The Jackie Robinson Story* (1950) and went on to appear in films such as *A Raisin in the Sun* (1961) and *Buck and the Preacher* (1972). She also enjoyed a successful theatrical career, highlights of which included an appearance as Kate in Shakespeare's *The Taming of the Shrew* in 1965. In 1988 she performed in a one-woman show, *My One Good Nerve*.

Like her husband, Dee spoke out on humanitarian and civil rights issues throughout her career. She received numerous major awards for her work, many of which were presented to her and Davis simultaneously. They included the National Medal of Arts in 1995, the Screen Actors' Guild Life Achievement Award in 2000, and Kennedy Center Honors in 2004. Both Dee and Davis were also inducted into the Theater Hall of Fame in 1988.

See also: Davis, Ossie; Lee, Spike

Further reading: Davis, Ossie, and Ruby Dee. *With Ossie and Ruby: In This Life Together.* New York, NY: HarperCollins Publishers, 2000.
http://www.npr.org/templates/story/story.php?storyId=1119605 (Audio interview with Dee and Davis).

KEY DATES	
1924	Born in Cleveland, Ohio, on October 27.
1943	Stars in the play *South Pacific*.
1948	Marries Ossie Davis.
1950	Makes first movie appearance alongside her husband in *No Way Out*.
1948	Appears in Shakespeare's *Taming of the Shrew*.
1980	Begins hosting *Ossie and Ruby!* a television show in which she appears with her husband.
2000	Receives the Screen Actors' Guild Life Achievement Award jointly with her husband.

DEFRANTZ, Anita L.
Athlete, Sports Rights Advocate

Anita L. DeFrantz is a renowned advocate for women in sports and a powerful woman in amateur sports. In 1984 she became the first president of the Los Angeles Amateur Athletic Foundation (AAF). In 1997 she became the first woman and the first African American elected as an International Olympic Committee (IOC) vice president.

Discovers rowing

Born on October 4, 1952, in Philadelphia, Pennsylvania, DeFrantz was raised in a middle-class home. Her father was a community activist, and her mother was a University of San Francisco professor.

DeFrantz graduated from Connecticut College in 1974. She attended the University of Pennsylvania Law School, graduating in 1977, and was admitted to the Pennsylvania state bar that year.

In 1973 DeFrantz accepted the invitation of the college crew coach, Bart Gulong, to join the team. In 1976 she won a bronze medal in rowing at the Olympic Games in Montreal, Canada, and was captain of the U.S. team. She won a silver medal in the 1978 World Championships in rowing, was a finalist in the World Championships four times, and won six National Championships. DeFrantz was determined to go for gold in the 1980 Olympics.

Olympic boycott

In 1980 President Jimmy Carter (1977–1981) announced that the United States would boycott the Olympic Games in response to the Soviet Union's invasion of Afghanistan. Attending the Moscow Olympics, he argued, would be dangerous for Americans. DeFrantz disagreed with the decision, arguing that it breached the rights of athletes, who should be able to choose whether or not to participate. DeFrantz cited the Amateur Sports Act of 1978,

▲ *Anita DeFrantz in 1997, when she became vice president of the IOC.*

which barred anyone from denying athletes the right to compete in the Olympics. She led a group of Olympians in a protest, suing the U.S. Olympic Committee (*Anita L. DeFrantz v. United States Olympic Committee*). Although DeFrantz lost the case, she was the only Olympian ever to challenge the USOC. She says, "If I had been able to compete in the 1980 Olympic Games, so much of this would be different. It was really my work to fight the boycott in 1980 that led to my work [of sports advocacy] in the IOC."

In 1984 DeFrantz became the first president of the AAF and in 1986 the first African American to be appointed to the IOC, becoming vice president in 1997. In 2001 she failed in her bid to become its first woman president.

Further reading: *Official Biography, Anita L. DeFrantz*. Los Angeles, CA: Amateur Athletic Foundation, 2005.
www.msmagazine.com/summer2004/anitadefrantz.asp (*Ms. Magazine* interview).

KEY DATES	
1952	Born in Philadelphia, Pennsylvania, on October 4.
1976	Wins Olympic Bronze Medal.
1980	Sues U.S. Olympic Committee (USOC).
1984	Becomes president of AAF.
1986	Becomes first African American appointed to IOC.

DELANEY, Beauford
Artist

Beauford Delaney is today considered one of the finest African American artists of the 20th century. During much of his lifetime his work was largely ignored, but it is now appreciated for its jazzlike exuberance and for its foreshadowing of abstract expressionism—the first great movement in modern American art.

▼ *Beauford Delaney in his studio in Paris, France, in August 1962.*

Beauford Delaney was born in 1901 in Knoxville, Tennessee. His father, Samuel, was a Methodist minister; but despite the strict atmosphere of the family home, he and his wife, Delia Johnson, encouraged their 10 children's artistic talents. Beauford's drawings and paintings won the admiration of white Knoxville artist Lloyd Branson, who helped him study painting in Boston at the Massachusetts Normal School of Art and the South Boston School of Art.

In 1929 Delaney moved to New York City, whose flourishing black arts scene was centered in Harlem. There Delaney became friends with some of the leading black writers, musicians, and artists of the day, including Ethel Waters and Louis Armstrong. Delaney recorded his friendships in a series of luminous portraits that often feature the color yellow. He also painted exuberant scenes of New York's street life. Delaney never made much money from his work, but he became a minor celebrity noted for

KEY DATES

1901	Born in Knoxville, Tennessee, December 31.
1929	Moves to New York City.
1953	Settles in Paris, France.
1979	Dies in Paris on March 26.

his high spirits, charm, and generosity. Nonetheless, Delaney's was a deeply troubled personality. He worried about his homosexuality, drank too much, and suffered from fits of delusion.

Inspired by Delaney's success, his younger brother Joseph (1904– 1991) moved to New York in 1930; but he found that Beauford had changed, and the two brothers drifted apart. Joseph spent the next 50 years painting realistic pictures of Manhattan's street life.

In the early 1940s a New York newspaper described Beauford as living without electricity in Greenwich Village in a condemned building, whose floors were sometimes coated with ice. By candlelight, he showed visitors the paintings that covered his walls.

The expatriate in Paris

In 1953 Delaney left New York for a short stay in Paris, France, which became permanent. Many African American writers, artists, and musicians had settled in Paris. There Delaney's paintings became increasingly abstract—color, light, and form were more important than subject matter. Although he continued to exhibit, he remained very poor and could often be found painting in his unheated studio wearing a parka and wool hat. His mental problems worsened, and he was institutionalized. Delaney died in 1979 without a will. Joseph paid to have his brother's paintings and effects shipped back to Knoxville.

See also: Armstrong, Louis; Harlem Renaissance; Waters, Ethel

Further reading: Leeming, David. *Amazing Grace: A Life of Beauford Delaney.* New York, NY: Oxford University Press, 1998.
www.cnn.com/2003/TRAVEL/DESTINATIONS/03/15/
delaney.yellow.ap (Exhibition review including examples of Delaney's works).

DELANY, Martin Robinson
Journalist, Abolitionist, Physician, Army Officer

Best known for his involvement in the "back to Africa" movement, Martin Robinson Delany was a prominent journalist, abolitionist, and intellectual who also practiced medicine for much of his life.

Born in Charlestown, Virginia, on May 6, 1812, Delany was the son of a slave and a free mother. In 1822 he moved with his mother and siblings to Chambersburg, Pennsylvania; a year later his father joined the family there after having purchased his freedom. Delany was taught to read by his mother. In 1831 he attended Bethel Church School in Pittsburgh, later serving as an assistant to the local doctor.

In 1843 Delany married Kate Richards, with whom he had 11 children. That same year he founded an antislavery newspaper called the *Mystery;* Delany later became coeditor, with abolitionist Frederick Douglass, of the *North Star*. Delany also actively helped slaves escape to the North along the Underground Railroad, a secret network of routes and safe houses.

"Back to Africa"

In 1849 Delany enrolled at Harvard Medical School; he set up practice in Pittsburgh in 1852. That same year Delany published his controversial work *The Condition, Elevation, Emigration and Destiny of the Colored People of the United States*, which promoted the settlement of black people outside of the United States. His writing stemmed from his interest in the "back to Africa" movement, which urged free slaves to emigrate to Africa. During the 1850s Delany dedicated much of his time to this issue, including helping organize the first National Emigration Convention in 1854. In 1959 he headed an expedition to Yorubas (now part of

▲ *Major Martin R. Delany was the highest ranking African American officer in the Civil War.*

Nigeria) to investigate the area as a possible resettlement location. He returned to the United States after the Civil War (1861–1865) had broken out and was appointed a major in charge of recruiting black soldiers. After the war Delany moved to South Carolina and later became a judge. He spent his last years supporting the emigration of blacks to Liberia, writing, and practicing medicine.

See also: Douglass, Frederick; Slavery

Further reading: Ullman, Victor. *Martin R. Delany: The Beginnings of Black Nationalism*. Boston, MA: Beacon Press, 1971.
http://www.libraries.wvu.edu/delany/home.htm (Comprehensive site dedicated to Delany).

KEY DATES

1812   Born in Charlestown, Virginia (now West Virginia) on May 6.

1847   Becomes coeditor of the *North Star* with Frederick Douglass.

1852   Publishes *The Destiny of the Colored People of the United States*.

1859   Visits Yorubas, West Africa.

1885   Dies in Wilberforce, Ohio, on January 24.

DEMBY, Edward T.
Bishop

Edward T. Demby was the first African American to be consecrated a bishop. He served in the African Methodist Episcopalian Church (AME) until his death.

Edward Thomas Demby was born on February 13, 1869, in a wagon on the way from Baltimore, Maryland, to Wilmington, Delaware. He graduated from Howard University, Washington, D.C., in 1893 and that same year took his divinity degree at Wilberforce University, Ohio.

In 1895 Demby left the Methodist Church in which he had been brought up and was ordained as a priest in the African Methodist Episcopalian Church. In 1896 he took charge of St. Paul's Church in Mason, Tennessee, the second largest black mission in the state, with a congregation of 50. Within a year Demby had increased membership by 18. He also ran the day school, which, although fee-paying, proved attractive to African Americans

KEY DATES	
1869	Born in Delaware on February 13.
1893	Awarded Bachelor of Divinity.
1895	Ordained a priest in African Methodist Episcopalian Church.
1918	Consecrated a bishop in September.
1957	Dies on October 14.

▼ *Edward T. Demby was the first African American to be consecrated a bishop.*

because of the poor education provided for their children in local public schools.

From 1899 to 1904 Demby worked in other churches in Tennessee and Missouri, sometimes in more than one at a time. He then moved to St. Peter's in Key West, Florida, where in two years he increased the congregation and doubled the size of the school to four teachers and 150 students. His reputation as an evangelical preacher and educator was now firmly established.

Fighting segregation

In 1909 the diocese of Tennessee made it a requirement that all congregations in the state be segregated. In 1912 Demby became archdeacon for "colored work" in Tennessee, and in 1917 the Episcopal government of the segregated mission in Arkansas offered him the job of suffragan (assistant) bishop for "colored work in the Southwest." He initially turned it down but later accepted the post. Consecrated in St. Louis, Missouri, in September 1918, Demby proposed to bring as many as possible of the 1,850,000 African Americans in his diocese into the Episcopalian Church. He was held back from achieving that mission by a constant lack of funds, however.

In 1932 Demby was one of the three bishops—the other two were white—who ousted the newly enthroned bishop of Little Rock, Arkansas; they argued that he had been elected on racist grounds. Demby remained in office until his death in October 1957.

Further reading: Beary, Michael J. *Black Bishop: Edward T. Demby and the Struggle for Racial Equality in the Episcopal Church.* Chicago: University of Illinois Press, 2001.
http://www.ube.org/history/bbishops.htm (Black bishops in America).

DEPREIST, James
Conductor

Widely considered to be one of the United States's finest conductors, James DePreist has served with many orchestras around the world. His name, however, is most closely associated with the Oregon Symphony, which under his musical directorship rapidly established itself as one of the United States's leading orchestras. He has made numerous recordings, including 15 with the Oregon Symphony alone.

DePreist was born on November 21, 1936, in Philadelphia, Pennsylvania. His childhood was steeped in classical music: His aunt was the celebrated opera singer Marian Anderson, with whom he remained close until her death in 1993. DePreist studied composition at the Philadelphia Conservatory of Music under the composer Vincent Persichetti and went on to earn BS and MA degrees from the University of Pennsylvania in 1958 and 1961 respectively.

DePreist's musical career was threatened in 1962 when he contracted polio while on a musical tour of Thailand and was left permanently disabled. He was able nonetheless to win first prize in the Dimitri Mitropoulos International Conducting Competition in 1964. Soon afterward he was chosen by composer and conductor Leonard Bernstein to be an assistant conductor of the New York Philharmonic for the 1965–1966 season.

DePreist subsequently worked with many orchestras in Europe, the United States, and Canada, holding musical directorships of both the Monte Carlo Philharmonic Orchestra and the Quebec Symphony Orchestra. In 1980 he was appointed music director and conductor of the Oregon Symphony, a position that he continued to hold until 2002.

Bringing classical music to the masses

Throughout his tenure in Oregon DePreist was committed to bringing classical music to as wide an audience as possible, and he expanded the orchestra's educational and community programs. He gained a reputation for championing modern American composers, from pioneering giants such as the German-born Paul Hindemith (1895–1963) to contemporary figures such as Joseph Schwantner (1943–). In 1995 he conducted the Oregon Symphony's recording of Schwantner's *New Morning for the World: Daybreak of Freedom* (1982), a tribute to civil rights leader Martin Luther King, Jr.

▲ *Conductor James DePreist is best known for his work with the Oregon Symphony.*

In 2005 DePreist was appointed musical director of the Tokyo Metropolitan Symphony Orchestra. In addition to his work as a conductor, DePreist has also written two books of poetry, *This Precipice Garden* (1987) and *The Distant Siren* (1989).

KEY DATES	
1936	Born in Philadelphia, Pennsylvania, on November 21.
1965	Appointed assistant conductor of the New York Philharmonic.
1980	Appointed musical director of the Oregon Symphony.
2005	Appointed musical director of the Tokyo Metropolitan Symphony Orchestra.

See also: Anderson, Marian; King, Martin Luther, Jr.

Further reading: DePreist, James. *This Precipice Garden.* Portland, OR: University of Portland Press, 1987.
http://www.jamesdepreist.com (DePreist's official site).

DEPRIEST, Oscar
Politician, Civil Activist

Respected politician and civil rights campaigner Oscar DePriest was the first African American to be elected to the House of Representatives in the 20th century. DePriest once said that "Politics was recreation to me. I always enjoyed a good fight."

Born in Florence, Alabama, on March 9, 1871, Oscar Stanton DePriest moved with his family to Salina, Kansas, at age six. DePriest attended the local public school, where he studied business and bookkeeping among other subjects. In 1889 DePriest ran away from home with two white friends to Dayton, Ohio, but ended up moving to Chicago, where he found employment as a painter and decorator. DePriest began to invest in the stock market and in real estate; he showed a talent for business, and he amassed a fortune.

Political career

DePriest entered politics in 1904 when he joined the Republican Party and served two terms as a Cook County commissioner. He was appointed alternate delegate to the Republican National Convention in 1908. Seven years later DePriest became Chicago's first African American alderman. He was accused of bribery in 1917 and in 1919 but was subsequently cleared of the charges.

In 1928 DePriest became the first black American of the 20th century and the first from the North to be elected to the House of Representatives. During his three terms in office (1928–1934) DePriest fought discrimination in government and the military, proposed an antilynching bill, recommended a monthly pension for former slaves aged 75 and over, and suggested

▲ **Oscar DePriest was the first black congressman to be elected from a northern state.**

that a reduced number of congressional seats be granted to the states that discriminated against African Americans. In 1933 he succeeded in adding an antidiscrimination amendment to the bill establishing the Civilian Conservation Corps.

In 1929 there was an outcry from white politicians and the press when First Lady Lou Hoover invited Jessie DePriest to one of her tea parties for congressional wives. Southern papers accused Mrs. Hoover of "defiling" the White House and the Texas legislature formally admonished her.

In 1934 DePriest lost his seat to Arthur W. Mitchell, after which he returned to his real-estate business. DePriest was elected to Chicago's City Council in 1943 and served as alderman until 1947. He died in 1951.

See also: Political Representation

Further reading: Ragsdale, Bruce A., and Joel D. Treese. *Black Americans in Congress, 1870–1989.* Washington, D.C.: U.S. Government Printing Office, 1990.
http://www.chicagotribute.org/Markers/DePriest.htm (Chicago Makers tribute site featuring a biography of DePriest).

KEY DATES

1871 Born in Florence, Alabama, on March 9.

1889 Moves to Chicago, Illinois, where he generates a fortune from his real-estate business.

1904 Serves as a Cook County commissioner for four years.

1915 Becomes the first African American to be elected to the Chicago City Council.

1928 Elected to the House of Representatives.

1951 Dies in Chicago, Illinois, on May 12.

DERRICOTTE, Toi
Poet

One of the best-known contemporary African American women poets, Toi Derricotte uses her work to explore her own and other people's painful experience of racism. In addition to four collections of her poetry, she has published a powerful and controversial memoir, *The Black Notebooks* (1997).

The color of skin

Derricotte was born into a middle-class family in Hamtramck, Detroit, Michigan, on April 12, 1941. She earned a BA in special education at Wayne State University and went on to teach in Detroit's public schools. Derricotte studied English literature and creative writing at New York University, where she received her MA. She published her first book of poetry, *The Empress of the Death House,* in 1978. Her other poetry collections were *Natural Birth* (1983), *Captivity* (1989), and *Tender* (1997).

Derricotte's poetry is fierce and unflinching. She often uses stories from her own life to examine society's racism as well as the complex feelings of guilt, shame, and confusion that African Americans can suffer because of their skin color. In "Brother," for example, she shows the difficulties encountered by her dark-skinned brother because both his father and sister look white. Perhaps, the poet wonders, this is why he has married a woman with such black skin "and brags to family, strangers,/ to anyone about that/blackness—so easily recognized, his."

In her memoir, *The Black Notebooks*, Derricotte has written about the anguish she has suffered because of her pale skin, which makes her feel as if she is not a "proper" African American. She also admits to having tried to pass as white, for example when trying to buy a house in a white, middle-class suburb, and has often had to listen to racist remarks because white people assume she is white.

A refuge for black poets

Derricotte is sensitive to the isolation that many black poets can feel in what is an overwhelmingly white discipline. In 1995 she joined with other black poets and academics to found Cave Canem, a retreat and writers' workshop where African American poets can feel safe and offer each other support. The name, which means "beware the dog," suggests the protection participants are offered from those who attack black poetry. Derricotte has won

▲ *Toi Derricotte has won several awards for her work, including a Pushcart Prize.*

many honors, including fellowships from the National Endowment for the Arts and the Guggenheim. In 2005 she was associate professor of English at the University of Pittsburgh.

KEY DATES	
1941	Born in Hamtramck, Michigan, on April 12.
1978	Publishes her first collection of poetry, *The Empress of the Death House*.
1997	Publishes her memoir, *The Black Notebooks*.

Further reading: Derricotte, Toi. *The Black Notebooks: An Interior Journey.* New York, NY: W. W. Norton & Co., Inc., 1999. www.poetrymagazine.com/archives/2003/Fall2003/derricotte.htm (Includes a short biography as well as some sample poems).

DETT, R. Nathaniel
Composer, Pianist

Nathaniel Dett received national acclaim as a pianist, composer, and conductor. He was an important force in the preservation and performance of African American folk music. As a composer Dett promoted a style of music that set African American folk music within a western European structure. He influenced several generations of classical musicians.

The road to success

Robert Nathaniel Dett was born on October 11, 1882, in Drummondsville, Ontario, Canada, a terminus of the Underground Railroad set up to help fugitive slaves. His family moved to Niagara Falls, New York, in 1893. Dett's family was musical; the boy learned to play the piano by ear at age three and started piano lessons at age five. In 1900 Dett published his first composition for piano, a ragtime piece titled "After the Cakewalk." Between 1901 and 1903 Dett studied at the Oliver Willis Halstead Conservatory in Lockport, New York, and then at Oberlin College, Ohio; in 1908 he became the first African

▼ **Composer, conductor, and teacher R. Nathaniel Dett influenced several generations of musicians.**

American to receive a BA in music from Oberlin. Dett taught at several black American colleges, but his longest tenure was at the Hampton Institute, Virginia, where he stayed for almost 20 years (1913–1932); he became director of the music department there and founded the Hampton Choir, which toured the United States and Europe and established Dett as a conductor and composer of spirituals. In 1919 Dett was also instrumental in founding the National Association of Negro Musicians; he was president of the organization between 1924 and 1926.

In addition to composing, conducting, teaching, and writing music, Dett carried on studying, attending several universities, including Harvard (1920–1921), from which he received the Francis Boott Music Prize for his choral work *Don't Be Weary, Traveler*, and the Bowdoin Literary Prize for the essay "The Emancipation of Negro Music." He was awarded honorary doctorates from Howard University (1924) and Oberlin College (1926). In 1929 Dett went to study with the French composer, conductor, and teacher Nadia Boulanger (1887–1979). He also received an MA in music from the Eastman School of Music in Rochester, New York, in 1932.

During World War II (1939–1945) Dett joined the United Services Organization. He was touring as choirmaster of the Women's Army Chorus when he suffered a fatal heart attack in 1943. The Nathaniel Dett Chorale was founded in 1998, and in 2000 Hampton University established the Robert Nathaniel Dett Music Society.

KEY DATES	
1882	Born in Drummondsville, Ontario, on October 11.
1900	Publishes first composition for piano.
1908	Becomes the first black American to receive a BA in music from Oberlin College.
1932	Receives MA in music from Eastman School of Music.
1943	Dies in Battle Creek, Michigan, on October 2.

Further reading: Simpson, Anne Key. *Follow Me: The Life and Music of R. Nathaniel Dett*. Metuchen, NJ: Scarecrow Press, 1993.
http://www.afrovoices.com/dett.html (Biography).

DEVERS, Gail
Athlete

The athletic success enjoyed by two-time Olympic 100-meter champion Gail Devers came in the face of tremendous physical adversity, in particular a potentially career-ending health crisis. Despite such obstacles, Devers persevered to win gold in the premier women's athletic event at two consecutive Olympic Games.

Early life

Yolanda Gail Devers was born in 1966 in Washington. As a young girl she moved to a small town near San Diego, California. Although she began her athletic career as a distance runner, she quickly shifted to shorter races, achieving considerable sprinting success in high school. Devers's athletic prowess led to her being pursued by several major universities, and she eventually elected to study at the University of California at Los Angeles (UCLA). While there she won the 100-meter sprint at the 1988 National Collegiate Athletic Association (NCAA) championships and also set a United States record in the 100-meter hurdles.

Devers's performances seemed to augur well for the Olympic Games, due to be held in Seoul, South Korea, later that year. However, she started to develop health problems, including migraine headaches, sleeplessness, and fainting spells, and performed disappointingly.

Fighting illness

Devers initially believed that her illnesses had been caused by the stress of preparing for such a major event. In 1990, however, she was diagnosed with Graves' Disease, a debilitating thyroid disorder. She undertook radiation therapy to treat the illness, but it caused her feet to become so blistered, swollen, and cracked that doctors considered amputating them.

Gradually, however, Devers regained her health and resumed her intense athletic training. At the next Olympic Games, held in Barcelona, Spain, in 1992, Devers's perseverance and training paid off. She won her first Olympic gold medal in the 100-meter sprint. She also reached the final of the 100-meter hurdles but stumbled while in the lead and finished fifth.

Devers's dominant form continued over the next few years. At the 1993 World Championships in Stuttgart, Germany, she won both the 100-meter sprint and the 100-meter hurdles, and further success followed at the 1995

▲ *Gail Devers on her way to gold in the 100-meter hurdles at the DN Galan Grand Prix meet in Stockholm in 2002.*

World Championships. At the 1996 Olympic Games in Atlanta Devers repeated her gold-medal performance in the 100-meter sprint; she was also part of the gold medal-winning 4 x 100-meter relay team, although success again eluded her in the hurdles.

Injury hampered Devers's attempts to defend her Olympic 100-meter title in Sydney, Australia, in 2000. In 2002 she won a gold medal in the 100-meter hurdles in Stockholm. In 2004 she qualified for the Olympic Games in Athens but failed to win a medal.

KEY DATES	
1966	Born in Seattle, Washington, on November 19.
1990	Diagnosed with Graves' Disease.
1992	Wins 100 meters at Olympic Games in Barcelona.
1993	Wins both the 100-meter and the 100-meter hurdles at World Championships in Stuttgart.
1995	Defends 100-meter hurdles title at World Championships.
1996	Defends Olympic 100-meter title in Atlanta.
1999	Wins third world title in 100-meter hurdles.
2004	Qualifies for Athens Olympics at 37 years of age.

Further reading: Plowden, Martha Ward. *Olympic Black Women*. Gretna, LA: Pelican Publishing Company, 1996. www.gaildevers.com (Devers's official site).

DICKERSON, Earl B.
Attorney

Earl B. Dickerson fought many battles during his lifetime. As a lawyer, businessman, and chair of the Supreme Liberty Life Insurance Company, the largest black-owned insurance company in the United States, Dickerson fought racial discrimination, particularly with regard to housing policy.

Early life
Born in Canton, Mississippi, on June 23, 1891, Earl Burrus Dickerson was still young when he saw his brother-in-law shot and crippled by the local police chief. Dickerson went to local schools, and after ninth grade he was sent to the preparatory school for the University of Mississippi. In 1907 he went to the University of Chicago, but lack of funds caused him to leave after only two semesters. He moved to Evanston Academy and Northwestern University, and graduated from the University of Illinois in 1913. Dickerson spent the following year teaching at Tuskegee Institute, Alabama. He began to study law at the University of Chicago but quit to fight as a commissioned officer in World War I (1914–1918), after which he returned to his studies. In 1920 Dickerson completed a doctorate in jurisprudence, becoming the first black American to obtain a law degree from the University of Chicago. He became chief attorney for the black-owned Supreme Liberty Life Insurance Company of America. He also served on the Chicago City Council from 1939 to 1943.

Hansberry v. Lee and after
In 1937 businessman Carl A. Hansberry, father of the playwright Lorraine Hansberry, challenged Chicago's restrictive housing covenants, which were designed to keep black Americans out of white residential areas. Hansberry bought a property in a restricted area; at the same time Harry Pace, an attorney and president of the

▲ *Earl B. Dickerson was chief attorney for the Supreme Liberty Life Insurance Company of America.*

Supreme Liberty Life Insurance Company purchased another building in the area. White property owner Anna Lee, who had signed the restrictive covenant, sued Hansberry and Pace for $100,000. On November 12, 1940, Dickerson successfully won *Hansberry v. Lee* when the Supreme Court ruled that the covenants were unconstitutional.

For the rest of his life Dickerson helped fight for improved black rights. He joined the board of the Hyde Park Savings and Loan Association, which loaned money to black house-buyers in Chicago. In 1941 he was appointed a member of the first Fair Employment Practices Commission set up by President Franklin D. Roosevelt. He also helped organize the NAACP Legal Defense and Education Fund. Dickerson died in Chicago in 1986.

See also: Hansberry, Lorraine; Pace, Harry; Supreme Court

Further reading: Blakeley, Robert J. *Earl B. Dickerson: A Voice for Freedom and Equality.* Evanston, IL: Northwestern University Press, 2006.
http://www.aaregistry.com/african_american_history/938/Earl_Dickerson_a_Chicago_leader (Biography).

KEY DATES	
1891	Born in Canton, Mississippi, on June 23.
1920	Becomes first African American to obtain a law degree from the University of Chicago.
1940	Supreme Court rules that restrictive covenants are unconstitutional in *Hansberry v. Lee*.
1986	Dies in Chicago, Illinois, on September 1.

DICKERSON, Eric
Football Player

During his 11-year career as a running back in the National Football League (NFL), Eric Dickerson gained a reputation as one of the game's most explosive players, famous for his remarkable acceleration. Commenting on Dickerson's contribution to the game, fellow running back O. J. Simpson described him as "the best I've seen, and I mean ever."

Journey to the top

Dickerson was born in Sealy, Texas, on September 2, 1960. He was raised by his great-great-aunt because his mother was too young to care for him. His athletic prowess became apparent in high school and college, where his exploits on the football field were soon legendary. Dickerson's professional career began in 1983, when he was selected as the second overall pick in the first round of the NFL draft by the Los Angeles Rams. Dickerson enjoyed a remarkable first season, setting rookie records for most rushing attempts (390), most touchdowns rushing (18), and most rushing yards (1,808). His performances earned him the Rookie of the Year award for 1983.

In his second year with the Rams Dickerson continued to put together remarkable back-to-back performances: He rushed for more than 100 yards in a game 12 times, breaking the record of 100-yard games in a season held by O. J. Simpson. The 1984 season also saw Dickerson set the all-time single season rushing record by posting 2,105 total rushing yards. Consequently, he was named the National Football Conference's Player of the Year for 1984. In his first four seasons with the Rams, Dickerson ran over 1,000 yards each season; in three of those seasons he rushed over 1,800 yards.

A dispute over payment led to Dickerson being traded to the Indianapolis Colts during the 1987 season. At

▲ *Running back Eric Dickerson set numerous records during the course of his 11-year NFL career.*

Indianapolis Dickerson became the first Colts running back to lead the NFL in rushing since Alan Ameche in 1955. In 1988 he became the first player in NFL history to gain more than 1,000 yards rushing in seven consecutive seasons. However, confrontations with management led to his being traded to the Los Angeles Raiders in 1992. After a short period with the Atlanta Falcons in 1993, Dickerson announced his retirement on October 20. After his retirement Dickerson began a media career, working as a game analyst for Fox and ABC television.

See also: Simpson, O. J.

Further reading: Dickerson, Eric, and Steve Delsohn. *On the Run.* Chicago, IL: Contemporary Books, 1986.
www.profootballhof.com/hof/member.jsp?player_id=55
(Biography).

KEY DATES	
1960	Born in Sealy, Texas, on September 2.
1983	Joins Los Angeles Rams.
1984	Sets record for most rushing yards in a single season.
1987	Traded to the Indianapolis Colts.
1993	Retires on October 20.

DICKEY, Eric Jerome
Writer

Sometimes referred to as the male Terry McMillan, Eric Jerome Dickey has become one of the United States's most successful modern African American writers.

Early life
Dickey was born in Memphis, Tennessee, on July 7, 1961. His mother abandoned him as a baby, and Dickey was raised by his grandmother and godparents, who lived on the South Side of Memphis. He attended local public schools and showed a talent for writing; but he was also good at science and technology and chose to major in computer systems technology, at the University of Memphis. After graduating in 1983, Dickey decided to move to Los Angeles, where he pursued a career as a computer software developer for the aerospace company Rockwell, which is now part of the Boeing Company.

New talent
While working in technology, Dickey began to perform stand-up comedy in local clubs, to act, and to write short stories. In the early 1990s he lost his job in a wave of firings that swept the aerospace industry, and he found himself struggling financially. Dickey made a living doing a variety of jobs, including acting, teaching, and stand-up work, and claimed that comedy and acting helped him hone his skill as a writer: "In comedy you learn to write with flow—segue, setup, and punch line.... And in theater you learn about character." Dickey took some development workshops with the International Black Writers and Artists (IBWA) organization and he won a creative writing scholarship to the University of California at Los Angeles (UCLA).

In 1994 Dickey's short story "Thirteen" was published in the IBWA collection _River Crossing: Voices of the Diaspora_. He published a second short story, "Days Gone By," shortly afterward in the magazine _A Place to Enter_. Dickey then wrote a screenplay called _Cappuccino_, which was produced in 1999. His first novel, _Sister, Sister_ (1996), which took several years to write, looked at relationships and the dating game. Dickey was particularly praised for his female characterizations, prompting comparisons with black female writers such as Terry McMillan. Dickey, however, claimed that his influences included detective writers Walter Mosley and Ed McBain. Most of Dickey's novels, such as _Friends and Lovers, Milk in My Coffee,_

▲ **Eric Jerome Dickey has acted and done stand-up comedy, but he is best known for his writing.**

Cheaters, and _Drive Me Crazy,_ have appeared on the _New York Times_ bestseller list, and between 1996 and 2004 his books sold about 15 million copies. Dickey's ready wit and sharp observations have also made him a familiar face on shows such as CNN's _Sunday Morning Live._

KEY DATES	
1961	Born in Memphis, Tennessee, on July 7.
1983	Graduates from the University of Memphis; begins working as a software developer for Rockwell.
1994	Publishes the short story "Thirteen."
1996	Publishes first novel, _Sister, Sister._
2004	Publishes his 15th literary work, _Drive Me Crazy._

See also: McMillan, Terry; Mosley, Walter

Further reading: Dickey, Eric Jerome. _Milk in My Coffee._ New York, NY: Signet, 1999.
http://www.ericjeromedickey.com (Dickey's site).

DIDDLEY, Bo
Musician

Although the singer and guitarist Bo Diddley had only one mainstream hit, he was one of the most influential African American musicians to emerge in the 1950s. Sometimes referred to as "the Originator," Diddley influenced several generations of black and white musicians with his raw form of rhythm and blues (R&B).

Diddley was born Ellas Bates near McComb, Mississippi, on December 30, 1928. He was adopted by his mother's cousin, Gussie McDaniel, and took her last name. When Diddley was a young boy, the family moved to Chicago, and he began to show an interest in music, learning classical violin at the local Baptist church. One Christmas Diddley's sister gave him an acoustic guitar, which changed his musical outlook. He became increasingly influenced by the blues scene that was flourishing in Chicago at the time. While learning the guitar as a teenager, Diddley developed his own distinctive style, in which he placed more emphasis on rhythm than melody, playing the guitar like a percussion instrument.

After leaving school, Diddley began to play blues in local clubs, supplementing his income by working on building sites and as a truck driver. He also boxed, and according to one account, it was as a fighter that he first started to use the name Bo Diddley, which is probably southern slang meaning "nothing at all." Diddley himself said that he was unaware when or why he acquired the name. By the time the guitarist had established himself as a musician in the early 1950s, it was the name by which he was known.

The road to fame

After several years of playing in Chicago clubs Diddley finally signed a record contract in 1955. In the first months of that year he approached Chess, a blues label based in Chicago, with a demo tape of two songs that he had recorded: "Uncle John" and "I'm A Man." The label was run by brothers Phil and Leonard Chess, who suggested changes to the lyrics and the title of the first song. When the songs were rerecorded in March, "Uncle John" had become "Bo Diddley." The two tracks were released as a double A-sided single and went straight to the top of the R&B chart.

The single was to be the first of a string of R&B hits for Diddley. Among the most famous of which were "Who Do You Love?" (1956), "Mona" (1957), and "Pretty Thing" (1958). Diddley's style is highly distinctive, marked by a raw, distorted guitar sound and a shuffling offbeat rhythm, sometimes known as the "hambone" rhythm. Although the rhythm had been used in a number of previous R&B songs, the style became so identified with Diddley that it eventually became known as the "Bo Diddley beat." It later appeared on a number of classic rock-'n'-roll songs, including "Not Fade Away" by Buddy Holly, "I Want Candy" by the Strangeloves, and "Magic Bus" by the Who.

▲ **Bo Diddley plays his trademark square-bodied guitar, which he designed and developed himself; it was the world's first square guitar.**

INFLUENCES AND INSPIRATION

Diddley's huge influence on generations of musicians was completely out of proportion to his own chart and commercial success. One of the first major stars to pay homage to him was Buddy Holly, who covered his autobiographical song "Bo Diddley" in 1956. A few years later Diddley was one of the key inspirations for the British R&B scene that spawned such successful bands as the Yardbirds, the Animals, and the Rolling Stones. The scene was centered on the Crawdaddy Club, in Richmond in the south of England, named for Diddley's song "Doing the Crawdaddy" (1960). The Rolling Stones later covered two of Diddley's songs, "Mona" and "I'm Alright" (1964).

Diddley's music also had an influence on punk rock. One of the first punk bands, the New York Dolls, covered Diddley's song "Pills" on their debut album, while Diddley was also a hero of Joe Strummer, lead singer of the British punk band the Clash. Strummer based his guitar style on that of Diddley; and in 1979, when the Clash made its first major U.S. tour, Strummer insisted that Diddley open for them. Despite promoters' reservations that Diddley was not suitable for white punk rock audiences, Strummer got his way.

Style

As well as having a highly individual sound, Diddley also had a very distinctive look. He wore thick black glasses and in later years a large black stetson hat. However, his most famous trademark was his oddly shaped guitar, which he designed and had built for himself. In the late 1950s and early 1960s Diddley was joined on stage by percussionist Jerome Green, and the sound of Green playing the maracas became an integral part of Diddley's music. Green also played a major role in Diddley's only mainstream hit, "Hey Man," which appeared in the Top 20 of the pop chart in 1959. The song revolved around banter between Diddley and Green.

Throughout the late 1950s and 1960s Diddley challenged the status quo by using women musicians in his band, the most famous of whom was Peggy Jones, better known as Lady Bo. Diddley hired Jones in 1957, and they played together until 1961, when she went on to form her own successful group, the Jewels. In the 1960s Diddley released a number of singles such as "Pills" (1961) and "You Can't Judge a Book by Its Cover" (1962), and the albums *Bo Diddley Is a Gunslinger* (1960) and *Two Great Guitars* (1964), on which he shared the limelight with fellow Chess R&B star Chuck Berry. By the early 1960s Diddley's records were popular in the United Kingdom, where they influenced rock-'n'-roll bands such as the Rolling Stones and the Yardbirds. Diddley toured the United Kingdom with the Stones in 1963. The shows also featured R&B legend Little Richard and the Everly Brothers.

Later years

After the mid-1960s Diddley did not hit the creative heights that he had achieved in the 1950s. He continued to record and perform, however, and from the 1970s his name was

KEY DATES	
1928	Born near McComb, Mississippi, on December 30.
1955	Debut single "Bo Diddley: I'm A Man" enters R&B chart at No. 1.
1979	Opens for the Clash on its tour.
1985	Opens the U.S. leg of Live Aid, playing with George Thorogood on July 13.
1987	Inducted into the Rock and Roll Hall of Fame.

kept in the spotlight by bands that covered his songs and claimed him as an influence. Diddley also played a number of high-profile concerts. In 1985 he performed at the Live Aid concert in Philadelphia in front of millions of TV viewers worldwide. Four years later he played at President George H. W. Bush's inaugural gala. He was inducted into the Rock and Roll Hall of Fame in 1987.

In the 1990s Diddley received numerous honors, including lifetime achievement awards from the Rhythm and Blues Foundation in 1996 and the Recording Academy in 1999 at the 41st annual Grammy Awards ceremony. In 2002 he received a Pioneer in Entertainment award from the National Association of Black Owned Broadcasters, and in 2005 he celebrated 50 years in music. Diddley continues to tour and play at charitable events.

See also: Berry, Chuck; Little Richard

Further reading: White, George. *Bo Diddley—Living Legend.* New York, NY: Sanctuary Publishing, 1998.
http:// members.tripod.com/~Originator_2/index_2.html (Biography).

DILLARD, Harrison
Athlete

Harrison Dillard was a runner and hurdler; he is still the only male runner to win Olympic gold medals in both sprinting and hurdle events (1948 and 1952).

William Harrison Dillard was born in Cleveland, Ohio, on July 8, 1923. He excelled in sports during his time at East Technical High School. Nicknamed "Bones" because of his thin frame, Dillard became interested in sprinting during the 1936 Berlin Olympics at which Jesse Owens (1913–1980), an alumnus of Dillard's school in Cleveland, won four gold medals. While Owens was a sprinter, Dillard emerged as both a flat runner and a hurdler. Some commentators were surprised at Dillard's talent as a hurdler given that he was only 5 feet 10 inches (1.78m) tall, which was considered too short to exel at the event. Despite this, Dillard won the Ohio State high- and low-hurdle championships while still at school. On graduating,

KEY DATES	
1923	Born in Cleveland, Ohio, on July 8.
1946	Equals world record in 220-yard hurdles.
1947	Equals world record in 120-yard hurdles.
1948	Wins gold medals at London Olympics in 100-meter dash and relay.
1952	Wins gold medals at Helsinki Olympics in 110-meter hurdles and relay.
1956	Retires from athletics.

he went to Baldwin-Wallace College, based in Berea, Ohio, before he was called up to fight in World War II (1939–1945). While on active service he won four gold medals in the GI Olympics.

Phenomenal achievement

After the war Dillard returned to Baldwin-Wallace, where he equalled a world record in the 220-yard low hurdles. In 1947 he equaled the world record for the 120-yard hurdles. Dillard looked certain to be selected for the U.S. team at the 1948 Olympics in London, England, but in the qualifiers he ran a disastrous 110-yard race and only made the team by coming in third in the trial 100-meter dash, which became his main event. Dillard won the gold and tied the Olympic record of 10.3 seconds. He also achieved a second gold medal as a member of the 4 x 100-meter relay team. On his return to the United States Dillard completed a degree in business and took a job as a public relations officer for the Cleveland Indians baseball team.

At the start of 1952 American athletes began competing in qualifiers for that year's Olympics in Helsinki, Finland. This time Dillard qualified for the 110-meter hurdles and took gold in the final. He also won another gold in the relay. After failing to qualify for the 1956 Olympics, Dillard retired and worked for the Cleveland School Board. He was inducted into the U.S. Olympic Hall of Fame in 1984.

Further reading: Wallechinsky, David. *The Complete Book of the Summer Olympics.* Wilmington, DE: SPORTClassic Books, 2004.
http://www.olympic.org/uk/athletes/heroes/bio_uk.asp?PAR_I_ID=1345 (Olympic page with pictures).

▲ *Harrison Dillard was nicknamed the "Ebony Streak" after skimming 120-yard high hurdles and winning the world record.*

DINKINS, David
Politician

Politician David Dinkins was the first African American mayor of New York City (1989–1993). He beat Edward Koch and Rudolph Giuliani for the post in what turned out to be a scandal-ridden race.

Born in Trenton, New Jersey, on July 10, 1927, Dinkins moved with his family to Harlem, New York City, during the early 1930s. Educated in local schools, Dinkins went on to serve in the Marines during World War II (1939–1945). He studied at Howard University, Washington, D.C., graduating in math in 1950. Dinkins went on to study law at Brooklyn Law School.

Following his graduation in 1956, Dinkins became involved in politics and joined the Carver Democratic Club. In 1966, while running his own private law practice, Dinkins ran for and was elected to the New York State Assembly. He campaigned for the establishment of such programs as the Search for Education, Elevation and Knowledge (SEEK), and for the provision of educational support to low-income students. Dinkins was also president of the New York City Board of Elections, a powerful position that he used to encourage voter registration, particularly among African and Hispanic American minority groups. In 1985, during the term of Mayor Ed Koch, Dinkins became president of the Borough of Manhattan. He succeeded Koch as the Democratic Party mayoral candidate and in 1989 was elected mayor of New York City, despite a series of commercials run by the Republican Party to discredit him by claiming among other things that he had avoided paying taxes between 1969 and 1972.

Breaking barriers
Dinkins became New York's first African American mayor at a time when the city's economy was in crisis: It had a budget deficit of $500 million, and about a quarter of its residents were classified as poor. Crime and drug addiction

▲ *David Dinkins was the first African American mayor of New York City.*

were also major city problems. Dinkins campaigned to reduce crime and combat the HIV/AIDS crisis in the city, as well as fighting for more support for low-income families. In 1993, however, when the mayoral elections took place, many of those problems still existed, and Republican Rudolph Giuliani defeated Dinkins.

Dinkins has remained active in city affairs and has campaigned on civil and human rights issues. He has also held several academic posts, including professor in the practice of public affairs at Columbia University School of International and Public Affairs.

Further reading: Colburn, David R., and Jeffrey S. Adler (eds.). *African-American Mayors: Race, Politics, and the American City.* Chicago, IL: University of Illinois Press, 2001. http://c250.columbia.edu/c250_celebrates/harlem_history/dinkins.html (Dinkins page on Harlem history site with video).

KEY DATES	
1927	Born in Trenton, New Jersey, on July 10.
1966	Elected to the New York State Assembly.
1985	Becomes president of the Borough of Manhattan
1989	Becomes mayor of New York City (until 1993).

DISCRIMINATION

The history of African Americans in the United States is full of discrimination suffered at the hands of the white majority. This discrimination is one of the major factors that have characterized racial inequality in U.S. history, alongside prejudice, racism, and segregation. Prejudice normally results from false stereotypes, as when a white person believes that most black males are prone to violence or when a black person is convinced that all white people are racist.

When prejudice results in action against other ethnic groups, particularly to deny them rights and benefits, it becomes discrimination. Discrimination based on race is known as racism.

Throughout U.S. history, racism has resulted in segregation, or the separation of races in such areas as schools, restaurants, theaters, transportation, water fountains, restrooms, courts, recreation, hospitals, shops, and employment establishments, as was common in the South during slavery and the Jim Crow era (1877–1965). Jim Crow laws enshrined the provision of unequal facilities to African Americans.

Slavery and discrimination
Discrimination began early in North America. After the official arrival of the first slaves at Jamestown, Virginia, in 1619, colony after colony, beginning with Virginia (which declared that the status of a child's freedom or perpetual slavery would be determined by that of its mother), passed laws to ensure the availability of labor by

KEY DATES	
1619	The first African slaves are brought to England's North American colonies.
1865	The Thirteenth Amendment ends slavery.
1896	*Plessy v. Ferguson*: "separate but equal" found constitutional.
1954	*Brown v. Board of Education*: "separate but equal" found unconstitutional.
1964	Civil Rights Act passed by Congress.
1965	Voting Rights Bill passed by Congress.

discriminating against the African American population. Defenders of slavery justified their attitude by asserting Africans' "human inferiority" and "lack of material and intellectual advancement."

End of the slave trade
By 1809, when the slave trade was abolished in the United States, more than 800,000 Africans and their descendants were held in bondage. The slave population in southern states rose from 700,000 in 1790 to 3.2 million in 1850, reaching four million in 1860.

Even though there were thousands of free and freed African Americans in various parts of the country, especially in the North, most remained enslaved in the South until the end of the Civil War in 1865. They were stripped of their right to worship freely, marry legally, move about, testify in court, own property, express themselves, attend school, and pursue individual economic goals. While exceptions existed, men could be arrested or beaten without cause, and women raped, taken away from their consorts, or separated from their children.

The Constitution, which upheld the principle that all men were born equal, and free to pursue liberty and happiness, declared an African American equal to three-fifths of a voting white American.

Roots of discrimination
The roots of the racially based policies of the United States in the 19th and 20th centuries, and the resulting discriminatory laws and practices, lay in the justification for slavery. They also reflected 19th-century evolutionary theories, which argued that humans did not all come from the same stock. Weaker groups or races were physically or intellectually inferior.

This pseudo-scientific thinking gave rise to theories of racial inequality and their tragic social consequences. It was reinforced by the European conquest of Africa and the introduction of exploitative colonial polices following the infamous Berlin Conference (1884–1885).

Resisting slavery
African Americans attempted to free themselves from the conditions of slavery mostly

through peaceful means, such as refusing to work, feigning ignorance and ill-health, and running away. They also sometimes used violence, such as poisoning the master or organizing an insurrection. There were an estimated 250 rebellions against slavery from the 17th century to the mid-19th century. The best-known were those led by Gabriel Prosser in Virginia in 1800, Denmark Vesey in South Carolina in 1822, Nat Turner in Virginia in 1831, and white abolitionist John Brown in Virginia in 1859.

Ending slavery

Even though the insurrections demonstrated the slaves' hatred for the institution of slavery, Southern whites grew more determined to protect it and heightened the repressive measures necessary to preserve it. In the industrialized North, however, slavery had become economically obsolete and abolitionists, such as Frederick Douglass, William Lloyd Garrison, Sojourner Truth, and Harriet Tubman, grew vocal in their campaigns against slavery. Several legislatures had earlier enacted laws to end the institution: Vermont in 1777, Massachusetts and Pennsylvania in 1780, New Hampshire in 1783, Rhode Island and Connecticut in 1784, New York in 1799, and New Jersey in 1804.

In addition, during the 1850s Congress had prohibited slavery in territories north of the Ohio and east of the Mississippi rivers. The Underground Railroad, which smuggled runaway slaves from the South to freedom in the North or in Canada, was running at full speed; antislavery societies had

been active in the North since 1775; and many communities refused to enforce the Fugitive Slave Acts of 1793 and 1850.

The 1860 election of Abraham Lincoln, whom the South saw as an abolitionist, was the last straw. In 1861 the South walked out of the Union to preserve its way of life and its institutions, of which slavery was core, leading to military conflict. The Civil War (1861–1865) ended with a clear victory for the North. Slavery, as an institution, was dealt the first major blow when Lincoln issued his Emancipation Proclamation in 1862, which declared "forever free" every slave in the rebel states. In 1865 Congress approved the Thirteenth Amendment to the Constitution declaring slavery illegal.

Discrimination continues

The end of slavery did not mean the end of discrimination and racial segregation. The federal government passed various laws and constitutional amendments in

Black customers outside a shop in the South in about 1925. African Americans were forced to use separate facilities until the Civil Rights Act of 1964.

the 1860s and 1870s designed to end all vestiges of slavery and reconstruct the South so that it could be fully integrated into the Union. The period from the end of the Civil War to 1877 is therefore known as Reconstruction.

The Fourteenth Amendment was ratified in 1866, declaring all African Americans citizens of the United States. The South continued to resist enfranchising black males, however, so the federal government passed the Civil Rights Act of 1866 (over the veto of President Andrew Jackson) and the Fifteenth Amendment (1868). They were followed, on March 1, 1875, by a Civil Rights Bill that prohibited discrimination in places of public accommodation. The law was struck down by the U.S. Supreme Court in 1883, when it ruled that the Fourteenth

Amendment did not give the government the power to outlaw discrimination by individuals.

Meanwhile the Freedman's Bureau, established by the federal government in 1865, helped freed blacks in matters of education, health, employment, and property ownership (even though it fell short of providing the former slaves with the promised "40 acres and a mule").

Political representation

Many former slaves remained on the plantations as sharecroppers, who were obliged to pay their landlords a share of their income, or as indentured servants, who were committed to remain in servitude for a contracted length of time. For the first time, however, public schools were open to blacks, and many states and counties in the South had a majority of black electors or a majority in the legislature, as occurred in Georgia, Mississippi, Louisiana, South Carolina, Florida, and Alabama.

In 1868 Oscar Duncan became the first black lieutenant governor in Louisiana; in South Carolina, the state legislature had a black majority (87 to 40) in 1868; and in 1870 and 1872, respectively, Alonzo J. Ransier and Richard H. Gleaves became Louisiana lieutenant governors. John Menard from Louisiana was elected to the U.S. House of Representatives in 1868, while Hiram R. Revels from Mississippi was sent to the U.S. Senate to fill the term vacated by senator Jefferson Davis, former president of the Confederacy.

Other political successes came when Joseph H. Rainey from South Carolina was elected to the U.S. House in 1870 and Blanche Bruce of Mississippi was elected to the U.S. Senate in 1875. J. R. Lynch became house speaker in Mississippi and served two terms in the U.S. House (1873–1877 and 1881–1883).

The Jim Crow era

Throughout the South such gains were slowly diluted through the reemergence of segregation, oppressive laws, intimidation, and lynching—between the 1870s and the 1930s, 5,000 African Americans were murdered by such hate organizations as the Ku Klux Klan and the Knights of White Camellia (see box on p. 100).

The reemergence of discrimination in the South was aggravated by a deal between the two main political parties in February 1877, whereby conservative Republican Rutherford Hays would be

JIM CROW LAWS

Date	Place	What the Law Tried to Do
1870	Georgia	Set up first Jim Crow school system.
1891	Georgia	Jim Crow railroad seating.
1900	South Carolina	Jim Crow railroad cars.
1905	Georgia	Separate parks for whites and blacks.
1906	Alabama	Jim Crow street cars.
1910	Baltimore, Maryland	Blacks and whites not allowed to live on the same blocks.
1914	Louisiana	Separate entrances and seating at circuses.
1915	South Carolina	Separate entrances, working rooms, water glasses, etc., for workers in the same factory. Amount voted to educate each white child 12 times that to educate each black child.
	Oklahoma	Separate phone booths for whites and blacks.
1922	Mississippi	Jim Crow taxicabs.
1926	Atlanta, Georgia	Black barbers could not cut white women's hair.
1932	Atlanta, Georgia	White and black baseball clubs could not play within two blocks of each other.
1933	Texas	Blacks and whites could not wrestle together.
1935	Oklahoma	Blacks and whites could not fish together.
1937	Arkansas	Segregation at race tracks.
1944	Virginia	Jim Crow waiting rooms at airports established.
1965	Louisiana	State money not to be spent on schools attended by both white and black students.

(Adapted from Benjamin DaSilva et al. *The Afro-American in United States History*. New York, NY: Globe Book Company, 1972, p. 215.)

declared U.S. president and Union troops withdrawn from the South, ending the Reconstruction era and giving way to Jim Crow laws (*see box on p. 97*).

Whites used literacy tests, intimidation at the polls, recitation of the Constitution, property ownership, grandfather clauses, and poll taxes to prevent blacks from voting against the Fifteenth Amendment. Legal (de jure) discrimination and discrimination in practice (de facto) were again the norm in the South. Desegregation laws were dealt a further blow when the Supreme Court ruled in *Plessy v. Ferguson* (1896) that the provision of "separate but equal" facilities was constitutional.

Fighting back
Black Americans mobilized to regain the rights they had lost after 1877. They created several organizations (the Niagara movement in 1905, the National Association for the Advancement of Colored People (NAACP) in 1909, the Urban League in 1911, and the Universal Negro Improvement Association in 1916–1917) to exert pressure on the government to enforce the old and enact new laws. Activists such as W. E. B. DuBois, David Walker, Ida Wells, and Marcus Garvey advanced the African American agenda.

The combination of lynching, lack of jobs, discrimination in schools, and segregation in housing led to an unprecedented number of blacks moving from the South to northern cities during the early 1920s. According to the Labor Department, the exodus reached 500,000 by October 1923. Historians call this northward movement the "Great Migration."

The first major breakthrough with the widest implications occurred at the U.S. Supreme Court in 1954. Arguments presented by Thurgood Marshall of the NAACP compelled the justices to unanimously declare that "separate but equal" was unconstitutional. The ruling was tested in Arkansas on September 25, 1957, when President Dwight Eisenhower sent troops to open the Little Rock High School to nine black students following Governor Orval Faubus's refusal to enforce desegregation laws.

The civil rights era
The mid-1950s through the 1960s experienced a new wave of direct action by activists and civil rights organizations, such as the Committee of Racial Equality (CORE), the Student Non-Violent Coordinating Committee (SNCC), and the Southern Christian Leadership Conference (SCLC). The movement was sparked by Rosa Parks's refusal to sit in the back of a bus in Montgomery, Alabama, in 1955, and the killing of Emmett Till in Mississippi in 1955.

A crescendo of boycotts, sit-ins, protests, voter registration, freedom rides, and civil disobedience culminated in the March on Washington in the summer of 1963, where Martin Luther King, Jr., made his famous speech, "I Have a Dream." Under pressure from presidents John F. Kennedy and Lyndon B. Johnson,

TURNING POINT

For a long time it was public knowledge that the defense industry discriminated against blacks. Elected president in November 1932, Franklin D. Roosevelt promised not only to announce a New Deal for America but also to tackle discrimination in the federal government. By 1940, however, the president had taken no action, and A. Philip Randolph, leader of the Brotherhood of Sleeping Car Porters, the only black labor union, scheduled a march on Washington for July 1, 1941. Roosevelt asked black leaders to call off the march. Randolph refused and threatened to lead 100,000 marchers to the capital. Unexpectedly, on June 25, 1941, the president issued Executive Order 8802, prohibiting "racial and religious discrimination in defense industries and government training programs." Randolph called off the march.

On July 19, 1941, Roosevelt created the Fair Employment Practices Commission to monitor discrimination against African Americans in the defense industry. Black leaders hailed the executive order and the new commission as the greatest civil rights action since the Emancipation Proclamation. Although the commission eventually failed in its aims, the episode demonstrated both the persistence of discriminatory practices and the potential power of an organized African American minority.

Congress passed the Civil Rights Act of 1964 and the 1965 Voting Rights Bill, which restored the basic citizenship rights of African Americans.

The laws were followed by several executive orders and laws during the 1970s, particularly Title VII, that justified affirmative action, which used quotas to overcome the effects of discrimination, and banned discrimination in the workplace and in housing and education.

Discrimination persists

Although many of the legal gains of the civil rights era were not fully enforced, and blacks still lagged behind whites in most aspects of civic life, there were improvements. Many schools were desegregated, sometimes through busing, upheld by the courts; exclusive neighborhoods were opened to black residents; professional sports admitted black athletes, while the film industry, impressed by such actors as Sidney Poitier and Bill Cosby, allocated better roles to blacks; and by 2005 more than 10,000 blacks had been elected to local, state, and national office (350 in 1964, 1,469 in 1970, and 9,040 in 2000). Political gains were more vividly reflected in the election of black mayors in major cities (Washington, D.C., Los Angeles, Cincinnati, Baltimore, Memphis, Atlanta, Houston, Cleveland, New Orleans, New York, Newark) and that of three African Americans to the U.S. Senate, Edward Brooke of Massachusetts, Carol Moseley-Braun of Illinois, and Barack Obama, also of Illinois. In 2005, they remained the only African American senators since Reconstruction.

African Americans stage a demonstration against Jim Crow segregation laws in 1944.

Black versus white America

After more than two centuries of action against discrimination, what was the actual condition of black America when contrasted with white America at the start of the 21st century?

In employment, blacks experienced an unemployment rate twice that of whites (12 percent versus 6 percent); their income was 10 percent lower than that of whites, just as it was during the 1970s. Fewer than 50 percent of blacks owned their homes; the percentage among whites was 70 percent. Blacks were denied mortgages and loans twice as often as whites. Blacks were over-represented in service-sector jobs, where employment was less secure.

Across the nation 33 percent of blacks (10 million people) lived in poverty, a similar percentage as 30 years earlier. Some 87 percent of young African Americans, with the median age of 27, lived in inner cities where conditions are often deplorable, contrasted to 34 percent of whites. This situation was brought home to many Americans in September 2005, when a disproportionate number of the victims of Hurricane Katrina were poor black residents of New Orleans and nearby communities.

In health, mortality rates among black children aged one to four years were twice those of white children; life expectancy for blacks was 72 years while that of whites was 78 years. Black adult mortality rates were 30 to 40 percent higher than those of white adults; blacks were five times more likely to die as victims of homicide, and 10 times more likely (20 times for women) to be HIV positive than whites.

In education, black children were three times more likely to be sent to special classes than their white counterparts because of indiscipline, learning disability, emotional instability, and low IQ (70 or less). Even though blacks made up only 13 percent of the

From 1901 to 1920, 16 antilynching bills failed in the U.S. Senate. From 1880 to 1930, 723 whites and 5,000 blacks had been lynched, mostly in the South. Since its inception in 1909, the NAACP had targeted ending lynching as one of its major goals. Its most vigorous antilynching campaigns started in 1918, when Missouri congressman Leonidas Dyer introduced a bill in the House of Representatives seeking to end lynching and punish state, county, and local authorities who condoned it. In May 1919 the NAACP took the issue as one of its priorities at the National Conference on Lynching at Carnegie Hall, New York. Dyer's bill passed the House on January 26, 1922, but stalled in the Senate. A filibuster and a call for states' rights prevented the bill from reaching the full Senate. Reintroduced in 1923, it failed once again in the Senate.

The women's wing of the NAACP led the sponsorship of the Dyer Bill and, in 1922, women founded the Anti-Lynching Crusaders, which sought to engage "one million women," black and white, asking them to contribute at least one dollar each, pray, and promote the bill. White women did not respond, however, and not much money was raised, forcing the Crusaders to disband in early 1923. The issue of lynching had been publicized, however, and had an impact on people of good will. In 1930 white women created the Association of Southern Women for the Prevention of Lynching.

population, their representation in special education programs was 28 percent. Teachers in segregated black schools lacked an average of

Homeless people and their supporters demand adequate housing in Detroit, Michigan, on December 27, 1991.

three years' experience compared to their counterparts working in more endowed schools. In addition, mostly as a result of lack of jobs, black youngsters volunteered for military service at a rate 1.4 times higher than their white cohorts. Black prisoners' average jail sentences were longer than those of whites by an average of six months, and the rate of black incarceration was higher, at 4,819 per 100,000 persons, but only 649 per 100,000 for whites.

A continuing struggle

The statistics clearly reveal that racism and discrimination are still very much a part of American society. Many African Americans succeed despite social attitudes and not because of them. The statistical profile of the nation reminds blacks—and whites, too—not to take anything for granted in assuming that discrimination has been defeated.

See also: Affirmative Action; Braun, Carol; Brooke, Edward; Bruce, Blanche K.; Cosby, Bill; Douglass, Frederick; DuBois, W. E. B.; Gabriel; Garvey, Marcus; Great Migration and Urbanization; Lynch, J. R.; Marshall, Thurgood; Obama, Barack; Parks, Rosa; Poitier, Sydney; Randolph, A. Philip; Revels, Hiram; Slavery; Supreme Court; Truth, Sojourner; Tubman, Harriet; Turner, Nat; Vesey, Denmark; Walker, David; Wells, Ida

Further reading: National Urban League. *The State of Black America*. New York, NY: National Urban League, 2000–2005.
Black Population in the United States. U.S. Government. Washington, D.C.: Government Printing Office, 2002
Kitano, H. *Race Relations*. Englewood Cliffs, NJ: Prentice-Hall, 1997
Gavin, R. "Slavery in the Diaspora," in Mario Azevedo. *Africana Studies*. Durham, NC: Carolina Academic Press, 1998
Zangrando, Robert. *The NAACP Crusade Against Lynching, 1909–1950*. Philadelphia, PA: Temple University Press, 1980.

DOBBS, Mattiwilda
Opera Singer

Along with her contemporaries Marian Anderson and Leontyne Price, Mattiwilda Dobbs was one of the leading African American opera singers of the 20th century. During the 1950s she broke the color bar in many opera houses across Europe and the United States, thrilling audiences with her rich, agile soprano voice.

From Atlanta to Paris

Mattiwilda Dobbs was born on July 11, 1925, in Atlanta, Georgia. Named for her grandmother Matti Wilda Sykes, Dobbs was one of six children. Her father, John Wesley Dobbs, a railroad postal clerk involved in the early Atlanta civil rights movement, was interested in music, and the Dobbs sisters were all taught piano from an early age; they were also taken to see touring opera companies. Theaters were still segregated in the South at the time, and Dobbs and her siblings had to sit in the balcony, which was set aside for African Americans. As an established singer, Dobbs later refused to play to segregated audiences.

Dobbs began singing in her church choir and eventually went to study music at Atlanta's Spelman College, a predominantly black institution. After

▼ *Opera singer and diva Mattiwilda Dobbs, pictured here with her father, John Wesley Dobbs, was the first black American to sing at La Scala, Italy.*

graduation she took singing classes in New York City and won a Marian Anderson Award in 1948. Other grants and scholarships followed and Dobbs used the money to pursue her studies in Europe, working with eminent baritone and teacher Pierre Bernac in Paris, France. Despite Anderson's achievements, there were still very few opportunities for black singers in the United States, and Dobbs focused her career on Europe.

In 1951 Dobbs won first prize in singing at the famous Geneva Conservatory competition, attended by many of the leading agents and musical directors of the time. Two years later Dobbs made her debut at one of the world's most illustrious opera houses, La Scala, in the Italian city of Milan. Dobbs was the first black woman to sing on its stage.

In 1954 Dobbs returned to the United States, giving her first major performance in New York City. Critically well received, Dobbs eventually won a role at New York City's Metropolitan Opera House (the Met), playing Gilda in its 1956 production of Giuseppe Verdi's *Rigoletto*. She was the second African American woman to perform at the Met; Marian Anderson had sung there just one year earlier. Dobbs only performed in her hometown of Atlanta in 1962 after segregation had been abolished. She continued to perform until her retirement in 1974, after which she taught at universities, including Spelman College and Howard University, Washington, D.C. Dobbs received many awards, including the Swedish Order of the North Star.

KEY DATES	
1925	Born in Atlanta, Georgia, on July 11.
1953	Becomes the first black woman to sing at La Scala, Milan, Italy.
1956	Sings at the Met, New York City.
1974	Retires from professional singing.

See also: Anderson, Marian; Price, Leontyne

Further reading: Story, Rosalyn M. *And So I Sing: African American Divas of Opera and Concert.* New York, NY: Amistad, 1993.
www.usoperaweb.com/2002/april/dobbs.htm (Interview).

DOBY, Larry
Baseball Player

Larry Doby racked up a series of honors during his lifetime, including being the first African American to play in the American League and the first African American to hit a home run in the World Series.

Lawrence Eugene Doby was born in South Carolina in 1924. His father was a semiprofessional baseball player but died when the boy was only eight years old. By the time Doby was a teenager and living in Paterson, New Jersey, he was already known as a star baseball player at the Eastside High School, as well as showing prowess in football and track.

Professional play

Doby began his semiprofessional career in 1942 with the Newark Eagles, playing in the Negro National League. He emerged as a phenomenal left-handed batter and fielder, but opportunities to step up into the major leagues were still limited for black players at the time. After the African American player Jackie Robinson broke into the major

▼ *Cleveland Indians' batter Larry Doby achieved many firsts, including being the first black American to hit a home run in the World Series.*

leagues early in 1947, Doby signed with the Cleveland Indians. He played for the Indians between 1947 and 1955, and was a major force behind their World Series win in 1948. Doby had league-leading stats in batting and runs for much of the early 1950s, and played alongside baseball greats such as Robinson and Roy Campanella. Between 1956 and 1957 Doby took a break from playing to become a coach for the Chicago White Sox, but he went back to the Indians in 1958 before playing for both the Detroit Tigers and the Chicago White Sox in 1959. He retired later that year with 253 career home runs.

Active life

During the 1960s and 1970s Doby coached teams such as the Montreal Expos and the White Sox; he also worked in advisory roles within the American League. Doby was also able to pursue his other great love, basketball. In 1977 he became director of community relations for the NBA's New Jersey Nets, working in particular in youth programs aimed at inner-city children. He was inducted into the National Black Sports Hall of Fame in 1973 and the Baseball Hall of Fame in 1998. Doby died on June 18, 2003, at age 78.

See also: Campanella, Roy; Robinson, Jackie

Further reading: Moore, Joseph Thomas. *Pride Against Prejudice: The Biography of Larry Doby.* Westport, CT: Greenwood *Press, 1988).*
http://www.baseballhalloffame.org/hofers_and_honorees/hofer_bios/doby_larry.htm (Baseball Hall of Fame page).

DOMINO, Fats
Musician

Fats Domino was a master of a variety of piano styles whose playing showed influences of the blues, stride piano, and boogie-woogie. Domino developed a unique vocal style, while his compositions made him an important link between rhythm and blues (R&B) and rock 'n' roll. With more than 20 gold records and 65 million record sales to his credit, Domino was one of the bestselling popular singers of the 1950s and early 1960s.

Born in New Orleans, Louisiana, on February 26, 1928, Antoine Domino grew up speaking French as his first language. The Domino family was musical; the boy's father played violin and his older brother-in-law, Harrison Verrett, was a well-known guitarist, who taught Domino to play the piano. He began to perform live at age 10; aged 14 Domino was so engrossed in music that he quit school and worked days in a factory so that he could perform at local bars and clubs at night. Early in his career he acquired the nickname "Fats" for his 200-pound (90kg) physique.

▼ *Fats Domino had five songs in the Top 40 in 1956, including "I'm In Love Again" and "Blueberry Hill."*

The Domino style

A regular performer at the New Orleans' Hideaway Club, Domino came to the notice of trumpeter, bandleader, and composer Dave Bartholomew (1922–). The two men made the first of numerous recordings together, an arrangement of "The Fat Man." It featured Domino's unique rolling piano style and his "wah-wah" vocalizing; he used the syllable "wah" to bend or alter musical notes to improve his expressiveness. Released in 1950, the recording was a enormous hit and by 1953 about one million copies had been sold. The songwriting partnership between Domino and Bartholomew lasted for many years.

In 1949 Domino had signed with Imperial Records, recording the traditional New Orleans "Hey La Bas," which was released after "The Fat Man." Following a number of other R&B hits in 1951, including "Rockin' Chair," "Please Don't Leave Me," and "Goin' Home," Domino had a huge hit with "Ain't That A Shame" in 1955. Although the song crossed into a new music market and reached a large rock-'n'-roll audience when it got to No. 10 on the charts, it had also been covered by white singer Pat Boone, whose version reached No. 1. Another

recording, "Blueberry Hill," was Domino's highest charting record, reaching No. 2 in 1956. He had five songs in the Top 40 in that year.

White cover songs

In the 1950s it became popular for larger record companies to use white musicians in their stables to rerecord or "cover" songs made popular by African American artists. In addition to "Ain't That A Shame," other Domino songs covered by white performers included "Blueberry Hill" by Glenn Miller, "I'm Walking" by Rick Nelson, and "Boll Weevil" by Teresa Brewer.

The decision of the big record companies to release the watered-down versions by white performers of the music created by African Americans was aimed partly at reducing the popularity of black artists and partly at protecting their monopoly on record sales from the independent labels, such as Chess Records in Chicago. In fact, the white singers' imitations of their black models also helped the black performers find mainstream acceptance.

KEY DATES

1928	Born in New Orleans, Louisiana, on February 26.
1949	First recording session with Imperial Records.
1956	Appears in rock-'n'-roll film *Shake, Rattle, and Roll*.
1986	Inducted into Rock and Roll Hall of Fame.
1987	Receives a Lifetime Achievement Award at the 29th annual Grammy Awards.
1993	Releases the album *Christmas is a Special Day*.
2005	Rescued from floodwaters of Hurricane Katrina in New Orleans.

Movie career

Domino also began to perform in films. He sang three songs in the landmark rock-'n'-roll film *Shake, Rattle, and Roll* (1956). A year later Domino appeared in another music film, *The Girl Can't Help It*, singing his hit "Blue Monday." He also toured for three months with *The Biggest Show of Stars for 1957*, which also featured some of the leading musicians of the time, including Chuck Berry, LaVern Baker, Clyde McPhatter, Bill Doggett, and the Moonglows.

During the next few years Domino continued to record a series of hits, including "I'm Walking," the cover of which helped establish the career of teen idol Ricky Nelson. In 1960 Domino's "Walking to New Orleans" was released; it became his last Top 10 pop hit, reaching No. 2 on the R&B chart.

Touring and honors

Over the next two decades Domino performed in casinos in Las Vegas, Nevada, and Europe, where his New Orleans-based musical style was immensely popular with audiences. In 1993 Domino released his first major-label album, *Christmas is a Special Day*. In 1995 he had to leave a tour in England with James Brown and Chuck Berry because of health problems. The recipient of many awards, including a Grammy Lifetime Achievement Award in 1987, Domino was inducted into the Rock and Roll Hall of Fame in 1986.

See also: Baker, LaVern; Berry, Chuck; Brown, James; Waller, Fats

Further reading: Henke, James, et al. (eds.). *The Rolling Stone Illustrated History of Rock & Roll*. New York, NY: Random House, 1992.
http://www.fatsdominoonline.com (Site about Domino with links).

DONEGAN, Dorothy
Musician, Singer

Dorothy Donegan was an exceptional and versatile pianist known for her ability to successfully blend a variety of musical styles in her performances, including jazz and European classical music. She was an artist recognized more for her flamboyant performances than for her recordings, of which there were few. Donegan had a unique and entertaining style of delivery in which she often acted out the songs that she was performing, parodied other musicians, and danced while playing the piano. Donegan's career as a classical pianist was stifled by the lack of opportunities for African Americans to perform with symphony orchestras, but her career as a jazz pianist has left a lasting impression. Dempsey J. Travis, author of the bestselling *Autobiography of Black Jazz,* described Donegan as simply the best pianist the United States has ever produced.

Early life
Born in Chicago, Illinois, on April 6, 1922, Donegan was encouraged by her mother to study music. She began piano lessons at age five. By the time she was 10, Donegan was performing as a church organist. While studying music in high school, Donegan began a career as a professional jazz pianist, playing in nightclubs on Chicago's South Side. Music teacher Walter Dyett, who taught at DuSable High School and helped many other performers, including Dinah Washington, tutored her.

▼ *Dorothy Donegan was known for her wild gesticulations during her performances.*

KEY DATES	
1922	Born in Chicago, Illinois, on April 6.
1942	Records first album on the Bluebird label.
1943	Performs in concert at Chicago's Orchestra Hall.
1949	Stars in show at Hollywood's Tom Breneman Café.
1992	Receives American Jazz Master Hall of Fame Award.
1998	Dies in Los Angeles, California, on May 19.

Aged just 17 Donegan was hired to play piano with the Bob Tinsley Band. Despite her budding jazz career, Donegan aspired to be a classical pianist and continued her musical education at the Chicago Conservatory of Music, the Chicago Musical College, and a decade later, at the University of Southern California.

A musical career
In 1942 Donegan recorded her first album of blues and boogie-woogie piano. A year later she became the first African American artist and the first jazz pianist to perform in concert at Chicago's Orchestra Hall. The concert, which featured both European classical music and jazz standards, drew the attention of the celebrated African American jazz pianist Art Tatum, who became her mentor.

During the 1940s Donegan performed in jazz clubs in Los Angeles, New York, and Chicago. She performed in a touring show with African American comedienne Moms Mabley and starred in the first all-black American show at the Tom Breneman Café in Hollywood, California. During the 1950s Donegan performed in clubs throughout the country and by the 1970s she had become a regular at jazz festivals in the United States and abroad, performing as a soloist or with her trio. Donegan performed until 1997, when she was diagnosed with cancer. She died in 1998.

See also: Tatum, Art; Washington, Dinah

Further reading: Placksin, Sally. *American Women in Jazz: 1900 to the Present—Their Words, Lives, and Music.* New York, NY: Wideview Books, 1982
http://www.umich.edu/~afroammu/standifer/donnegan.html (Interview with Donegan).

DORSEY, Thomas A.
Musician

Thomas A. Dorsey was a singer, songwriter, and pianist who blended elements of the blues with the traditional religious music of his upbringing, a style that became known as gospel. He is often called the "father of gospel."

Early life

Thomas Andrew Dorsey was born on July 1, 1899, in Villa Rica, Georgia. The son of a revivalist preacher, Dorsey was the eldest of 10 children. He learned to play the church organ as a child and began writing his own music when he was about eight years old. The family lived in the poorest part of town, and it was there that Dorsey met blues singer Ma Rainey and slide guitarist Tampa Red Whitaker. Dorsey played the piano and sang to help support his family.

In 1916 Dorsey moved to Chicago, where he attended the College of Composition and Arranging and worked as a pianist, arranger, and vocalist. Performing under the stage name Georgia Tom, he wrote "hokum" songs, which had lyrics with a double meaning, for stag parties and clubs. Dorsey also began to collaborate with Whitaker, and in 1928 they released "It's Tight Like That," which sold around seven million copies.

Changing tack

From 1919 onward Dorsey began to write religious-oriented songs with a blues flavor—what would become known as gospel songs. Many of his most successful songs were inspired by personal tragedy—"If You See My Savior,

▼ *"Father of gospel" Thomas A. Dorsey was taught to play the piano by his mother.*

Tell Him You Saw Me" (1926) was written after the death of a friend, and "Precious Lord, Take My Hand" (1932) was written after the death of his wife and baby. "Precious Lord" was extremely successful. Singers Mahalia Jackson and Elvis Presley helped popularize it, Martin Luther King, Jr., said that it was his favorite song, and President Lyndon B. Johnson (1963–1969) requested that it be sung at his funeral.

Making a difference

Dorsey was greatly discouraged by his efforts to publish and sell his songs through the popular method of peddling songsheets on the streets, and he was dissatisfied with the treatment given to black American composers by the music-publishing industry. In 1932 he set up his own publishing company. The Chicago-based company the Dorsey House of Music became the first independent publisher of black gospel music.

In 1932 Dorsey became choral director of the Pilgrim Baptist Church in Chicago. He also founded the National Convention of Gospel Choirs and Choruses in 1933, remaining its president for 40 years. He stopped recording in 1934, but he continued to write songs and toured widely until well into the 1940s. Dorsey received many honors before his death in January 1993. He was the first African American to be elected to the Nashville Songwriters International Hall of Fame (1979) and to enter the Gospel Music Association's Living Hall of Fame (1982).

KEY DATES	
1899	Born in Villa Rica, Georgia, on July 1.
1928	Has a hit with "It's Tight Like That."
1979	Becomes the first African American to be elected to Nashville Songwriters International Hall of Fame.
1993	Dies in Chicago, Illinois, on January 23.

See also: Jackson, Mahalia; King, Martin Luther, Jr.; Rainey, Ma

Further reading: Haskins, Jim, et al. *Black Stars of the Harlem Renaissance.* New York, NY: Wiley, 2002.
http://www.umich.edu/~afroammu/standifer/dorsey.html (Interview with Dorsey).

DOUGLAS, Aaron
Painter, Illustrator, Educator

Aaron Douglas is considered the foremost artist of the Harlem Renaissance, the literary and arts movement that flourished in New York during the 1920s; he was also at the center of the intense creative activity taking place among the artists, writers, and intellectuals of the New Negro Movement. His successful attempts to combine African imagery with a modernist aesthetic earned him an important place in the history of American art.

Rise to fame
Douglas was born in Topeka, Kansas, on May 26, 1899; his father was a baker, and his mother painted. From an early age Douglas was interested in education; he attended local segregated schools and graduated from Topeka High School in 1917. He went on to receive a BA in fine art from the University of Nebraska in 1922, after which he taught art at Lincoln High School in Kansas City (1923–1925).

Douglas moved to New York in 1925, interested in the artistic ambition and political commitment of the artists and intellectuals of Harlem. After studying with the German illustrator Fritz Winold Reiss, Douglas was hired by W. E. B. DuBois to provide innovative illustrations for his magazine *Crisis*. He was interested in establishing a connection between African art and African American culture, and drew inspiration from Ethiopian, Egyptian, and Ivory Coast art in particular. Douglas quickly became one of the most popular illustrators of the Harlem Renaissance; he worked on books such as *The New Negro* (Alain Locke, 1925), *God's Trombones* (James Weldon Johnson, 1927), and *Black Magic* (Paul Morand, 1929).

In 1928 Douglas and Gwendolyn Bennett became the first African American artists to receive a scholarship to study at the Barnes Foundation in Merion, Pennsylvania. Douglas went on to spend a year in Paris, France, at

L'Académie Scandinave in 1931, where he met the black American painter Henry Ossawa Tanner.

During the 1930s Douglas completed many murals, including *Aspects of Negro Life* (1934) for the Harlem Branch of the New York Public Library and murals for Fisk University in Nashville, Tennessee. In 1940 he founded the art department at Fisk University, where he taught until his retirement in 1966. He believed that his work at Fisk was among his greatest achievements. Before his death in 1979 Douglas received many honors and awards.

▼ *Harlem Renaissance artist Aaron Douglas worked with the influential W. E. B. DuBois during the 1920s.*

See also: Bennett, Gwendolyn; DuBois, W. E. B.; Harlem Renaissance; Tanner, Henry O.

Further reading: Kirschke, Amy Helene. *Aaron Douglas: Art, Race, and the Harlem Renaissance*. Jackson, MS: University Press of Mississippi, 1995.
http://www.pbs.org/wnet/aaworld/arts/douglas.html (Biography).

KEY DATES

1899	Born in Topeka, Kansas, on May 26.
1925	Joins the Harlem Renaissance movement
1931	Studies in Paris, France.
1934	Creates murals for the Harlem Branch of the New York Public Library.
1979	Dies in Nashville, Tennessee, on February 3.

DOUGLASS, Frederick
Abolitionist, Writer

A powerful orator, eloquent author, and leading civil rights activist of the 19th century, Frederick Douglass escaped slavery to champion the abolitionist cause and become the first African American to be appointed to a high-ranking government post.

Early life

Born Frederick Baily in 1818, Douglass was raised by his grandmother, having been separated from his slave mother. He never learned the identity of his white father. Sent to live with the slave children belonging to the Maryland estate of Aaron Anthony when he was six, he endured the harsh cruelty of slavery: feeding from a trough, sleeping without a bed or blanket, and observing, and being himself subjected to, fierce beatings.

Douglass's engaging personality resulted in his being chosen as a companion for the plantation owner's youngest son. Later he was sent to the household of Hugh Auld in Baltimore, where he ran errands and looked after Auld's infant son. When Auld's wife inadvertently broke state law by teaching him the alphabet, Douglass discovered that education would make him unfit for slavery. Auld stopped the reading lessons, but Douglass continued learning secretly, swapping pieces of bread for reading lessons from local white boys.

Escape from slavery

As a teenager Douglass returned to the plantation to work as a field hand. Following a foiled escape attempt and a week in prison in 1833, Douglass was apprenticed as a ship caulker in Baltimore. His second escape attempt, aged 20, was more successful. Disguised as a sailor, Douglass escaped to New York. Eventually he reached Bedford, Massachusetts, where he worked as a laborer and changed his surname from Baily to Douglass to evade the slave hunters.

Douglass became a member of the American Anti-Slavery Society and regularly attended abolitionist lectures. In August 1841 he delivered an impromptu speech to an antislavery convention, detailing his experiences as a slave. His dignity and sincerity so moved and impressed his audience that the Anti-Slavery Society invited Douglass to become one of their agents.

Over the next six years Douglass toured the northern states, tirelessly giving lectures against slavery, regardless

▲ *Frederick Douglass was an escaped slave with a gift for making moving and powerful speeches in support of civil rights for African Americans and all women.*

of the verbal and physical abuse the work frequently earned him. His lectures impressed all who heard them; one Massachusetts newspaper applauded his "wit, arguments, sarcasm, pathos," adding that "as a speaker, he has few equals."

To answer those who doubted a former slave could speak so articulately, Douglass wrote a comprehensive account of his life, including the name and location of his former owner, published in 1845 as *Narrative of the Life of*

INFLUENCES AND INSPIRATION

As a young man Douglass eagerly sought out every educational opportunity, spending his spare time honing his debating skills at the East Baltimore Mental Improvement Society, an educational association formed by free blacks. Later, aged 60, Douglass decorated the library of his home with portraits of inspirational figures from his life. Foremost among them was his hero and mentor William Lloyd Garrison (1805–1879), leader of the American Anti-Slavery Society and editor of its crusading newspaper, the *Liberator*, which Douglass called his "meat and drink." Douglass toured with Garrison, following his moral, pacifist stance, until he met militant abolitionist John Brown. While Douglass did not agree with Brown's call for violent action, he was persuaded that pacifism alone could not effect change. Another portrait depicted Susan B. Anthony (1820–1906), abolitionist and pioneer of the women's movement, who supported Douglass in his early days as a newspaper editor in Rochester, developing his fervent belief in equal rights for women. Also represented was President Abraham Lincoln, who, as well as seeking advice from Douglass throughout the Civil War, had personally welcomed him, the only African American to attend his second inaugural address, as "my friend."

Frederick Douglass, An American Slave: Written by Himself. Becoming an international sensation, Douglass embarked on a lecture tour of Britain and Ireland to use his success to win support for the American Anti-Slavery movement and to avoid recapture. Douglass refused to recognize Auld's right to own him and so was unable to return home until two of his English friends purchased his freedom for $710.96.

A free man

In 1847 Douglass returned to the United States and established his own forthright abolitionist newspaper, the *North Star*, afterward known as *Frederick Douglass's Paper*, which he published until 1860.

Douglass was tenacious in his pursuit of equality for all; at the invitation of Elizabeth Cady Stanton (1815–1902) he addressed the first Women's Rights Convention in 1848, urging political equality for women. From 1850 Douglass became active in the Underground Railroad, helping runaway slaves reach places of safety and sometimes providing sanctuary for as many as 11 people in his own home. He also successfully fought to end segregation in the schools in Rochester, New York.

Convinced that political activism as well as moral persuasion was essential to abolish slavery, Douglass split from his mentor William Lloyd Garrison (see box). Douglass remained a pacifist, however, opposing a violent attack on Harpers Ferry, Virginia, led by abolitionist John Brown in 1859.

Throughout the Civil War (1861–1865) Douglass acted as an adviser to President Abraham Lincoln (1809–1865). He helped recruit two African American regiments but then campaigned against the discrimination experienced by black soldiers in the Union Army. Following the abolition of slavery in 1865, Douglass fought relentlessly for African American civil rights, writing to local newspapers to protest whenever he encountered discrimination.

Douglass was honored with a series of political appointments: assistant secretary of the Santo Domingo Commission in 1871, federal marshal for the District of Columbia in 1877, recorder of the deeds in 1881, and U.S. minister resident and consul general to the Republic of Haiti from 1889 to 1891. He died in 1895.

KEY DATES	
1818	Born in Easton, Maryland, on February 14.
1838	Escapes to New York.
1841	First speaks at an abolitionist meeting and is employed as a lecturer for the Anti-Slavery Society.
1845	Publishes *Narrative of the Life of Frederick Douglass, An American Slave*.
1846	English friends purchase his freedom.
1847	Publishes the *North Star*.
1861	Becomes an adviser to Abraham Lincoln.
1895	Dies in Washington, D.C., on February 20.

See also: Slavery

Further reading: Blassingame, John W., et al. (eds.). *Narrative of the Life of Frederick Douglass, An American Slave: Written by Himself*. New Haven, CT: Yale Nota Bene, 2001.
http://www.nps.gov/frdo/freddoug.html (Site dedicated to preserving the legacy of Frederick Douglass).

DOUGLASS, Sarah Mapps
Teacher, Abolitionist

Sarah Mapps Douglass dedicated her life to improving the lives of African Americans, particularly women. A committed teacher and abolitionist, Douglass was also an important figure in the women's movement.

Early life

Douglass was born in Philadelphia, Pennsylvania, on September 9, 1806, to Robert Douglass, Sr., a wealthy hairdresser, and Grace Bustill, a milliner. The Douglasses and Bustills were prominent members of Philadelphia's African American community. Douglass's grandfather Cyrus Bustill had been a leading figure in the Free African Society, one of the first black benevolent organizations.

Douglass, who spent most of her life in Philadelphia, was educated privately in the school founded by her mother and the philanthropist James Forten, grandfather of educator Charlotte Forten, to offer African American children a better education. She therefore received a much more comprehensive education than many young women of the time. After a brief period of teaching in New York, Douglass returned to Philadelphia to take over the running of the school in the 1830s.

Although raised a Quaker by her mother, Douglass despised the racism that many white Quakers showed toward black Americans. While Douglass dressed in the Quaker style and was close friends with prominent Quakers such as the abolitionist and women's rights activist Lucretia Mott (1793–1880), she was openly critical of Quaker intolerance.

Working toward a better world

During the 1830s Douglass began to contribute poetry and prose under the pseudonyms Sophanisba and Ella to such magazines as the *Liberator, Anglo-African Magazine,* and the *National Enquirer*. Her writing was often critical of slavery, prejudice, and injustice.

Douglass also helped form various societies, the most important of which was the Philadelphia Female Anti-Slavery Society, a multiracial group of women abolitionists. Through the group she met Sarah and Angelina Grimké, with whom she formed a life-long friendship. When Douglass and her mother attended Angelina's wedding in 1838, the Philadelphia press condemned their attendance on the grounds of race. Douglass worked for the Anti-Slavery Society in different capacities over the next four decades. In 1838 the society offered to financially support her struggling school. The arrangement was not a success, however, and Douglass took back control of the school two years later.

Douglass witnessed the race riots that raged through her beloved Philadelphia in the 1830s and 1840s. Despite attacks on African American people and property, Douglass continued to attend Quaker meetings at the Meeting House on Ninth and Spruce streets. Having no choice but to accept the enforced segregation, she took charge of the Quaker-supported girls' primary department at the Institute for Colored Youth in 1853. She remained there until her retirement in 1877.

In 1855 Douglass married the Reverend William Douglass, a widower with nine children. Although the marriage was not successful it did open up certain opportunities for Douglass. She used her status as a married woman to enroll at Pennsylvania Medical University, where she studied basic medical training and female health, both of which had long interested her. As a married woman she was also able to teach subjects considered unsuitable for unmarried women. Her lectures to female audiences in New York City and Philadelphia were popular. She continued to lecture and work for reform throughout the 1860s and 1870s. She died in 1882.

KEY DATES

1806   Born in Philadelphia, Pennsylvania, on September 9.

1833   Establishes the Philadelphia Female Anti-Slavery Society.

1853   Takes charge of the girls' primary department at the Institute for Colored Youth.

1855   Marries Reverend William Douglass; enrolls at Pennsylvania Medical University.

1882   Dies in Philadelphia, Pennsylvania, on September 8.

See also: Forten, Charlotte; Forten, James; Slavery

Further reading: Sterling, Dorothy (ed.). *We Are Your Sisters: Black Women in the Nineteenth Century.* New York, NY: W. W. Norton, 1984.
http://voices.cla.umn.edu/vg/Bios/entries/douglass_sarah_mapps.html (Biography and links).

DOVE, Rita
Poet

The first African American to be appointed Poet Laureate Consultant in Poetry by the Library of Congress, Rita Frances Dove was born on August 28, 1952, in Akron, Ohio. Her father, Ray A. Dove, was the first black chemist at the Goodyear Tire and Rubber Company in Akron, and her mother, Elvira, was a housekeeper.

Dove developed a love of poetry at a young age. She was an outstanding high school student and was invited to the White House as a Presidential Scholar in 1970. She went on to study English at Miami University, Oxford, Ohio, graduating in 1973. She then traveled to Germany on a Fullbright Scholarship to study at the University of Tübingen before returning to join the Writers' Workshop at the University of Iowa, where she obtained an MA in 1977.

Published work

Dove continued to write after leaving Iowa, and her first collection of poetry, *The Yellow House on the Corner*, was published in 1980. It was followed by *Museum* (1983), *Thomas and Beulah* (1986), *Mother Love* (1995), *On the Bus with Rosa Parks* (1999), and *American Smooth* (2004). *Thomas and Beulah,* which contained a series of loosely connected poems based on the lives of Dove's grandparents, earned her the 1987 Pulitzer Prize for Poetry; she became the second African American poet to received the award, after Gwendolyn Brooks in 1950.

▲ *Rita Dove has won numerous awards for her work, including a Pulitzer Prize in 1987.*

Dove also wrote a novel, *Through the Ivory Gate* (1992), and a play, *The Darker Face of the Earth* (1994), a reworking of the Greek myth of Oedipus set in the Deep South in the days of slavery.

In 1993 Dove was appointed Poet Laureate Consultant in Poetry, a position in which she served until 1995. Other awards that Dove won include the NAACP Great American Artist Award (1993) and the Duke Ellington Lifetime Achievement Award (2001). Dove taught at Arizona State University (1981–1989) and the University of Virginia, Charlottesville, where she has been professor of English since 1989.

See also: Brooks, Gwendolyn

Further reading: Pereira, Malin. *Rita Dove's Cosmopolitanism.* Chicago, IL: University of Illinois Press, 2003. http://www.people.virginia.edu/~rfd4b (Dove's site).

KEY DATES	
1952	Born in Akron, Ohio, on August 28.
1970	Invited to White House as Presidential Scholar.
1977	Obtains MA from the University of Iowa.
1980	Publishes first poetry collection, *The Yellow House on the Corner.*
1981	Begins teaching at Arizona State University.
1987	Wins Pulitzer Prize for Poetry for *Thomas and Beulah.*
1989	Joins University of Virginia, Charlottesville, as professor of English.
1993	Appointed Poet Laureate Consultant in Poetry by the Library of Congress.

DOZIER, Lamont
Composer, Musician

Lamont Dozier, also known as Lamont Anthony, gained distinction as a songwriter and producer along with brothers Brian and Eddie Holland. Known as Holland-Dozier-Holland, the songwriting and production trio created more than 200 bestselling songs. Between the years of 1963 and 1968 they were instrumental in creating what has become known as the "Motown sound." They were the most successful songwriting team at Motown Records, producing 25 Top 10 pop hits.

Born to be in music

Dozier was born in Detroit, Michigan, on June 16, 1941. He began his musical career in the gospel choir of his Baptist church. By age 13 Dozier had written his first songs and had decided that he wanted to be a singer. While in his teens Dozier sang with two Detroit vocal groups, the Romeos and the Voicemasters.

By 1962 Dozier had joined Detroit's most famous record label, Berry Gordy's Motown Records, as an artist, songwriter, and producer. He started to work with the Holland brothers in 1963. Their first collaborative song was the Supremes' "Where Did Our Love Go," which went to No. 1 on the rhythm-and-blues (R&B) charts. Over a five-year period Holland-Dozier-Holland wrote hits for such Motown artists as Martha and the Vandellas, the Four Tops, and Marvin Gaye.

In 1968, after arguments over royalties, among other things, the trio left Motown and formed Hot Wax and Invictus Records. Dozier decided to rekindle his performing career, releasing "Why Can't We Be Lovers" on Invictus, which reached No. 6 on the R&B charts. In 1973 he recorded a duet with Eddie Holland, "New Breed Kinda Woman," which reached No. 61 on the R&B charts. Dozier and the Holland brothers split up soon after.

Dozier released the album *Out Here on My Own* later

▲ *Lamont Dozier performs songs from his own repertoire at a Motown Review in 2001.*

in 1973, for which he won *Billboard* magazine's best new artist award. He had a number of hits in the 1970s and 1980s, including "Going Back to My Roots." In 1984 he formed a record label with the Holland brothers to oversee their back catalog of work and develop a new roster of talent. During the 1980s and 1990s Dozier also wrote for and produced many British artists such as Eric Clapton and Simply Red. He received an Oscar nomination for his collaboration with Phil Collins on "Two Hearts" for the movie *Buster* (1988). Dozier and the Holland brothers received many awards and honors and were inducted into the Rock and Roll Hall of Fame in 1990.

See also: Gaye, Marvin; Gordy, Berry; Ross, Diana

Further reading: http://www.lamontdozier.com/home.html (Official site).

KEY DATES

1941	Born in Detroit, Michigan, on June 16.
1962	Signs with Motown Records.
1988	Receives Grammy Award for "Two Hearts" (cowritten with Phil Collins).
2004	Receives the Ivor Novello Award for lifetime songwriting achievement.

DR. DRE
Producer, Rapper

Gangsta rap pioneer, inventor of G-Funk, and remarkable record producer, Dr. Dre (Andre Young) is probably best known for producing music for rapper Eminem (Marshall Mathers). However, he is increasingly viewed as a star in his own right and as one of the most influential artists and producers in hip-hop.

Emerging talent

Born Andre Ramelle Young in South Central Los Angeles on February 18, 1965, Dre was raised in a South Compton housing project by his mother and grandmother. He attended Centennial High School in Compton and was exposed to gang culture at an early age—an experience that is reflected in his tough, uncompromising attitude.

Dre became interested in hip-hop as a teenager. He worked as a DJ at L.A. nightclub Eve after Dark, and after forming the World Class Wreckin' Cru at age 17, he played at house parties in his neighborhood. Around this time he began using the DJ name "Dr. Dre" in honor of basketball star Julius "Dr. J" Erving.

In 1986 Dre met Ice Cube (O'Shea Jackson), and the two wrote songs for Ruthless Records, which was run by Eazy-E (Eric Wright). The following year the duo decided to perform with Eazy-E, and they formed Niggaz With Attitude (NWA). By the time they released their second album, *Straight Outta Compton*, NWA had become notorious for its hardcore sound and violent, misogynistic lyrics.

Despite Ice Cube's acrimonious departure from NWA in 1989, Dre and Eazy-E built on NWA's success, with Eazy's distinctive rap style and comic-book lyrics set against Dre's funky, sonic musical backdrop. Meanwhile, Dre also acted as resident producer for Ruthless Records, putting out seven platinum-selling albums between 1983 and 1991. Around this time Dre planned a change in direction and met former football player and celebrity bodyguard Suge Knight, who wanted to set up a West Coast record label to challenge the hip-hop scene on the East Coast.

Rise and fall of Death Row Records

In 1992 Dre and Knight formed Death Row Records, and Dre released his first solo single "Deep Cover," the title song from the film *Deep Cover*, and an album, *The Chronic*, named for a strong type of marijuana. The album marked the debut of G-funk, a sound Dre developed from the musical style called P-Funk, invented in the 1970s by George Clinton with his two bands Funkadelic and the Parliament. It was also the beginning of Dre's collaboration with rapper Snoop Dogg, whom Dre met through his stepbrother Warren G. *The Chronic* sold over one million copies, spent eight months on the Billboard Top 10, and became enormously influential over the next four years as G-funk came to dominate hip-hop. At Death Row Dre produced a number of albums, including *Doggystyle* (1993) by Snoop Dogg and *Regulate* (1994) by Warren G.

▼ *Rapper and producer Dr. Dre was part of the infamous rap group NWA (Niggaz With Attitude), along with Ice Cube and Eazy-E.*

INFLUENCES AND INSPIRATION

Dre's first musical influences came from listening to his mother's record collection of R&B and funk. He was most inspired by George Clinton and his band Funkadelic. As he said himself, "Back in the '70s that's all people were doing: getting high, wearing Afros, bell-bottoms, and listening to Parliament-Funkadelic.... His [music] was a big influence on my music. Very big."

At age 16 Dre heard a song by groundbreaking DJ Grandmaster Flash that inspired him to become a full-time DJ himself.

Dre's childhood in the projects and later the "gangsta vibe" at Death Row Records led to frequent run-ins with authority and the law. They included an assault on television presenter Denise "Dee" Barnes in 1991, which was settled out of court;

a conviction for breaking the jaw of record producer Damon Thomas, for which he served a house arrest sentence; and a drunk-driving conviction following a police chase in 1994, for which he served a six-month jail sentence. Dre's time in jail was a wakeup call, and he decided to move away from the negative influence of Death Row Records and pursue a calmer lifestyle.

KEY DATES

1965	Born in South Central Los Angeles on February 18.
1987	Forms NWA with Eazy-E and Ice Cube.
1992	Cofounds Death Row Records; releases solo album, *The Chronic*.
1996	Leaves Death Row and forms Aftermath Records.
1999	Coproduces *The Slim Shady LP* for Eminem; releases second album, *Dr. Dre 2001*.
2000	Produces Eminem's *The Marshall Mathers LP*.
2001	Becomes first hip-hop producer to win a Grammy for producer of the year.

By 1996 Dre had become disillusioned working at Death Row Records, in particular with Knight's aggressive attitude. He wanted to focus on producing music. Declaring gangsta rap dead, he left Death Row Records at a time when tensions between East and West Coast rappers were at a dangerous level. In 1997 a long-running dispute boiled over between Death Row rapper Tupac Shakur and the Notorious B.I.G., who had contracts with East Coast record company Bad Boy Records. Both artists were killed in shootings that remain unsolved.

Aftermath

On his departure from Death Row Dre formed his own label, Aftermath Records, and released a debut album, *Dr. Dre Presents... The Aftermath* (1996), a compilation that received much media attention but little commercial success. Dre became a household name after working with Eminem. He is often credited with discovering the Detroit

rap star, coproducing Eminem's 1999 debut *The Slim Shady LP*, which went on to sell three million copies, and producing the phenomenally successful *The Marshall Mathers LP* the following year. Meanwhile, Dre continued to work on his own music, releasing his hugely successful second solo album *Dr. Dre 2001*, featuring Eminem, Snoop Dogg, and Mary J. Blige. By 2005 it had sold more than six million copies. Dre once said that in order to complete a successful album, he often records around 100 songs and selects the best.

Films and the future

Dre has also turned his hand to acting. First appearing in *Who's the Man* in 1993, he went on to play supporting roles in films such as *Training Day* (2001). Admitting that he prefers to be behind the scenes rather than in the spotlight, Dre has also composed scores for such recent films as *Bad Boys II* (2003). Following a period producing Aftermath artists Busta Rhymes and Eve, Dre restarted work on his third solo album, *Detox*.

Dre married Nicole Young in 1996; the couple have four children. Dre also has one other child from a previous relationship.

See also: Black Identity and Popular Culture; Busta Rhymes; Clinton, George; Ice Cube; Eazy-E; Grandmaster Flash; Knight, Suge; Notorious B.I.G; Shakur, Tupac; Snoop Dogg

Further reading: Kelly, Kenyatta. *You Forgot About Dre: The Unauthorized Biography of Dr. Dre and Eminem—From N.W.A. to Slim Shady, a Tale of Gangsta Rap, Violence, and Hit Records*. Phoenix, AZ: Busta Books, 2001. www.dre2001.com (Official site).

DREW, Charles
Surgeon, Scientist, Educator

Charles Richard Drew was an influential scientist, surgeon, and educator. His development of the blood bank revolutionized modern medicine.

Early life

Born on June 3, 1904, and raised in working-class, multicultural Foggy Bottom in Washington, D.C., Drew was the eldest of five children born to Richard T. Drew, a carpet layer, and Nora Drew, a Howard University-trained teacher.

Drew attended the Paul Laurence Dunbar High School, in Washington, D.C. An exceptional student who excelled particularly in the sciences, Drew was also a natural athlete. He won a medal for his performance in football, basketball, and track. After graduating from school in 1922, Drew attended the then all-male Amherst College on an athletic scholarship. He was captain of the track team there and received the Most Valuable Player award on the football team. After graduating from college in 1926, he postponed his plan to attend medical school in order to repay student loans and save money for his studies. Drew was employed as an athletic director and instructor in biology and chemistry at the black educational institution Morgan College, now Morgan College University.

A change in direction

After being rejected by Howard University because of a lack of English credits, Drew attended McGill University Medical School in Montreal, Canada. Many of Drew's colleagues and friends at McGill came from completely different backgrounds: They were wealthy and white, and their studies were funded by their families. At first demoralized by his experiences at McGill, in 1930 Drew wrote to what he called "The Spirit of the New Year," stating, "Here I am, a stranger amongst strangers in a strange land, broke busted, almost disgusted, doing my family no good, myself little that is now demonstrable… I must go on. I must finish what I have started."

In the end McGill actually gave Drew all kinds of new opportunities. He was particularly impressed by John Beattie (*see box on p. 116*), a visiting scholar from the United Kingdom who became his mentor. Beattie was a leading blood-storage expert, and Drew assisted him in his research. After watching a blood transfusion that saved a patient's life, Drew decided to specialize in blood, an area to which he devoted the rest of his life.

▲ *Charles Drew helped save millions of soldiers' lives during World War II (1939–1945) through his development of dried plasma.*

In 1933 Drew graduated from McGill University Medical School with a doctor of medicine and master of surgery (MCDM) degree. He also won a prize in neuroanatomy and the J. Francis Williams Prize in Medicine. After a year's internship at Royal Victoria Hospital in Montreal Drew tried to find a residency in surgery at an American medical facility, but he found himself discriminated against on the grounds of his race.

In 1935, following his father's death, Drew took a job lecturing in pathology at Howard University Medical

At McGill University in Canada Drew came under the influence of John Beattie, a visiting professor from the United Kingdom who taught anatomy. Beattie's field of specialization was blood plasma. Drew subsequently became interested in blood research; he continued his blood work during the two years that he was an intern and resident doctor at Montreal General Hospital and during his time at Columbia University's medical school. At Columbia Drew met John Scudder, who was researching fluid balance, chemistry, and blood transfusion, and Drew's 1940 thesis focused on banked blood and blood preservation. In the same year Drew was appointed medical supervisor of the Blood for Britain Project, which supplied the liquid plasma used to save the lives of soldiers wounded in World War II. In 1941 he also served as the medical director of a three-month program set up by the American Red Cross, which involved the mass production of dried plasma. Drew was able to help his former mentor Beattie, who was head of research laboratories for the Royal College of Surgeons in London, England. Beattie requested 5,000 ampules of dried plasma to use in transfusions. Drew's work helped save many people's lives.

School, where he stayed for a year. Drew impressed Mordechai Johnson, Howard's first black president, and Numa P .G. Adams, the dean of the medical school, so much that they recommended him for a two-year fellowship in medicine at Columbia University.

A revolutionary idea

Drew was the first black American to be trained at Columbia's Presbyterian Hospital. He continued to conduct research into blood, especially after meeting John Scudder, who was investigating blood chemistry and blood transfusions (*see box*). He helped Scudder set up the Presbyterian Hospital's first blood bank. While supervising the bank, Drew conducted postgraduate research that focused on the storage, transportation, and preservation of plasma—blood from which the cells have been removed. Drew discovered, as explained in his dissertation, "Banked blood: A Study in Blood Preservation," that plasma could be sustained longer than whole blood and therefore could be used for transfusion.

In 1940 Drew became the first African American to receive a PhD in science. In the same year he briefly taught surgery at Howard University before returning to New York City. World War II (1939–1945) had broken out in Europe, and Drew was offered a job as medical director of the Blood for Britain Project (*see box*), aimed at developing and transporting liquid blood plasma for use in the treatment of British soldiers injured in combat. Drew coped with the challenge of supplying liquid plasma abroad in quantities far bigger than any needed before; he also developed the use of refrigerated trucks to transport the plasma. The process saved many lives. In 1941 Drew became the first medical director of a program set up by

KEY DATES	
1904	Born in Washington, D.C., on June 3.
1940	Becomes the first black American to receive a PhD in science from Columbia University.
1942	Becomes the first African American surgeon to serve as an examiner on the American Board of Surgery.
1950	Dies in a car accident on April 1.
1966	The Martin Luther King/Charles R. Drew University opens in Los Angeles, California.

the U.S. Red Cross Blood Bank to provide dried plasma. Drew later famously opposed the exclusion of African American donors to the blood collection program set up by the Red Cross following the United States's entry into the war in 1941. The Red Cross continued that practice until 1950, however.

In April 1941 Drew returned to Howard University as chair of the department of surgery and chief surgeon in the Freedman's Hospital. In 1950 Drew's life was cut tragically short after he was fatally injured in a car accident. Rumors spread that the white-run hospital where Drew died had refused to give him a blood transfusion, but the black doctors traveling with Drew said that his injuries were far too severe to be treated.

Further reading: Wynes, Charles. *Charles Richard Drew: The Man and the Myth.* Chicago, IL: University of Illinois Press, 1988.
http://www.princeton.edu/~mcbrown/display/charles_drew.html (Biography and list of Drew's achievements).

DUBOIS, W. E. B.
Intellectual, Civil Rights Leader

A brilliant scholar, writer, editor, academic, and political activist, W. E. B. DuBois had a profound and long-lasting influence on the development of African American thought. He led the Niagara movement, one of the earliest black organizations fighting for political and civil rights, and was cofounder of the National Association for the Advancement of Colored People (NAACP).

DuBois's sociological studies of African Americans and his analysis of African political development influenced politics and race relations worldwide. He stated at the end of the 19th century that the greatest "problem facing the 20th century would be the problem of the color line." He also explained the psychological aspect of being a black American in terms of what he described as "double consciousness." He said, "One ever feels his twoness—an American, a Negro; two warring souls, two thoughts, two unreconciled strivings; two warring ideals in one dark body, whose dogged strength alone keeps it from being torn asunder."

Early life

The only child of Alfred DuBois and Mary Burghardt, William Edward Burghardt DuBois was born on February 23, 1868; he grew up in the white, middle-class, puritan community of Great Barrington, Massachusetts. Both his parents were of mixed white and black backgrounds, and his skin was so light that he was often mistaken for white.

Even as a child DuBois thought about matters deeply; he was intellectual and extremely inquisitive. DuBois attended the local integrated high school and in 1884 became the first black American to graduate. He contributed to several newspapers, including the black-owned New York *Globe*. Although DuBois gained a place at Harvard University after graduating from high school, he could not afford to take it up. Instead, he won a scholarship to Fisk College (now Fisk University) in Nashville, Tennessee.

A Fisk man

After graduating in 1888 with a BA, DuBois enrolled at Harvard University; he received a second BA in 1891, and an MA in 1892. Between 1892 and 1894 he studied history, economics, and sociology at the University of Berlin in Germany, after which he returned to the United States to teach classics at Wilberforce University, Ohio. He finished a PhD at Harvard in 1895, becoming the first African American to receive a doctorate from the university. His dissertation title was "The Suppression of the African Slave Trade in America."

Despite his varied educational experience, DuBois always considered Fisk to be his true alma mater. He said, "I was in Harvard but not of it. I was a student at Berlin but still the son of Fisk." At Fisk he was inspired by a "world centering and whirling about [his] race in America." At Fisk he achieved a life of nearly perfect happiness in which he admired both his classmates and his professors.

Studies

DuBois greatest effect was in the field of sociology. He and his wife, Nina Gomer, moved to Philadelphia, Pennsylvania, where DuBois was invited to work on a sociological study

▲ *Activist, writer, and educator W. E. B. DuBois influenced generations of leaders and intellectuals, including Martin Luther King, Jr., and Cornel West.*

INFLUENCES AND INSPIRATION

As a student at Harvard University DuBois was influenced by the German-trained American historian Albert Bushnell Hart (1854–1943) and the philosopher William James (1842–1910), both of whom became friends and mentors. James in particular followed DuBois's debate with Booker T. Washington over the development of African Americans and believed that both men had important and useful points of view. DuBois's work in turn had a tremendous influence on the lives and work of numerous African American artists, musicians, business professionals, and political leaders, ranging from Langston Hughes, Zora Neale Hurston, and James Weldon Johnson to the Reverend Adam Clayton Powell, Sr., and Congressman Adam Clayton Powell, Jr. Contemporary African American leaders who credit DuBois with stimulating their intellectual development and way of thinking include Michael Eric Dyson, Cornel West, and Maulana Karenga. Martin Luther King, Jr., commenting on DuBois's legacy, said he was a "tireless explorer and a gifted discoverer of social truths. His singular greatness lay in his quest for truth about his own people. There were very few scholars who concerned themselves with [the] honest study of the black man and [DuBois] sought to fill this immense void. The degree to which he succeeded disclosed the great dimensions of the man."

at the University of Pennsylvania,. After conducting interviews in over 2,000 households in Philadelphia, DuBois completed a study called *The Philadelphia Negro* (1899) that looked at the "Negro Problem" and political responses to it.

In 1897 DuBois moved to Atlanta University, where he became a professor of economics and sociology. In 1903 he published *The Souls of Black Folk.* In it DuBois demanded full civil and political rights for African Americans and accused black educator Booker T. Washington of ignoring the brutality of white violence against black citizens in his policies of political conservatism and racial accommodation. From then on the two men were bitter and often vocal rivals.

Intellectual development

In a direct challenge to Washington's leadership DuBois gathered other African American leaders and intellectuals together for a conference at Buffalo, New York, in 1905.

KEY DATES

1868   Born in Great Barrington, Massachusetts, on February 23.

1895   Becomes first African American to earn a PhD from Harvard University.

1903   Publishes *The Souls of Black Folk.*

1905   Initiates Niagara Movement.

1963   Dies in Accra, Ghana, on August 27.

They opposed Washington's argument that developing African American vocational skills would bring economic growth to the community and was more important than providing them with a college education. The group founded the Niagara movement, named after their meeting place, which advocated civil justice and the abolition of discrimination.

Many of the group's ideals became the aims of the NAACP, founded in 1909. In 1910 DuBois was appointed editor of the association's monthly magazine *Crisis,* where he remained for 25 years. Having moved to New York City, DuBois, together with poet and activist James Weldon Johnson, encouraged the flowering of black creativity in the 1920s that became known as the Harlem Renaissance. DuBois used *Crisis* to advocate many black causes, to explore his own interest in pan-Africanism—a nationalist movement that emphasized African unity—to promote equality between the races, and to publish a new generation of talented black novelists and poets. In 1961, frustrated with government policies, DuBois moved to Accra, Ghana, and joined the Communist Party. In 1962 he renounced his American citizenship. DuBois died in 1963.

See also: Civil Rights; Dyson, Michael Eric; Hughes, Langston; Hurston, Zora Neale; Johnson, James Weldon; Karenga, Maulana; King, Martin Luther, Jr.; Powell, Adam Clayton, Jr; Washington, Booker T.; West, Cornel

Further reading: Rudwick, Elliot M. *W. E. B. DuBois: Propagandist of the Negro Protest.* New York, 1969. http://www.duboislc.org (DuBois Learning Center).

DUMAS, Henry
Writer

Despite his tragically short career, Henry Dumas created a substantial body of work—including poems, short stories, and an unfinished novel—that continue to provide inspiration for black writers. Almost all of his work was published after his death.

Early life

Dumas was born on July 20, 1934, in Sweet Home, Arkansas, where he was strongly influenced by the black community's intense religious feeling and love of folklore. At age 10 he moved with his family to Harlem in New York City, where he graduated from Commerce High School in 1953. Soon after he joined the Air Force and was based mainly at Lackland Air Force Base in San Antonio, Texas, although he also spent a year on the Arabian Peninsula. During his military service he began publishing his poetry in Air Force magazines.

A life cut short

In 1955 Dumas married Loretta Ponton. The couple had two sons. In 1958 Dumas left the Air Force and enrolled part time at Rutgers University, New Jersey. He also studied with jazz artist-philosopher Sun Ra (1914–1993). In 1961 Dumas left Rutgers without completing his degree. At the time he was deeply engaged with the civil rights movement, which was at its height, transporting food and clothing to protesters in Mississippi and Tennessee.

In 1967 Dumas became a teacher at Southern Illinois University near East St. Louis. He was appointed as the director of language workshops in the Experiment in Higher Education Program. While living in East St. Louis, he became friendly with the black poet Eugene B. Redmond, a fellow teacher.

In May 1968 Dumas's career was cut short when he was shot and killed by a New York City Transit policeman in what appeared to have been a case of mistaken identity. He was 33 years old. The circumstances surrounding his death remain unclear, since there was little investigation into the incident at the time.

Myth and black power

After Dumas's death Redmond worked hard to publish the trove of writings that his friend had left behind. Both *"Ark of Bones" and Other Stories* and a collection of his soaring, blues- and jazz-inspired poetry, *Play Ebony, Play*

KEY DATES	
1934	Born in Sweet Home, Arkansas, on 20 July.
1955	Marries Loretta Ponton.
1967	Begins teaching at Southern Illinois University.
1968	Killed in New York City on May 23.
1974	Publication of *Play Ebony, Play Ivory* (poems) and *"Ark of Bones" and Other Stories*.

Ivory, were published in 1974. Dumas was immediately heralded as one of the finest African American writers of his generation and, by fellow black poets, as a "prophet" of black liberation. Redmond also helped publish Dumas's unfinished novel *Jonah and the Green Stone* (1976), along with *Rope of Wind and Other Stories* (1979), *Goodbye, Sweetwater* (1988), and *Knees of a Natural Man: The Selected Poetry of Henry Dumas* (1989).

In 1972 Kent State University set up the Henry Dumas Memorial, which included a small research library and reading room in the Center of Pan-African Culture.

In his writing Dumas blended African folklore and everyday life to create a distinctive "black" literature that was outside the European tradition. In one of his best-known stories, "Ark of Bones," for example, a young African American boy discovers and then becomes one of the caretakers of an ark full of the bones of victims of racism. In embodying forgotten or neglected African and Christian myths in contemporary black life, Dumas sought to reempower and offer hope to an oppressed African American nation. Academic Molefi Asante describes Dumas as "one of the most centered of African American authors … a profoundly honest writer who tells his and his people's special truth to the world."

See also: Civil Rights; Redmond, Eugene B.

Further reading: Ishmael Reed. "Henry Dumas: The Poet of Resurrection." *Black American Literature Forum.* Volume 22, Number 2 (Summer 1988).
www.english.uiuc.edu/maps/poets/a_f/dumas/dumas.htm (Biography plus appreciations).
http://hierographics.org/hdumaspoetandseer.htm (Biography).

DUNBAR, Paul Laurence
Poet

Paul Laurence Dunbar was the first African American poet to receive national critical acclaim. He was a prolific writer of poems, essays, novels, and short stories that often focused on the struggle of black Americans. He used both standard English and the dialect of the black community in his work, and was popular with black and white audiences alike.

Road to success

Dunbar was born on June 27, 1872, in Dayton, Ohio, to Matilda and Joshua Dunbar, both former slaves. His parents separated when he was two years old, and his mother worked as a washerwoman to support her four children. Matilda Dunbar was a huge influence on her son. She loved poetry and passed on her passion to him.

Dunbar attended Dayton Central High School, where he was the only nonwhite pupil. He performed well and became editor of the school paper. After leaving school, he worked as an elevator operator to support himself, writing poetry and newspaper articles in his spare time. He soon came to the attention of fellow poet James Newton Matthews, who wrote to an Illinois newspaper praising Dunbar's work. The letter was reprinted in several other publications. Dunbar's reputation grew, and he published a book of poems, *Oak and Ivy*, in 1892.

In 1895 Dunbar moved to Toledo, Ohio, where he published his second book of poetry, *Majors and Minors*. A review by the respected author, critic, and editor of *Harper's Weekly* William Dean Howells further enhanced Dunbar's reputation. A New York publisher subsequently put out Dunbar's first two collections in a single edition entitled *Lyrics of a Lowly Life*. In 1898 Dunbar married Alice Ruth Moore, a writer, teacher, and political activist. He moved to Washington, D.C., where he worked for the Library of Congress for a year. He resigned to concentrate on his poetry and other writing. Over the next few years his work appeared in newspapers and journals. Poetry collections published in this period included *Poems of Cabin and Field* (1899) and *Candle Lightin' Time* (1901).

In 1902 Dunbar and his wife separated, and Dunbar began to develop alcoholism, stemming from depression. In 1904 he went back to live in Dayton and died there of tuberculosis two years later.

See also: Dunbar-Nelson, Alice

Further reading: Dunbar, Paul. *The Complete Poems of Paul Laurence Dunbar*. New York, NY: Dodd, Mead, 1993. http://www.english.uiuc.edu/maps/poets/a_f/dunbar/dunbar.htm (Biography).

▲ **The poet Paul Laurence Dunbar was one of the foremost African American writers of his generation.**

DUNBAR-NELSON, Alice
Writer

Alice Dunbar-Nelson was a civil rights activist, educator, novelist, poet, and essayist, and also a perceptive critic of African American literature.

Early life
Born in New Orleans, Louisiana, on July 19, 1875, Alice Ruth Moore was of mixed black, white, and Native American parentage. From a young age she identified strongly with her African roots despite her light appearance and middle-class status. Dunbar-Nelson joined the teacher's training program at Straight University (now Dillard University). She later studied at Cornell University, the Pennsylvania School of Industrial Art, and the University of Pennsylvania, specializing in educational psychology. She taught in New Orleans between 1892 and 1897 before moving to Brooklyn, New York City, where she taught between 1897 and 1898.

Love affair with literature
Although Dunbar-Nelson was a committed teacher, her first love was literature, and she wrote short stories and poems. Her first collection of work, *Violets and Other Tales*, was published in 1895, when she was barely 20 years old. The book was well received critically. Dunbar-Nelson came to the notice of Paul Laurence Dunbar, who saw her photograph in a Boston journal and began corresponding with her: The couple married in 1898. A year later Dunbar-Nelson published her second book, *The Goodness of St.*

Rocque and Other Stories, as a companion volume to her husband's collection *Poems of Cabin and Field*. Although the couple attracted much attention, particularly in literary circles, they were not happy together, and Dunbar's violence and alcoholism led to their separation in 1902: Dunbar died four years later.

Much of Dunbar-Nelson's writing in her later life was published in newspapers and journals; she edited and wrote for the influential *A. M. E Review* (1913–1914) and published *Masterpieces of Negro Eloquence* (1914). She also published in *Crisis, Ebony, Topaz, Negro Poets, Harlem: A Forum for Negro Lift*, and *The Journal of Negro History*. Dunbar-Nelson wrote columns for several papers, including the *Pittsburgh Courier* and *Washington Eagle*.

Dunbar-Nelson married two more times, briefly in 1910 to teacher Henry Arthur Callis, and in 1916 to journalist Robert J. Nelson. Her third marriage was a happy one, and Nelson provided her with emotional and professional support. Between 1920 and 1922 the couple published a black liberal newspaper called the *Wilmington Advocate*, which campaigned against inequality and for civil rights. Dunbar-Nelson had strong political opinions. Poems such as "I Sit and Sew" and essays express her belief in racial and gender equality. Dunbar-Nelson was a suffragist and was involved in several women's organizations. She helped found the Industrial School for Colored Girls in Marshalltown, Delaware. She also wrote passionately about the rights of black people in the United States and actively campaigned against lynching. From 1928 to 1931 Dunbar-Nelson was the secretary of the American Friends Inter-Racial Peace Committee. Her essays highlighted intolerance within black society toward lighter-skinned African Americans. Following Nelson's appointment to the Pennsylvania Athletic Commission in 1932, the couple moved to Philadelphia, where they mixed with such literary figures as W. E. B. DuBois and Langston Hughes. Dunbar-Nelson died of heart problems in 1935.

KEY DATES	
1875	Born in New Orleans, Louisiana, on July 19.
1892	Graduates from Straight College.
1895	Publishes *Violets and Other Tales.*
1898	Marries poet Paul Laurence Dunbar.
1899	Publishes *The Goodness of St. Rocque and Other Stories.*
1914	Publishes *Masterpieces of Negro Eloquence.*
1916	Marries Robert J. Nelson.
1935	Dies in Philadelphia, Pennsylvania, on September 13.

See also: DuBois, W. E. B.; Dunbar, Paul Laurence; Harlem Renaissance; Hughes, Langston

Further reading: Hull, Gloria (ed.). *The Works of Alice-Dunbar Nelson* (3 vols.). New York, NY: Oxford University Press, 1988. http://www.english.uiuc.edu/maps/poets/a_f/dunbar-nelson/about.htm (University page on Dunbar-Nelson).

DUNCAN, Tim
Basketball Player

Tim Duncan is a giant on the modern basketball court, both in terms of his play and his physique—he is 6 feet 11 inches (2.1m) tall and weighs 260 pounds (118kg).

Duncan was born on April 25, 1976, in St. Croix, part of the U.S. Virgin Islands. As a child he was a talented swimmer, producing competitive times in the 400-meter freestyle. He switched to basketball, however, in 1989 after Hurricane Hugo destroyed his training facilities along with much of the infrastructure of the Virgin Islands.

Pro career

Duncan did not start playing formal basketball until the ninth grade; but once he did, he dominated the court. In 1993 he graduated from high school and went to Wake Forest University, North Carolina, on a basketball scholarship. His playing singled him out as one to watch, and he set collegiate records for shot blocking. In 1997, when he graduated from college with a degree in psychology, he was drafted into the National Basketball Association (NBA) by the San Antonio Spurs.

Demonstrating remarkable speed and leaping dunk shots, Duncan was named NBA Rookie of the Year in 1998; the following year the Spurs went on to the NBA finals and beat the New York Knicks to take the championship. Following the game, Duncan was named as finals Most Valuable Player (MVP). He received further MVP titles in 2000, 2002 and 2003—the last award following Duncan's amazing performance in another NBA final against the New Jersey Nets.

Duncan's accolades as a basketball player continued to increase. He was the second player in NBA history to be named to an All-NBA team and an All-Defensive team in his first five seasons, and he has been on the All-NBA first

▲ *Tim Duncan brings the ball upcourt in San Antonio, Texas, in October 2003. He scored 24 points in the Spurs' 83–82 defeat of the Phoenix Suns.*

team for seven seasons. In 2004 Duncan was on the U.S. team that won a bronze medal at the Olympics Games in Athens, Greece.

Charity activities

Duncan is deeply involved with charity work alongside his wife Amy (they were married in 2001). The Tim Duncan Foundation promotes health awareness and recreational activities among young people, supporting nonprofit organizations and programs in south Texas, the U.S. Virgin Islands, and North Carolina. In addition, Duncan's charity bowling and golf events have raised hundreds of thousands of dollars for cancer research. Duncan also arranged for St. Croix to build its first professional-standard wooden basketball court.

Further reading: Finkel, Jon. *Greatest Stars of the NBA 2004: Tim Duncan*. Los Angeles, CA: Tokyopop, 2004.
http://www.nba.com/playerfile/tim_duncan/ (Duncan's NBA player file).
http://www.slamduncan.com/ (Duncan's official site).

KEY DATES	
1976	Born in St. Croix, U.S. Virgin Islands, on April 25.
1989	Begins playing basketball.
1997	Drafted by the NBA San Antonio Spurs.
1998	Named NBA Rookie of the Year.
1999	Named NBA Finals Most Valuable Player.
2004	Wins a bronze medal at the Athens Olympics.

DUNCANSON, Robert Scott
Artist

Robert Scott Duncanson was one of the first African American artists to earn a living as a painter and to receive international acclaim for his work.

Early life

Duncanson was born in Seneca County, New York, in 1821, into a family of free African Americans, many of whom worked as housepainters and carpenters. His mother was of African descent, and his father was a Canadian of Scottish descent. Duncanson spent his early childhood in Canada. He learned about art by studying and copying engravings of famous paintings.

In the late 1830s Duncanson moved to Mount Healthy, a small town north of Cincinnati, Ohio—a city known for its large free black population and active abolitionist movement—to embark on a career as a painter. In Cincinnati he was able to participate in the city's free art education programs. In 1839 the Freedman's Aid Society of Ohio raised enough money to send him to Glasgow, Scotland, to study painting. He returned to Cincinnati in about 1842.

Artistic career

Duncanson's early works included still lifes and portraits of abolitionists whose support helped secure his success. He received his first substantial commission from the wealthy entrepreneur and abolitionist Nicholas Longworth, in whose mansion (now the Taft Museum of Art) he painted 12 mural-landscapes (1850–1852). They were the first murals painted by an African American. In later years they were covered with wallpaper, but in the 1990s they were rediscovered and restored.

In the 1850s Duncanson came to specialize in romanticized views of American landscapes of the type made popular by Thomas Cole and the painters of the Hudson River School. *Blue Hole, Flood Waters, Little Miami River* (1851) is one of Duncanson's best-known works of this type. His paintings are usually horizontal and do not have a particular viewpoint; they emphasize light, clouds, and sky. Patrons felt comfortable with these reflective landscapes, which seemed to carry no overt political messages, and they sold well.

In 1853 Duncanson traveled to Italy, where he was inspired by the idealized landscapes of the 17th-century painter Claude Lorrain. On his return to the United States,

KEY DATES	
1821	Born in Seneca County, New York.
1851	Paints *Blue Hole, Flood Waters, Little Miami River.*
1850s	Produces 12 mural-landscapes for the abolitionist Nicholas Longworth between 1850 and 1852.
1853	Travels around Italy.
1861	Paints *Land of the Lotus Eaters;* goes to Canada, where he remains until 1865.
1865	Travels to Ireland, Scotland, and England, where his work is acclaimed.
1872	Dies in Detroit, Michigan, on December 21.

he produced scenes inspired by literary works, as well as paintings based on real places. One such painting, *Land of the Lotus Eaters* (1861), based on a poem by British poet Alfred Tennyson, brought him international acclaim. Exhibited in his home city in 1861, it prompted the *Cincinnati Gazette* to praise Duncanson as "the best landscape painter in the West." In 1863 Duncanson left the United States for Europe in order to escape the racial tensions provoked by the Civil War (1861–1865).

Although Duncanson worked within the tradition of idealized landscapes that encapsulated the national American style, his paintings often included subtle references to black life, slavery, and freedom. When he died in 1872 in Detroit, Michigan, he left behind a large body of work. He was the first African American painter to attain international acclaim; some of his paintings were purchased by the king of Sweden and Britain's Queen Victoria. Today his works can be seen in both national and international collections, and his paintings fetch high prices at auction. In 2000, for example, *Still Life with Fruit and Nuts* sold for $222,500.

Further reading: Ketner, Joseph D. *The Emergence of the African American Artist: Robert S. Duncanson.* Columbia, MO: University of Missouri Press, 1993.
www.artcyclopedia.com/artists/duncanson_robert_scott.html (Links to pictures by Duncanson in art museums).
http://www.hammondshouse.org/index.php?pid=31 (Biography).

DUNGY, Tony
Football Coach

Tony Dungy became fascinated by football at school. In 1980 he gave up playing to become a coach. He was an excellent coach, gaining a reputation for turning around losing teams and making them winners.

Anthony Kevin Dungy was born on October 6, 1955, in Jackson, Michigan. Growing up, he was surrounded by an atmosphere of academic achievement at home, but he began playing football at Parkside High School and went on to play quarterback at the University of Minnesota from 1973 to 1976. Dungy's performance was good, but he lacked size, and hence power, as well as throwing ability, which meant that he initially had trouble finding an NFL team after college. He was eventually signed to the defense of the Pittsburgh Steelers.

From playing to coaching

Dungy remained with the Steelers until 1979 as part of the team's famous defensive wall. However, Dungy did not provide the big-hitting performance that the Steelers required; he was traded to the San Francisco 49ers and then to the New York Giants. His playing career ended in 1980, but his deep understanding of tactics led him to become an assistant coach for the Pittsburgh Steelers.

Between 1981 and 1992 Dungy acted as assistant coach for the Steelers, the Kansas City Chiefs, and the Minnesota Vikings, usually specializing in defensive tactics. However, he wanted to be a head coach. In 1996 he achieved his goal with the Tampa Bay Buccaneers, at the time a hugely unsuccessful team near the bottom of the league. Dungy's coaching almost singlehandedly changed the fortunes of the Buccaneers. The 1996 season ended with a series of wins, and then the 1997 season saw the

▲ *Tony Dungy in the second half of an AFC Championship game against the New England Patriots on January 18, 2004, in Foxboro, Massachusetts.*

team win its first five games and make the playoffs, only losing to Super Bowl champions the Green Bay Packers.

Under Dungy the Buccaneers reached three playoffs; but after team performance declined in 2001, Dungy was fired, to the disappointment of many of the players. Dungy became head coach of the Indianapolis Colts from January 2002. Under Dungy the Colts were also revitalized, achieving playoff positions in his first two seasons.

Dungy's style of coaching is quiet and respectful, and his deeply held Christian beliefs are central to his decision-making and player relations. Dungy also set up Mentors for Life, which supplies tickets for Buccaneer games to mentored young adults and their mentors. He is involved in charity work and speaks at family football clinics and Christian-related events. In 2002 Dungy, who had five children with his wife, was awarded the National Fatherhood Initiative Fatherhood Award. The family was struck by tragedy in December 2005, when Dungy's son James committed suicide at age 18. Dungy sought comfort in work, returning to the Colts only a week later.

KEY DATES	
1955	Born in Jackson, Michigan, on October 6.
1976	Signs to play defense for the Pittsburgh Steelers.
1981	Becomes assistant coach of the Pittsburgh Steelers.
1996	Becomes head coach of the Tampa Bay Buccaneers.
2001	Fired from the Buccaneers when the team's performance declines.
2002	Becomes head coach of the Indianapolis Colts.

Further reading: http://www.colts.com/ (Official site of the Indianapolis Colts).

DUNHAM, Katherine
Choreographer, Dancer

A pioneer of African American modern dance, Katherine Dunham created vibrant, dynamic choreography inspired by the traditional black dances of the Caribbean and Central and South America. Her influence on younger black dancers and choreographers, most notably Alvin Ailey, has been enormous.

Early life
Dunham was born on June 22, 1909, in Glen Ellyn, a village close to Chicago, and raised in nearby Joliet. Her mother, an assistant principal in a Chicago school, died when Dunham was five years old, and she and her older brother were brought up first by cousins and later by their stepmother. In 1928 Dunham went to study anthropology at the University of Chicago, where she also took dance lessons.

Dunham's love of dance led her to focus her studies on traditional black dances, and in 1935 she won a

scholarship to visit the Caribbean as part of her MA research. She was especially fascinated by the sacred dances of the vodun (voodoo) religion of Haiti. Returning to the United States, she used her research to create a series of dazzling dance revues, including the hugely successful *Le Jazz Hot—From Haiti to Harlem* (1940). She also found time to perform in dance sequences in films such as *Stormy Weather* (1943).

▼ *Choreographer Katherine Dunham created routines inspired by traditional Caribbean dances.*

A lifetime of achievement
In 1940 Dunham founded her own dance company, which toured throughout the world to great acclaim and became the first African American troupe to be fully self-supporting. She also founded dance schools in Chicago and New York City, developing a ground-breaking dance technique based on Caribbean dance moves that is still practiced today. Among her students were Alvin Ailey and the entertainer Eartha Kitt. In 1962 she became the first African American woman to choreograph works for New York City's Metropolitan Opera Company.

Dunham has always been politically and socially active. In 1967, for example, she opened the Performing Arts Training Center in East St. Louis, Illinois, offering dance classes to the city's disadvantaged black teenagers. In 1992 she went on a hunger strike after the U.S. government deported Haitian refugees fleeing a military coup in their native country.

See also: Ailey, Alvin; Kitt, Eartha

Further reading: Aschenbrenner, Joyce. *Katherine Dunham: Dancing a Life*. Urbana, IL: University of Illinois Press, 2002.
www.black-collegian.com/african/dunham9.shtml (Biography).

DUNJEE, Roscoe
Publisher, Activist

As owner and editor of the *Black Dispatch*, one of the leading African American newspapers of the early 20th century, Roscoe Dunjee campaigned for civil rights both in his home state, Oklahoma, and across the United States. For over 40 years his weekly editorials for the newspaper offered eloquent and passionate commentary on the injustices suffered by black men and women. Dunjee was also president of the Oklahoma City branch of the National Association for the Advancement of Colored People (NAACP).

Dunjee (or Dungee) was born in 1883. His father was a wealthy West Virginian Baptist minister, John William Dunjee, a former slave who had escaped to freedom in Canada.

Printer and editor

Dunjee entered the printing business at an early age and in 1915 established his own newspaper, the *Black Dispatch*, in Oklahoma City. Its banner included a black angel and the headline "Mouthpiece for All Better Thinking Colored People." The *Black Dispatch* built up a nationwide readership, reaching a circulation of about 26,500.

The newspaper quickly gained a reputation for its editor's outspoken views as well as the high quality of its journalism. Dunjee used the paper to address events and issues that were, by and large, ignored by the mainstream white press, such as the lack of recognition given to black soldiers who had fought during World War I (1914–1918) or the widespread segregation on buses and trains.

As well as attacking white racism, Dunjee also sought to raise the political consciousness of his black readers. He was intolerant of the political apathy he observed in many of his contemporaries: "The most disgusting and senseless Negro that we know, " he wrote in one fiery editorial in 1920, "is the fellow who stands around and says, 'Oh I never vote; I'm not registered....'"

Dunjee's older sister, Drusilla Dunjee Houston (1876–1941), was a frequent contributor to the *Black Dispatch,* for which she wrote thousands of articles, as well as being an influential Oklahoma educator and the author of an important history of ancient Ethiopia.

Dunjee continued to edit the *Black Dispatch* until 1955, when after 41 years as its editor he sold the paper to John Dunjee, his nephew. Despite this Dunjee continued to edit and write for the paper until his death in 1965. The *Dispatch* remained in the Dunjee family until it folded in 1982. Today Dunjee is remembered as one of the pioneers of modern black journalism and an important precursor of the civil rights activists of the 1950s and 1960s.

▲ *Roscoe Dunjee (left) goes over some work with his fellow employees in 1948.*

Further reading: Burke, Bob, et al. *Roscoe Dunjee: Champion of Civil Rights.* Oklahoma City, OK: Oklahoma Heritage Association, 1998.
http://wings.buffalo.edu/dunjeehouston/history/blkdisp.htm (Page on the *Black Dispatch*).

KEY DATES	
1883	Born in West Virginia.
1915	Founds the *Black Dispatch*.
1965	Dies.

DURNHAM, James
Physician

Former slave James Durnham (sometimes known as Derham, Derum, or Durham) was the first known African American licensed physician.

Early life
The details of the life and death of Durnham are very sketchy. He was born a slave on May 1 or 2, 1762. His masters, thought to be doctors, were enlightened for the time and taught Durnham how to read and write. Doctors at that time received their training through apprenticeships, and the young Durnham got some kind of medical training from age eight, when he became the slave of John A. Kersley, Jr.

A rigorous form of training
Durnham acquired more medical knowledge through other masters who were also thought to be doctors. He eventually became the property of a surgeon named George West, who was in the British Sixteenth Regiment during the American Revolution. Durnham helped West perform amputations on wounded soldiers and treated illnesses such as smallpox. In 1781, however, Durnham was taken prisoner by the Spanish following their defeat of the British at Pensacola, Florida; he was taken to New Orleans, Louisiana, which was under Spanish control.

Dow and New Orleans
Following his purchase by the Scottish physician Robert Dow, Durnham's life changed substantially. Dow treated Durnham with respect, and the two men became friends as well as colleagues despite the fact that Durnham remained Dow's slave. Dow allowed Durnham to perform various medical services in the French Quarter of New Orleans. Durnham, or "Santiago Derum" as he was alternatively known, quickly established himself as a popular doctor. He built up a flourishing practice, and in 1783 Dow allowed Durnham to purchase his freedom for the sum of 500 pesos.

In 1788 Durnham returned to Philadelphia to look for his relatives and friends. He met Benjamin Rush, one of the country's most eminent physicians, who was also an abolitionist. Rush, along with other leading liberal intellectuals of the time, was vehemently against the idea promoted by some slavery advocates that black people were intellectually inferior to white people. Rush became

KEY DATES	
1762	Born a slave in Philadelphia, Pennsylvania, on May 1 or 2.
1783	Buys freedom in New Orleans; practices medicine with Dow on and off until 1801.
1788	Returns to Philadelphia for a year, where he meets Dr. Benjamin Rush; the two men correspond for 16 years.

interested in Durnham and his achievements, which rebutted such racist theories. He was also impressed by Durnham's medical knowledge, especially in the treatment of diseases common to Louisiana; he subsequently published an article about Durnham in the *American Museum*. Rush also introduced Durnham to members of the Philadelphia College of Physicians and Surgeons. Although Durnham returned to New Orleans in 1787 to work with Dow, he corresponded with Rush until at least 1805, and the men exchanged ideas on the treatment of such diseases as yellow fever.

Changes
It seems likely that Durnham would have spent the remainder of his life working in New Orleans had not the Spanish authorities intervened. In August 1801 Durnham was one of six physicians named in a report that denounced unlicensed medical practices in New Orleans. However, Durnham was allowed to continue working because he was seen as an expert on throat conditions. The lack of information about Durnham's life makes it difficult to confirm what he did in the last years of his life or the year of his death. It is thought that Durnham decided to return to his native Philadelphia, where he soon acquired a reputation for his work with yellow fever victims. What is remarkable about Durnham is that, as a black man, he was allowed to successfully practice medicine in late 18th-century America and also gained the respect of some of the leading physicians of the time. The date of his death is unknown.

Further reading: Cox, Clinton. *African American Healers.* New York, NY: Wiley, 2000.
http://www.aaregistry.com/african_american_history/1574/James_Durnham_a_pioneering_physician (Short biography).

DU SABLE, Jean Baptiste Pointe
Trader, Settler

Jean Baptist Pointe Du Sable founded the first trading posts and settlements in the area that later became the city of Chicago in about 1779.

Early life
Much of the detail of Du Sable's life, particularly his early life, remains unknown. Du Sable, who was also known as Pointe de Sable, Au Sable, Pointe Sable, Sabre, and Pointe de Saible, was born in St. Marc, in present-day Haiti, probably in about 1745. His father was a French sea captain, and his mother was an ex-slave. It is thought that his mother died when Du Sable was young, and he was sent to France to be educated, after which he worked on his father's ships. How he came to America remains unclear; some accounts claim that he arrived in New Orleans, others that he originally migrated to French Canada with his friend Jacques Clemorgan.

Trading post
Around 1779 Du Sable arrived in the Chicago River area with Clemorgan and a Native American named Choctaw; they established a trading post on the sites of Peoria and Michigan City. Du Sable also established a trading post at the mouth of the river at a place the local Native Americans called Echecagou (Chicago). Du Sable acted as an agent for the British during the American Revolution (1775–1783), but he was temporarily imprisoned by them after they suspected he was working with the French. After the British released him, Du Sable traded with them, supplying their fort with goods.

▲ *Jean Baptiste Pointe Du Sable established the first settlements in the area that later became Chicago. This engraving dates back to the 18th century.*

In 1784 Du Sable returned to Eschecagou and reestablished his trading post. He built a cabin, the first house ever built in what is now Chicago. For the next 16 years Du Sable ran a very successful trading post. In 1788 he married Catherine, a Potawotomi Indian, with whom he had two children. In 1800 Du Sable sold his assets in Chicago for $1,200—the reasons prompting him to sell range from his defeat in an election for chief of the local Native Americans to the death of his wife and son. Du Sable is thought to have moved to Missouri with his daughter and grandchildren. In 1814 he is believed to have declared himself bankrupt. When Du Sable died in 1818, he was virtually penniless. In 1961 the Du Sable Museum of African American History, the oldest private nonprofit African American museum in the country, opened. Du Sable's importance in the founding of Chicago was overlooked until 1968, however.

KEY DATES

1745	Probably born in St. Marc, Haiti, at about this time.
1779	Travels to the Chicago River area to establish trading posts; temporarily imprisoned by the British.
1784	Returns to Echecagou (Chicago), where he reestablishes a successful trading post.
1788	Marries his long-time Native American companion.
1800	Sells his Chicago business for $1,200.
1814	Declared bankrupt.
1818	Dies in St. Charles, Missouri, on August 28.

Further reading: Altman, Susan. *Extraordinary African Americans*. New York, NY: Children's Press, 2001.
http://www.kreyol.com/xhistory/1history.html (Overview of Du Sable's importance as the founder of Chicago).

DYSON, Michael Eric
Educator, Minister, Critic

Michael Eric Dyson is a scholar, Baptist minister, and popular culture commentator. Calling him a "new intellectual," the *Philadelphia Inquirer* book critic Carlo Romano also referred to Dyson as a "crown prince ... to the two most established black male intellectuals: [Cornel] West and ... scholar Henry Louis Gates, Jr." Dyson has written on a variety of subjects, from race and civil rights issues to hip-hop and movies.

Rocky road to success

Born in Detroit, Michigan, on October 23, 1958, Dyson grew up in a middle-class family. He went to public schools until age 16, when he briefly attended a predominately white boarding school. He was expelled after defending himself against repeated racial assaults. At age 17 Dyson was single, expecting a child, and living on welfare. After a variety of jobs, including being a laborer and working in auto sales, Dyson also became involved in street gangs.

Recognizing the need to improve his life and set a good example for his young son, Dyson tried to change direction. Religion had always been important to him, and his Baptist pastor encouraged Dyson to train to be a minister; he was ordained by the time he was 21. Dyson attended divinity school at Knoxville College in Tennessee but transferred to Carson–Newman College, graduating in 1982. He went on to get an MA (1991) and a PhD (1993) in philosophy from Princeton University, New Jersey, where he also taught.

A man of diverse interests

Dyson has referred to himself as a feminist and has admitted to being inspired by such women as his second wife, the Reverend Marcia Dyson, and the writer Toni Morrison. A gifted educator, Dyson claims that his teachers were his early role models, including Mrs. Jones, his fifth grade teacher at Wingert Elementary School, who gave him a sense of who he was: "For one year, and in stark contrast to what we learned before, we breathed black, thought black, saw black, learned black, believed black—and for the first time for many of us, felt black."

Dyson's first published book, *Reflecting Black,* was a collection of essays on subjects such as the filmmaker Spike Lee and musician Michael Jackson. He has since published several critically acclaimed books, including

▲ *Michael Eric Dyson has been described as one of a group of "new intellectuals."*

Making Malcolm: The Myth and Meaning of Malcolm X (1995) and a popular study of gangsta rap entitled *Between God and Gangsta Rap* (1996). Dyson has taught at several eminent universities, including Brown. In 2002 he became the Avalon Foundation Professor in Humanities and African American Studies at the University of Pennsylvania.

KEY DATES	
1958	Born in Detroit, Michigan, on October 23.
1993	Receives a PhD from Princeton University.
2002	Appointed Avalon Professor in Humanities and African American Studies at the University of Pennsylvania.

See also: Black Identity and Popular Culture; Gates, Henry Louis, Jr.; Jackson, Michael; Lee, Spike; Malcolm X; Morrison, Toni; West, Cornel

Further reading: Dyson, Michael Eric. *Michael Eric Dyson Reader.* New York, NY: Basic Civitas Books, 2004. http://www.gale.com/free_resources/bhm/bio/dyson_m.htm (Biography).

EARLEY, Charity Adams
Army Officer

Charity Adams Earley was the first African American woman to become a lieutenant colonel in the U.S. Army. A graduate of the Women's Army Corps (WAC), she commanded the only battalion of African American women, the 6888th Central Postal Delivery Battalion, whose responsibility was to deliver mail to American soldiers stationed in Europe during World War II (1939–1945).

Road to the Army

Born Charity Edna Adams in Columbia, South Carolina, on March 20, 1918, Earley was the daughter of a minister, who spoke Greek and Hebrew, and a teacher. The family house was full of books, and Earley graduated from Booker T. Washington High School as the school valedictorian. In 1938 Earley completed her BA in mathematics from Wilberforce College, Ohio. She taught in Columbia for about four years while attending graduate summer school at Ohio State University.

In 1942 Early was invited to join the Women's Army Auxiliary Corps (WAAC), which later became the WAC. She joined the first batch of women officer candidates for the army. In August 1942 Earley became the first African American woman officer in the WAAC. She was assigned to the Third Company, stationed in Des Moines, Iowa; in 1943 she became the training supervisor at the base. A year later Earley, who was now a major, was posted overseas to Europe; she traveled to England, Scotland, and France training personnel. In March 1945 she became commander of the 6888th Battalion, whose job it was to deliver mail to the seven million U.S. troops based in Europe. Following the end of the war, Earley left military service in 1946; she was the highest-ranking African American in the WAC.

Life as a civilian

As as civilian Earley took advantage of the GI Bill to study for an MA in vocational psychology at Ohio State University. She married Stanley A. Earley in 1949 and moved with him to Switzerland before they settled in Dayton, Ohio. Earley served on the boards of organizations such as United Way, the Black Leadership Development Program, the American Red Cross, the Urban League, and the YWCA. Before her death in 2002 she was inducted into the Ohio Women's Hall of Fame (1979) and the South Carolina Black Hall of Fame (1991). Earley's memoirs, *One Woman's Army*, were published in 1989. She died in Dayton, Ohio, in 2002.

▼ *Charity Earley in 1945, when she was commanding officer of the WAC Postal Battalion, which was stationed in Britain during World War II.*

KEY DATES	
1918	Born in Columbia, South Carolina, on March 20.
1942	Becomes first African American officer in the WAAC.
1944	Posted to Europe; becomes commander of the 6888th Battalion (1945).
1946	Leaves military service as a lieutenant colonel.
2002	Dies in Dayton, Ohio, on January 13.

See also: Military

Further reading: Earley, C. E. A. *One Woman's Army.* College Station, TX: Texas A & M University Press, 1989.
http://www.scafricanamericanhistory.com/
currenthonoree.asp?month=5&year=1997 (Biography).

EAZY-E
Rapper, Entrepreneur

Eazy-E was a gangsta-rap pioneer, founder of Ruthless Records, and member of NWA (Niggaz With Attitude). In 1995 he died at age 31, shortly after having been diagnosed with AIDS. He was the first rapper to admit to having the disease.

Born in Compton, one of the roughest parts of Los Angeles, on September 7, 1964, Eric Wright dropped out of school at an early age. He used some of the profits from dealing drugs to start up the rap label Ruthless Records. The label was largely unsuccessful until Ice Cube and Dr. Dre began to write songs for it. When HBO, the signing company of Ruthless, turned down one of their compositions, "Boyz-N-the-Hood," the pair teamed up with Eazy to record it themselves, using the acronym NWA (Niggaz With Attitude). DJ Yella later joined the group.

Straight Outta Compton

Although their first album, *NWA and the Posse* (1987), met with little success, the addition of Lorenzo "MC Ren" Patterson, combined with violent lyrics and a more hard-edged sound, helped turn things around. NWA's second album, *Straight Outta Compton* (1988), shot the group to stardom and notoriety. That same year Eazy-E released what was to prove his only complete solo album, *Eazy-Duz-It*, which went on to sell more than two million copies.

Before long the Ruthless camp was beset by infighting and disputes over money. Ice Cube left NWA amid acrimony toward the end of 1989, leaving Eazy-E to take on an increasing share of the rapping and songwriting duties. This caused further discord since some people believed that Eazy's distinctive, high-pitched rap style and taste for vulgar comic-book lyrics undermined the group's credibility. Shortly after the release of 1991's Eazy-E-dominated *Efil4zaggin* (*Niggaz4life*), NWA broke up.

▲ *Eazy-E (Eric Wright) of the gangsta rap group NWA was famous as much for his attitude and style as for his music.*

This time Eazy-E and Dr. Dre feuded over past royalties. The two embarked on a brutal war of words: Dre's solo album *The Chronic* (1992) poked merciless fun at Eazy, while Eazy replied with some "dissing" of his own on 1993's *It's On (Dr. Dre) 187um Killa*. Eazy-E continued to make records but saw his status and credibility decline, even as Ruthless managed to maintain a successful roster, in particular with Bone Thugs-N-Harmony.

Early in 1995 Eazy-E was admitted to the hospital with breathing difficulties. He was shocked to find that he had full-blown AIDS but went public with the news, becoming the first rapper to do so. Eazy-E had time to marry his girlfriend, Tomika Wood, and to make peace with Dr. Dre and Ice Cube before he died on March 26, 1995.

See also: Black Identity and Popular Culture; Dr. Dre; Ice Cube

Further reading: Light, Alan. (ed.) *The Vibe History of Hip Hop*. New York, NY: Three Rivers Press, 1999.
http://www.eazy-e.com (Official Eazy-E/Ruthless Records site).

KEY DATES

1964   Born in Compton, Los Angeles, on September 7.

1988   *Straight Outta Compton* shoots NWA to stardom; releases solo album *Eazy-Duz-It*.

1991   NWA releases its fourth album, *Efil4zaggin*; the group splits.

1995   Dies in Los Angeles, California, on March 26.

EDELMAN, Marian Wright
Civil Rights Activist, Lawyer

Marian Wright Edelman, founder and president of the Children's Defense Fund (CDF), has long been an advocate for disadvantaged Americans, particularly children. Under her leadership the Washington-based CDF has become the most powerful children's lobby group in the United States. It secured the 1990 Act for Better Child Care, bringing more than $3 billion into daycare facilities and other programs.

Early life
Born Marian Wright in Bennettsville, South Carolina, on June 6, 1939, Edelman was the daughter of Arthur Jerome Wright, a Baptist minister, and Maggie Leola Bowen, who was active in the church. The Wrights had a strong sense of civic responsibility and often took in people who could not care for themselves; they built a black children's playground for young people denied access to white facilities and set up a home for the aged. The Wright children grew up with strong female role models; Edelman has referred to them as "lanterns" in her life (see box).

Edelman's father taught his children to respect influential African Americans such as Mary McLeod Bethune and Marian Anderson, for whom his daughter was named.

In 1956 Edelman went to Spelman College, Georgia, where she became aware of Martin Luther King, Jr. Edelman decided while she was studying that she wanted to dedicate her life to a cause larger than herself. She won a scholarship to study in Europe for a year and traveled to France, Switzerland, and several East European nations, an experience that she later said opened her eyes to the possibilities of what life could be like for racial minorities in other societies. Edelman returned home to Spelman, where Professor Howard Zinn helped get her involved in the civil rights movement. She said, "This was the South of the late 1950s, where the first attempts at social and political change in the struggle for civil rights originated.

▼ *Marian Wright Edelman was lucky enough to have very good role models when she was growing up. She has promoted the mentoring of young children.*

INFLUENCES AND INSPIRATION

Edelman has always claimed that her major influences were her parents, family, teachers, members of her local community, and civil rights leaders such as Ella Baker and Fannie Lou Hamer—the "lanterns" to whom she paid tribute in her 2000 book *Lanterns: A Memoir of Mentors.* Edelman's dedication to children and family rights has inspired other people, including Hillary Rodham Clinton, who also attended Yale University

Law School. Edelman was Clinton's mentor, and the two women formed a close and lasting friendship. Through Edelman Clinton developed a keen interest in child-related issues and welfare. In 1973 Clinton worked for a year at the CDF as a staff attorney, and she later served on the organization's board. Following Bill Clinton's 1992 election as president of the United States, Edelman's

relationship with the Clintons became the focus of media attention and some commentators speculated that the CDF would receive preferential treatment from the White House. In 1996 Edelman showed that her commitment to children's rights came before friendship when she organized the "Stand for Children" rally in Washington, D.C., to fight Clinton's proposed changes to the welfare program.

Professor Zinn would take us outside the sheltered stone wall of the Spelman gates to the realities of interracial dialogues and protests. The activism we initially took part in preceded the regional and national movements that are usually referred to as the civil rights era."

In 1960 Edelman took part in sit-ins to protest segregation. She wrote a paper called "An Appeal for Human Rights," which was published in both white- and black-owned newspapers. Edelman also took part in activist Ella Baker's meeting at Raleigh, North Carolina, initiated by the Southern Christian Leadership Conference (SCLC); she joined the Student Nonviolent Coordinating Committee (SNCC) shortly afterward.

Following her graduation from Spelman in 1960, Edelman went to Yale University Law School, from which she graduated in 1963. She directed the NAACP Legal Defense and Educational Fund office in New York before moving to Jackson, Mississippi, in 1964, arriving during the voter-registration campaign. She became friends with fellow activists Unita Blackwell and Fannie Lou Hamer. Edelman became the first black American woman to be admitted to the Mississippi Bar. She filed and won a school integration suit that began the process of fully desegregating Mississippi schools. She also worked on poverty-prevention programs there. Edelman testified before the Senate in 1967 on hunger and poverty in the

state and advised Senator Robert Kennedy on the same issues when he visited Mississippi. She also helped Martin Luther King, Jr., launch the "Poor People's Campaign," which highlighted poverty in the United States. She stayed on as attorney for the campaign after King's assassination in 1968. Later that year Wright married Peter Edelman, an aide to Senator Kennedy.

Children's advocate

In l968 Edelman moved to Washington, D.C., where she founded the Washington Research Project, a law firm concerned with child and family issues, and poverty; it was the parent body of the CDF. In 1971 Edelman moved with her family to Boston, Massachusetts; she became director of the Center for Law and Education at Harvard University, where she stayed for two years. In 1973 she began CDF with the intention of giving every child a head start in life. The organization dealt with welfare, health care, immunization, and education, it became the leading child advocacy agency and received a lot of political support from people like Hillary Clinton.

Edelman has received honorary degrees from over 30 colleges and universities, and her awards include the Albert Schweitzer Humanitarian Prize, the Heinz Award, and the prestigious Presidential Medal of Freedom. She is the author of several bestselling books.

KEY DATES

1939	Born in Bennettsville, South Carolina, on June 6.
1968	Founds Washington Research Project.
1973	Founds the Children's Defense Fund.
1993	Inducted into the Women's Hall of Fame.

See also: Anderson, Marian; Baker, Ella; Bethune, Mary McLeod; Blackwell, Unita; Hamer, Fannie Lou; King, Martin Luther, Jr.

Further reading: Edelman, Marian Wright. *Lanterns: A Memoir of Mentors.* New York, NY: Harper Paperbacks, 2000. http://bss.sfsu.edu/edelman (Marian Wright Edelman Institute).

EDMONDS, Kenneth "Babyface"
Singer, Songwriter

Kenneth "Babyface" Edmonds was one of the formative musical influences of the 1990s. A singer, songwriter, producer, and entrepreneur, Edmonds had a successful solo career and also wrote and produced hits for artists as varied as Eric Clapton, Celion Dion, Madonna, and Aretha Franklin. Edmonds won several Grammys, including three consecutive awards for producing between 1995 and 1997.

Road to success
Edmonds was born in Indianapolis, Indiana, on April 10, 1959. Music was an early love, and by his teens Edmonds was performing in several local rhythm-and-blues (R&B) bands. In the late 1970s he worked as a backing performer for funk star Bootsy Collins, who gave Edmonds his "Babyface" nickname. In 1977 Edmonds signed up as guitarist with the band Manchild. When the band split up in the early 1980s after producing three albums, he went on to form the urban funk band Deele, with Antonio "L.A." Reid. Although the Deele was quite successful, Edmonds and Reid also wrote and produced songs for other artists. In 1987 Edmonds recorded the solo album *Lovers,* which was a commercial success and yielded four chart singles.

In 1988 Edmonds and Reid left Deele; a year later they set up the record label LaFace, which took off. Edmonds wrote and produced records for many of the leading stars of the time, including Sheena Easton, Paula Abdul, and Bobby Brown. In 1989, the same year he released his second solo album *Tender Lovers*, Edmonds was nominated for a Grammy award and named the BMI (Broadcast Music Incorporated) Songwriter of the Year. In

▲ **Kenneth "Babyface" Edmonds's and "L.A." Reid's company LaFace has been responsible for launching the careers of OutKast and Usher.**

the 1990s and early 21st century his success continued and he worked with leading musicians such as Whitney Houston, Madonna, OutKast, Michael Jackson, and Usher.

Edmonds's 1993 solo album *For the Cool in You* sold over two million copies. Edmonds also wrote 15 of the 16 tracks on the soundtrack album from the movie *Waiting to Exhale*, which sold seven million copies and spawned three Top 10 singles. In 1997 Edmonds and his wife, Tracey, formed a film production company, Edmonds Entertainment, which released the acclaimed drama *Soul Food.* By 2005 Edmonds's successful solo and songwriting work had yielded sales of more than 100 million albums and singles, with 90 Top 10 hits.

See also: Brown, Bobby; Franklin, Aretha; Houston, Whitney; Jackson, Michael; Usher

Further reading: Southern, Eileen. *The Music of Black Americans: A History.* New York, NY: W. W. Norton & Co., 1997. http://www.babyfacemusic.com (Official site).

KEY DATES	
1959	Born in Indianapolis, Indiana, on April 10.
1987	Releases his first solo album, *Lovers.*
1989	Receives the BMI Songwriter of the Year award.
1995	Wins first of three consecutive Grammys for producing.
1997	Edmonds Entertainment releases its first movie, *Soul Food.*
2005	Career sales top 100 million albums and singles, including 90 Top 10 hits.

SET INDEX

Set Index

Set Index

Set Index

Picture Credits